PENGUIN BOOKS

SRI LANKA AND THE DEFEAT OF THE LTTE

K.M. de Silva held the chair of Sri Lanka History from 1969 to 1995 at the University of Ceylon, later the University of Peradeniya. He was foundation director and executive director of the International Centre for Ethnic Studies, Colombo/Kandy, 1982–2008.

Among his several books are *A History of Sri Lanka, Managing Ethnic Tensions in Multi-Ethnic Societies: Sri Lanka, 1880–1985* and *Regional Powers and Small State Security: India and Sri Lanka, 1977–1990*. He has edited two volumes of the *Sri Lanka: British Documents on the End of Empire* series, *Conflict and Violence in South Asia: Bangladesh, India, Pakistan and Sri Lanka* and *Pursuit of Peace in Sri Lanka: Past Failures and Future Prospects*. He also wrote *Reaping the Whirlwind: Ethnic Politics, Ethnic Conflict in Sri Lanka*.

Sri Lanka and the Defeat of the LTTE

K.M. de SILVA

PENGUIN BOOKS

An imprint of Penguin Random House

PENGUIN BOOKS

USA | Canada | UK | Ireland | Australia
New Zealand | India | South Africa | China | Singapore

Penguin Books is part of the Penguin Random House group of companies
whose addresses can be found at global.penguinrandomhouse.com

Published by Penguin Random House India Pvt. Ltd
4th Floor, Capital Tower 1, MG Road,
Gurugram 122 002, Haryana, India

Penguin
Random House
India

First published by Penguin Books India 2012

Copyright © K.M. de Silva 2012

ISBN 9780143416524

Not for sale in Sri Lanka

Typeset in Adobe Caslon Pro by InoSoft Systems, Noida
Printed at Repro India Limited

for Chandra and Ravi (Rajiv)
and
for Anne, Marisa, Sohan and Sanjay

Contents

Acronyms   ix

Maps   xi

Introduction   1

Sri Lanka:
The Travails of a South Asian Democracy

Separatism and Terrorism in South Asia
and Sri Lanka   13

Sri Lanka's Prolonged Ethnic Conflict:
Negotiating a Settlement   39

Mediation and the Indian Intervention   63

Sowing the Wind

Sri Lanka: From Demilitarization to Militarization   85

Appraisals of the Conflict   100

University Admissions Policy   108

Language Policy   134

State Sector Employment   147

The Defeat of the LTTE

A Weak Government and a Resurgent LTTE   161

The LTTE's Last Phase: 'No War No Peace'   180

The Collapse of the LTTE   192

After the Defeat of the LTTE   205

The Challenges of Militarization: 1986–2011   219

After the Rout of the LTTE:
Reconciliation and Reconstruction

The Passage to Reconciliation   241

Reconstruction   254

Conclusion   273

Notes   290

Select Bibliography   312

Acknowledegements   327

Index   328

Acronyms

ADB	Asian Development Bank
CFA	Cease Fire Agreement
CWC	Ceylon Workers' Congress
DK	Dravida Kazhagam
DMK	Dravida Munnetra Kazhagam
EBP	Eksath Bhikkhu Peramuna
EPDP	Eelam People's Democratic Party
EPRLF	Eelam People's Revolutionary Liberation Front
EROS	Eelam Revolutionary Organization of Students
EU	European Union
FACT	Federation of Associations of Canadian Tamils
FBI	Federal Bureau of Investigation
FP	Federal Party
GCE (A/L)	General Certificate of Education (Advanced Level)
GNP	Gross National Product
HSZs	High Security Zones
HUM	The Hizbul Mujahideen
IFT	International Federation of Tamils
IPKF	Indian Peace Keeping Force
ISI	Inter-Services Intelligence Directorate
ITAK	Ilankai Thamil Arasi Kachchi
JHU	Jathika Hela Urumaya

JKLF	Jammu and Kashmir Liberation Front
JVP	Janatha Vimukthi Peramuna
LSSP	Lanka Sama Samaja Party
LTTE	Liberation Tigers of Tamil Eelam
MEP	Mahajana Eksath Peramuna
MoU	Memorandum of Understanding
NCHE	National Council of Higher Education
NCP	North-Central provinces
NCPC	North-Central provincial council
NUA	National Unity Alliance
PA	People's Alliance
PLOTE	People's Liberation Organization of Tamil Eelam
P-TOMS	Post-Tsunami Operations Management Structure
RAW	Research and Analysis Wing
SAARC	South Asian Association for Regional Co-operation
SEAC	South East Asia Command
SLFP	Sri Lanka Freedom Party
SLMC	Sri Lanka Muslim Congress
SLMM	Sri Lanka Monitoring Mission
STF	Special Task Force
TC	Tamil Congress
TELO	Tamil Eelam Liberation Organization
TMVP	Tamileela Makkal Viduthalai Pulikal
TNA	Tamil National Alliance
TUF	Tamil United Front
TULF	Tamil United Liberation Front
UF	United Front
UGC	University Grants Commission
UNF	United National Front
UNP	United National Party
UPFA	United People's Freedom Alliance
WTA	World Tamil Association
WTM	World Tamil Movement

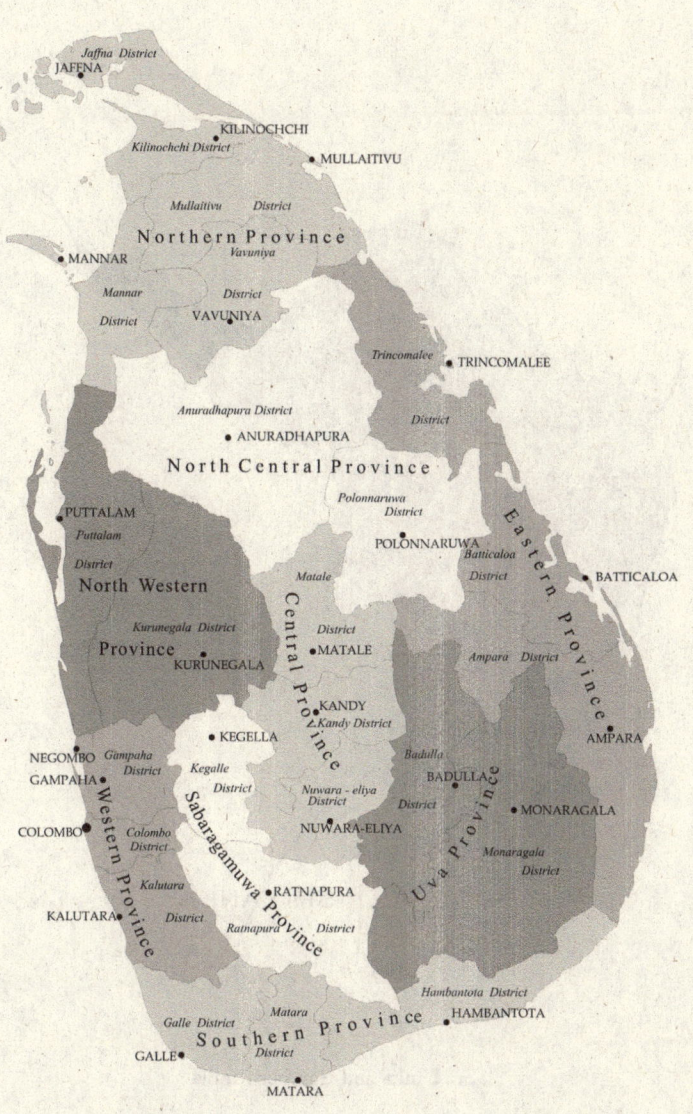

Sri Lanka: Provinces, Administrative Districts and Main Cities

Sri Lanka and Southern India

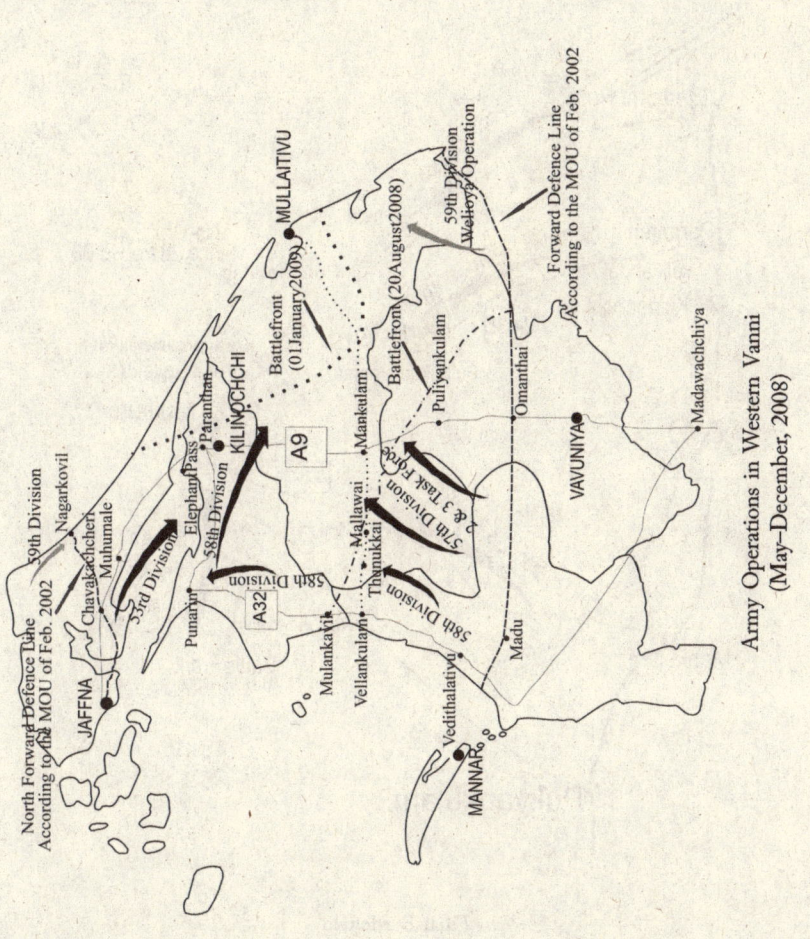

Army Operations in Western Vanni
(May–December, 2008)

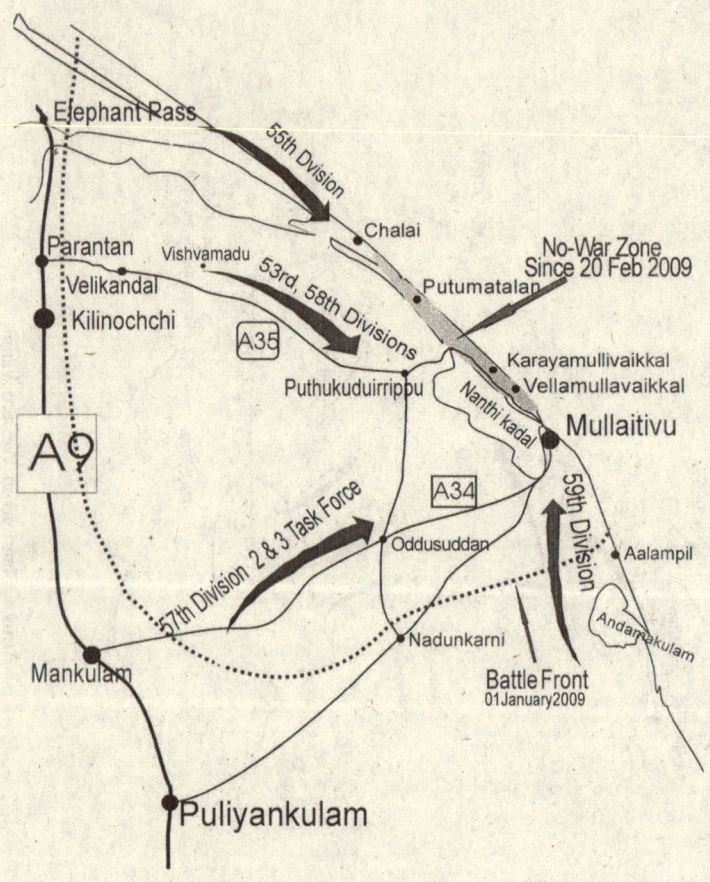

Final Battlefield
(January–May, 2009)

Introduction

This volume is a sequel to my *Reaping the Whirlwind: Ethnic Conflict, Ethnic Politics in Sri Lanka*, published by Penguin India in 1998. At the time I completed writing *Reaping the Whirlwind* in the late 1990s, I did not believe that we would see a decisive defeat of the Liberation Tigers of Tamil Eelam (LTTE) as early as 2009 despite the fact that I was aware of the rout of the LTTE at the hands of General Cyril Ranatunga's newly reconstituted Sri Lankan security services in May 1987. On that occasion, the LTTE and its leadership had fled in disarray, with its leader Velupillai Prabhakaran and some of his close associates in the leadership ranks moving desperately by sea from the Jaffna peninsula to hideouts in Tamil Nadu provided by the regional government there. Having defeated the LTTE forces on that occasion in the Vadamarachchi campaign, General Cyril Ranatunga had planned to move into Jaffna town, its suburbs and to other locations close by in order to destroy the LTTE's administrative structures there. He had been prevented from doing so by the intervention of the Indian government who warned President J.R. Jayewardene that it would not accept this projected entry of the Sri Lankan forces into the town of Jaffna and its environs.[1] The excuse it had given President Jayewardene was that such a move into Jaffna and its neighbourhood would be resisted by the Tamils and that the inevitable efforts to overcome this resistance would lead to a bloodbath.[2] The Indian government's concern about such a bloodbath had been on account of the inevitable outburst of protests to New Delhi by the regional government in Tamil Nadu and by Tamil agitators there and elsewhere. This had been something that New Delhi was acutely concerned about. New Delhi thus succeeded in persuading President Jayewardene to get General Ranatunga to desist from his proposed campaign of crushing the LTTE in Jaffna town and its suburbs as he had earlier done on the battlefield in the Vadamarachchi area. The Indian intervention on that occasion had saved the LTTE who lived to fight another day. As this present volume would show, it took the Sri Lankan armed services twenty-two more years before they could complete what General Ranatunga had started in May 1987. Ranatunga's successful campaign had been halted abruptly before it reached the conclusion he had in mind. Those of us who knew what had happened were disappointed at the consequences of this Indian intervention but always felt that the LTTE could be defeated militarily and that a military defeat would halt their terrorist attacks in the country. That was something we had in mind whenever we were told in later years by defeatist academics, defeatist politicians and defeatist generals that the campaign against the LTTE was an 'unwinnable war'. Those claims that the LTTE could not be defeated became more frequent in the 1990s and well into 2000 and beyond, every time the LTTE inflicted a defeat on the Sri Lankan forces or escaped defeat at the hands of the Sri Lankan army. General Ranatunga's Vadamarachchi campaign was one of the forgotten episodes of the struggle against the LTTE, forgotten by the politicians in Sri Lanka, including heads of government.

After a brief spell in public service outside the army after 1986–87, General Ranatunga[3] retired to live the life of a gentleman-farmer on the block of land he had inherited in Mawanella, near Kegalle, on the road from Colombo to Kandy. To visitors there, especially those whom he trusted to be discreet, he would talk of the Vadamarachchi campaign and how he had Prabhakaran and the LTTE on the run and how the Indians had prevented him from completing the campaign he had embarked upon. In retirement, he carefully collected the papers that would form part of the *Memoirs* he would publish in 2009. He had kept a record of the events of the Vadamarachchi campaign even when the official memories of it had become dim indeed, as politicians and soldiers kept telling themselves and others that the campaign against the LTTE was a futile struggle, an unwinnable war. General Sarath Fonseka who led the Sri Lankan forces to an overwhelming victory in the years 2006 to 2009 had been a lieutenant colonel in the Vadamarachchi campaign. He remembered how the LTTE had been routed on that occasion and was confident it could be done again. And indeed, the Sri Lankan armed forces did it again in 2009.

Written at a time when the LTTE was clearly on the verge of another—perhaps a decisive—defeat[4], this present work of mine begins with reflections on Sri Lanka's episodes of political violence as part of the larger issue of political violence in post-Independence South Asia, a larger theme on which not much has been written about. For many years Sri Lanka had been one of the principal trouble spots of South Asia, and the LTTE, who were in battle in the 1970s and 1980s with Sri Lankans and their governments, were both a formidable separatist force and, more to the point, became, in time, one of the most fearsome terrorist groups in the world. The most appropriate comparison with the Sri Lankan situation in the wider South Asian scene seemed to be with separatism in India, especially in Jammu and Kashmir. I have left Pakistan out of this exercise of comparison of types of political violence. True, Pakistan today is not merely one of the principal trouble spots of South Asia but also home to violent terrorist groups. But there was no Pakistani attempt to influence the terrorist struggle in Sri Lanka except in the sense that it was one of the sources of weaponry for the Sri Lankan governments in the struggle against the separatist, terrorist forces in the island.

One of the themes this present book seeks to explore is the complex relationship between the so-called moderates in Sri Lankan Tamil politics and the Tamil terrorist groups, especially the LTTE. The separatist programmes of the Tamil terrorist group, the LTTE, had sprung from the separatism of the Tamil United Liberation Front (TULF) as did the LTTE's enthusiastic commitment to the concept of a Tamil homeland or homelands in Sri Lanka. As we shall see, the LTTE not only took over the TULF's separatist programme and its policy of adherence to the concept of a Tamil homeland but also shared its acceptance of a programme of political violence. The LTTE's commitment to political violence was more wholehearted, and there was no attempt on its part to conceal its commitment to violence as had been the case with the TULF. The LTTE's violence was primarily directed against the Sri Lankan state and its security services, in particular the army, and also against Sinhalese villages in the east and close to the east, and in the north and close to the north. The violence was also systematically directed against the principal Tamil political organizations such as the TULF with whom it had earlier been associated or had worked with. A close examination of the relationship between the LTTE and the TULF, as well as with smaller separatist groups, shows that from the outset the LTTE was intent on eliminating all these groups—including the TULF—overlooking the political objectives and campaigns they had in common. The LTTE's aim was to become the sole representatives of the Tamils of Sri Lanka. The terrorist tactics of the LTTE treated these Tamil political groups and parties as essentially expendable. The Sri Lankan experience of the LTTE's unmistakable hostility to other Tamil groups who shared its separatist programmes, and its determination to impose its leadership on the forces of separatism—to the extent of it physically eliminating the leadership of these groups and occasionally the groups themselves—forms one of the themes in our study of terrorism in Sri Lanka. The TULF's founder and leader S.J.V. Chelvanayakam died in 1976 when the LTTE was operating in its earliest phase. All the leaders of the TULF after Chelvanayakam were killed by the LTTE. This was done over a ten-year stretch from 1989 onwards.

This present volume is a case study in the emergence, maturation and eventual collapse of a separatist and terrorist movement, and as such it is one of the very few such studies available. Part one of this volume also provides an introduction to the practice of negotiations among the principal political parties in Sri Lanka's political evolution as a South Asian democracy. These negotiations began with the so-called moderates among the Tamil political groups and individuals and parties of Sri Lanka, and continued when the LTTE became the principal Tamil political force. We also examine Sri Lanka's transition from a situation of virtual demilitarization to a state with a large army—larger in terms of its proportion to the civilian population—than other states of South Asia, including India and Pakistan. This important transformation in Sri Lanka—entirely in response to the challenge posed by the LTTE—has not been studied, so far, in any great detail. There has been no monograph on the Sri Lankan army and on its role in Sri Lanka's public life, including on its role in the defeat of the LTTE. There have been a few perceptive articles[5] but not much more than that.

Part two of this monograph deals with some of the controversial issues, issues that were prominent in the contention between the Sri Lankan state and the advocates of Tamil rights and claims. Most of such issues have been dealt with in some detail in *Reaping the Whirlwind*. Two particular issues are dealt with here, incorporating material not available in *Reaping the Whirlwind*. These involve studies of Sri Lanka's policy or policies on language change and the modification and the near transformation of these policies. This important theme is analysed in much greater detail here than was possible in *Reaping the Whirlwind*. The other theme—and one that is new—is a detailed study of the controversial issue of university admissions. Herein, we take a detailed look at the debates on this issue, the modifications made in the government policies on university admissions in response to criticisms made, as well as the rivalries between Tamils and Muslims regarding the issue, and between Tamil groups themselves and of course between the Tamils and various Sinhalese groups.

Part three of the present study deals with the issues that contributed to the defeat of the LTTE. I have attempted to link this defeat of the LTTE with the dynamics of Sri Lankan politics and rivalries among the country's political parties. In doing so, I examine how these rivalries had some effect on the state's efforts at defeating the LTTE. From 1994 to the present day, the Sri Lanka Freedom Party (SLFP) has been in power, controlling both the presidency and the Parliament. From 1994 to 2000, we see the last days of the Bandaranaike family's control of the SLFP. The Bandaranaikes were the founding family of the SLFP and held power in it from 1951 onwards. In 2000, the power in the SLFP moved reluctantly to Mahinda Rajapaksa and with him to the Rajapaksas. The LTTE was defeated in 2009, and the Rajapaksas went on to be in charge of the presidency and the Parliament. Although the victory over the LTTE was really an achievement of the army, and not really that of the political leadership, we shall see in this volume how the political leadership successfully claimed the victory as its own.

Part four of this volume deals with the problems of reconstruction and reconciliation after the rout of the LTTE and the deaths of Prabhakaran and other LTTE leaders. The processes of reconstruction include the rehabilitation of the political parties of the Tamils after their virtual destruction at the hands of the LTTE. The encouragement of a Tamil political movement or movements committed to democratic modes of activity would be an essential feature of the post-LTTE reconstruction process. The domination of the LTTE, over the political parties and groups that existed in Jaffna and the north and the east of the island from the time the LTTE emerged, had been so complete that a recovery to a state of independent activity for Tamil political parties would be a long-drawn-out process, and is dependent as much on the Tamils themselves as on the Sri Lankan government and on national political parties which would inevitably seek to move into the Tamil areas as part of their political activity.

The process of reconstruction of the Tamil political parties would need them to adopt a more modest set of objectives than those of the TULF and the LTTE. In brief, it would involve an acceptance of their role as a minority in a democratic Sri Lankan political system with all the responsibilities and limitations this would involve. The TULF had operated as a minority with a majority complex, while the LTTE had no limitations in the scope of their activities and objectives. With the LTTE now virtually extinct, except for the survival of some of their associates in the form of the Tamil National Alliance (TNA) who had played a limited role in Tamil politics before the collapse of the LTTE, the scene is wide open for other and newer Tamil political parties and groups. Some Tamil politicians still identify themselves as members of the TNA but with little or no mention of their previous subordinate role as the associates of the LTTE. There is then, of course, the whole question of the Tamil diaspora and their activities.

A key feature of the processes of reconstruction is a revival of the economy of those parts of the north and the east of the island that had been dominated, if not controlled, by the LTTE. A feature of these processes of economic recovery now in progress is the support it receives from the Indian government. The funding from the Indian government, so far, has been generous. A part of this process of reconstruction is the rehabilitation of infrastructure, including the railways and the roads damaged by the LTTE, and also those neglected by the LTTE.

However, the processes of reconciliation are more complex than those of reconstruction. Reconciliation has to do with the government of Sri Lanka, and the Sinhalese majority for the most part and their handling of relations with the Tamils and other minorities but at the same time reconciliation also depends on the Tamil minority and other minorities—the Tamil minority in particular.

SRI LANKA:
THE TRAVAILS OF A SOUTH
ASIAN DEMOCRACY

The core of the problems reviewed in this monograph is an explanation of how a dynamic democracy—with a vibrant multiparty political system based on universal suffrage since 1931, and demonstrating a strong commitment to social welfare, providing its citizens with wider access to education and health and living standards—became in time a leading trouble spot in South Asia and the centre of a violent separatist movement. It also became the centre of a terrorist movement.

In part one of this monograph, the situation in Sri Lanka—known as Ceylon up to 1972—is set in the context of the problems of political violence in South Asia. The point of comparison is with parts of India, not Pakistan. The Indian analogies are more appropriate for Sri Lanka than Pakistan.

Sri Lanka had a long tradition of discussion of contentious issues, and even negotiations on occasion. This pre-Independence tradition of discussions and negotiations continued after Independence. These discussions and negotiations were between what may be called 'moderates' in the political system. The tradition continued even after the separatist and terrorist Liberation Tigers of Tamil Eelam (LTTE) entered the political scene on its own and later proceeded to eliminate the 'moderates' among the Tamils. Another theme is discussed here—the Indian interest in the affairs of Sri Lanka, an interest which became in time an intervention. Yet another theme discussed is Sri Lanka's transformation from a demilitarized state to a militarized one.

1

Separatism and Terrorism in South Asia and Sri Lanka

Over the last two decades of the twentieth century and the first decade of the twenty-first, Sri Lanka was one of the most prominent trouble spots of South and South East Asia. Through most of this period, its deep-rooted and increasingly violent ethnic conflict eluded settlement till the middle of May 2009 when the armed forces of the Sri Lankan government inflicted a decisive defeat on the principal separatist group, the Liberation Tigers of Tamil Eelam (LTTE). The LTTE was one of the most prominent terrorist groups in the world.

Some questions relating to terrorism need to be raised here; and some answers are attempted. We need to begin the process of answering some of these questions by pointing out that the term 'terrorism',[1] like 'ethnicity', eludes precise definition. Some writers on the theme would do without a definition of terrorism at all and proceed to describe or discuss it in its many manifestations as a harsh reality in modern and contemporary world politics. In many ways, this is preferable to the comfortable but bland moral neutrality of those who argue that one man's terrorist is another man's freedom fighter, and move from there to blur the distinction between terrorism and war, and terrorism and ordinary criminal acts.[2]

Walter Laquer, one of the most respected experts on terrorism asserts that:

> One of the better definitions of terrorism was provided by the US Department of Defence, which in 1990 described terrorism as 'the unlawful use of, or threatened use of force or violence against individuals or property, to coerce and intimidate governments or societies, often to achieve political, religious or ideological objectives'. But even this working definition has not found acceptance among those studying the subject. Perhaps the only characteristic generally agreed upon is that terrorism always involves violence or the threat of violence.[3]

Two American political scientists writing in 1982 attempted to explain the difference between terrorism and civil disobedience:

> The obvious and most essential difference between civil disobedience and terrorism is clearly the latter's unswerving commitment to violence as a means of achieving the terrorist's goal, where civil disobedience uncompromisingly forswears all forces of violence. Both may require breaking the laws of a nation, but for civil disobedience the law that is broken as an act of protest must always be somewhat relevant or appropriate to the object of the protest. Terrorism has no such restraint.[4]

Now we turn to Fred Halliday's perceptive commentary on terrorism, published in 1993, for a convenient identification of some crucially important aspects of terrorism. For him, its

> central meaning is the use of terror for furthering of political ends, and it was originally used to denote the use of terror by the French revolutionary government against its opponents ... This usage of the term to cover terror by governments, has become less common, though by no means irrelevant, and in

most contemporary usage the term covers acts of terror by those opposed to governments. The range of activities which the term covers has been wide, but four main forms of action tend to be included: assassination, bombings, seizures of individuals as hostages, and [in recent times], the hijacking of planes.[5]

Halliday adds that 'in the 1970s the term began to be used to cover acts of violence committed by political groups outside the country in which they were primarily active'.[6] One could include in this the 'suicide bombers'—human beings with explosives attached to their bodies, killing themselves but more importantly killing others in the process, often prominent political figures identified for assassination; provocative attacks on places of religious worship, including those of great historical importance; and in all of this, a total lack of concern for the lives of the civilian population who happen to be around when the human bombs go off.

In illustrating the links between terrorism and political agitation in South Asia, two countries have been chosen—India and Sri Lanka—presently among those most affected by terrorism. In particular the book focuses on Jammu and Kashmir (J&K) in the north-west of India, and Sri Lanka, in its recent ethnic conflict between the Tamil separatists in the north—and to a lesser extent in the east of the island—and the forces of the government. In J&K the recent phase of terrorism began in the mid and late 1980s, just as it did in Sri Lanka where terrorism grew in intensity in the 1980s and 1990s. J&K is not the only part of India affected by terrorist attacks by separatist forces; it is only the most prominent. Terrorism is a feature of politics in parts of the troubled north-east of India, but our focus of attention here is on terrorism in J&K.

Terrorism in South Asia

Over the last sixty years, i.e., in the postcolonial phase of its history, South Asia has had a record of violence in public life, unusual even for states and societies breaking free of colonial rule in any part of the world. One feature of this is the large number of heads of government/heads of state, senior politicians and other public figures killed by assassins. No other part of the world has seen so many heads of state and heads of government, so many prominent personalities, political and national, become the victims of assassin's bullets and bombs as South Asia has over the last sixty years. In India it began with the assassination of Mohandas K. Gandhi in 1948. After a lull of over thirty-five years came the assassination of a prime minister, Indira Gandhi (in 1984), and seven years later of her son and successor as prime minister, Rajiv Gandhi,[7] leader of the Opposition at the time he was killed. In the first two cases, the assassins came from within the country—M.K. Gandhi was assassinated by a Hindu extremist, while in the case of Indira Gandhi, Punjabi Sikhs were reacting against her government's rigorous policies against the burgeoning separatist agitation in that part of the country. Rajiv Gandhi's assassins came from outside the country, from Sri Lanka, belonging to the LTTE.

In Pakistan, that country's first prime minister was assassinated within four years of Independence. It was followed—almost as in the case of India—by a lull of over twenty-five years till the violent elimination of two heads of government/heads of state, beginning with the hanging of Zulfiqar Ali Bhutto in what is widely seen as a judicial murder. But if this would not qualify as a terrorist act, the mysterious and violent death of Zia ul Huq—the man who put Bhutto in jail and set in motion the train of events that led to his execution—would qualify as one because the plane crash in which he was killed may have been due to a bomb planted in the plane. And we have in more recent times the assassination of Benazir Bhutto. When we turn to Bangladesh where its founder and several members of his family were killed (in 1975) to be followed thereafter (1981) by the assassination of his successor[8], we are back to terrorism as a feature of South Asian politics. The shadow of these assassinations still lies across the political landscape of Bangladesh like some sinister natural force seeking to regain dominance in public life.

Sri Lanka's record has been equally grim, perhaps even more so, beginning with the assassination of its third prime minister in 1959. Nearly thirty-five years later came the next assassination, of R. Premadasa, the island's second executive President (in 1993). In fact, three of Sri Lanka's most prominent politicians were assassinated between March 1991 and October 1994, each of them a head of government or a potential head of government—all of them, including Premadasa, assassinated by the LTTE. Among other victims of LTTE assassinations were several Tamil politicians including A. Amirthalingam, the head of the Tamil United Liberation Front (TULF) in 1990, and the heads of Tamil separatist groups who were rivals of the LTTE. All of them were eliminated in a deliberate policy pursued by the LTTE of securing primacy in the leadership of Tamil politics through a campaign of terror.

There is no parallel for such a series of assassinations in the postcolonial states of South East Asia. The only exceptions are Myanmar (Burma) in the earliest phase of its independence—when Aung San, its prime minister designate, and several ministers of his provisional government were assassinated (in July 1947)[9]—and Vietnam during the years of its long civil war.

Political assassination of leaders have been elevated to a macabre art form in South Asia. So too the exploitation for political advantage, by the closest relatives of the victim of the assassins, of the grief and sense of loss that often flows from the killings—or more particularly, of the public expressions of such grief. Developed into an elaborate ritual and high political theatre, the ultimate objective of the use of these sentiments is to gain personal or party advantage in the electoral process or both. In the intensely competitive electorates of South Asia, sorrow has become an eminently marketable commodity. Principally, the beneficiaries have been the wives or daughters of a murdered leader and occasionally a son (Rajiv Gandhi, for instance) but not, so far, a husband (except for Asif Ali Zardari in Pakistan). In this, if in nothing else, Sri Lanka was the pacesetter, beginning in 1960[10], where the assassination of S.W.R.D. Bandaranaike helped to bring his widow, Sirimavo Bandaranaike, to power (1960–65, 1970–77) and to national prominence as a political personality. Her first political campaign of July 1960 is a classic study in the deliberate exploitation of public expressions of sorrow for personal and party benefit.

Only one of these assassinations in South Asia did not have an overt political motive—the assassination of Sri Lanka's third prime minister, S.W.R.D. Bandaranaike, in September 1959. There the motive was a personal one. The man who planned the assassination—a *bhikkhu*, a member of the Buddhist order—had been closely associated with Bandaranaike in the latter's eventually successful bid for electoral success in the mid 1950s. The monk had been one of the principal figures in an unusual movement of bhikkhus, who converted what might have been a normal electoral campaign in 1956 into a moral crusade on Bandaranaike's behalf. The man who did the shooting, also a bhikkhu, had been a minor figure in that campaign. He was a human instrument directed and driven by the personal enmity of the principal conspirator towards the man he had helped bring to power. But even this murder with a personal rather than a political motive was not without links to the swings in the country's political moods of the mid 1950s and the late 1950s. In any event, it had profoundly important political consequences—in the emergence of Mrs Bandaranaike to power, the first of South Asia's many political widows, who was to be followed a decade or so later by 'political orphans', if one may use that term to describe the Benazir Bhutto-s, Rajiv Gandhi-s, Sheikh Hasina Wajed-s and Khaleda Zia-s of this world. In this context, Sri Lanka's Chandrika Kumaratunga, a recent executive President (1994–2005)[11], could be described as being both a political widow and a political orphan.

With the one exception of S.W.R.D Bandaranaike, every other assassination referred to above has had political motives. Some of them, especially the ones that took place in India and Sri Lanka, bore symptoms of a deep malaise in the political system—having to do with the politics of Partition in India and Pakistan in their very early years, and thereafter with separatist agitation and ethnic conflict. Rajiv Gandhi's violent death was a unique example of an assassination directed by separatists from a neighbouring state, a consequence nevertheless of an ethnic conflict claiming a presumed mediator as a victim.

A Case Study in Terrorism: Jammu and Kashmir

The crisis in J&K continues to be South Asia's—indeed Asia's—most dangerous, unresolved international dispute. That danger stems from two factors: the prolonged nature of the crisis, and, secondly, its record of several episodes of warfare between the neighbouring states of India and Pakistan. The conflict in the Kargil sector in J&K which brought India and Pakistan to the brink of war in 1999, and the December 2001 attack on the Indian Parliament attributed to Kashmiri separatists, are among the latest manifestations of the perilous situation. In the case of the Parliament attack, Indian troops were amassed in Kashmir on the border with Pakistan. It took several weeks before the tensions eased. The conflict in J&K has two phases, with the mid 1980s as the dividing timeline. In the second phase, terrorism has become a distinctive factor.

The Kashmir region was part of the Himalayan frontier of the Raj, and the roots of the Kashmir conflict go back to the imperial conflicts of the nineteenth century as the Raj continued to build a buffer zone between itself and the Tsarist empire. But while the British established control over J&K, they let it remain a princely state and did not exercise direct rule over it. Even when they sought to establish boundaries with China and Afghanistan in the Kashmir region, these were never clearly or fully demarcated.

The core of the current crisis can be identified as stemming from the diametrically opposite views held by the two sides on the legitimacy of the procedures through which the state of J&K acceded to India. While India claims these procedures were legally sound, Pakistan insists that they violated the principles which had guided the absorption of the princely states into India or Pakistan during the partition of the Raj in 1947.[12] The Kashmir dispute arose out of a conspicuous reluctance on the part of the British at the time of Partition to adhere strictly to the rules and policies by which the princely states were absorbed into the two successor states of the Raj. The failure to resolve the J&K problem at the time of Partition was either the most egregious of blunders that occurred at that time or was a matter of a calculated choice in an effort to strengthen the principal successor state to the Raj, India. From the outset, the leaderships of both India and Pakistan compounded the original problem by turning the Kashmir issue into a symbol of their respective national identities. For Pakistan, Kashmir was part of the unfinished business of the partition of the Raj, the completion of the separate state its founders had dreamed of in the 1930s and 1940s. For India, control over J&K was an assertion of the secularity of the Indian state. These diametrically opposite positions have left the issue an even more intractable one than the dispute between India and China over their border areas. Today, more tension prevails over the actual line of control between the Indian- and Pakistani-held parts of J&K than over the disputed boundary between India and China.

The Kashmir dispute has had an important military dimension for both countries. Ever since India crossed the international frontier of 1947 in response to an attack by Pakistani tribesmen inside Kashmir proper, the ceasefire line has become an extension of the international border. Nevertheless, this international frontier leaves both India and Pakistan dissatisfied. India insists on its rights to regions in Kashmir, which it claims should belong to it as a right, as heir to the erstwhile rulers of J&K. Large extents of territory in Ladakh are held by China, which India claims as belonging to her. There are the territories under Pakistani control in what is known as Azad Jammu and Kashmir: Swat, Gilgit and the so-called Northern Territories. As for Pakistan, it aspires to absorb much of the Kashmir Valley, and other parts of J&K now controlled by India. Whenever an opportunity to assert their rights presents itself, both India and Pakistan are quick to exploit it.

In the first two wars between India and Pakistan, in 1947 and 1965, Pakistan sought to challenge, if not reverse, the decision to convert J&K into a state of the Indian Union. One result of the first of these wars was that about a third of J&K was brought under Pakistani control. The second war, however, gave Pakistan no advantage at all. The third took place in 1971 against the background of India's successful intervention in support of the East Pakistani separatist movement and the emergence of Bangladesh as an independent state. It gave unmistakable diplomatic and political advantages to India.[13] The Simla Accord of 1972 which brought the 1971 war to an end was as much of an unequal treaty as anything the British had signed with weaker or weakened neighbours in the days of the Raj.

Following the 1972 Simla Accord, the Kashmir problem lost some of its salience as a territorial dispute between Pakistan and India for a decade or so. But the policy of benign (or not so very benign) neglect which India pursued over J&K since the early 1970s began to confront a severe test in the changed situation in Kashmir in the 1980s through a new development: the stirrings of a growing radicalization among the Kashmiri Muslims. Certainly the turmoil in Punjab, which culminated in the seizure of the Golden Temple by the most violent of separatists and eventually the attack on the temple by the Indian army and the assassination of Indira Gandhi, had its lessons for the Kashmiri militants.

It is this stage that saw the beginnings of Kashmiri terrorism and the rise to prominence of separatist groups who resort to terrorist tactics. Once this new form of radicalism reached Kashmir, the struggle was joined in by radicalized Islamist groups from outside—from Afghanistan, for instance. This was to have its impact on Indo-Pakistan relations and on regional security. Pakistan refused to be restrained with regard to events across the border on the basis of the Simla Accord, an agreement it had signed during a period of extreme weakness. Kashmiri Muslims had begun to look beyond Pakistan to Afghanistan, Iran and the Middle East. Equally important, the forces of nationalism that led to the prolonged resistance to the invasion of Afghanistan by the Soviet Union were soon at work in J&K, transforming the nature of politics there. The J&K issue then returned to its pre-Simla Accord form of an emotional factor in the domestic politics of India and Pakistan, especially in the case of the latter. For both civilian and military leaders in Pakistan, Kashmir became a useful rallying cry, and a readily available issue with which to divert attention from failures in the realm of social and economic policies. This profound change in the attitude of the Kashmiri population in the 1980s illustrated the interaction between the national, regional (South Asian) and international factors in exacerbating an already tense situation.

The Soviet invasion of Afghanistan was only one of the international factors that affected the situation in J&K. The second, the Iranian revolution, was just as important.

By the mid 1980s, the drift towards violence was virtually inexorable. The defeat of the Soviet forces in Afghanistan, and their departure from that country, led to a dramatic increase in violence in Kashmir. Kashmiris trained by the Afghan mujahidin, and the mujahidin groups themselves, had a major impact on the politics of J&K, and on the separatist groups there. The mujahidin included mercenaries from all parts of the Islamic world—Libya and Iran, Sudan and Egypt, and Bangladesh—who, having secured a victory over the Soviet forces, turned their attention towards J&K.

They had an enormous influence on the Kashmiri separatist forces, from the Jammu and Kashmir Liberation Front (JKLF)[14] to other and more violent groups—some smaller, some larger than the JKLF[15]. They were often in conflict with each other but more often in conflict with the Indian security forces present in J&K in enormous numbers. Separatism now got linked with terrorism through the adoption of the techniques of resistance and aggression popularized by the mujahidin in Afghanistan. Dissidents were targeted for elimination and more Kashmiri Muslims were killed in the process than others. Over 1,00,000 Kashmiri Pandits moved out of the Kashmir Valley to Jammu, Delhi and elsewhere. Their lives had become too insecure in the Kashmir Valley.

Pakistan facilitated the transfer of the mujahidin from Afghanistan to the Indian-controlled J&K. The assistance from Pakistan has taken several forms: provision of military training, the supply of weapons, and establishing safe houses and 'bases' for the separatist guerrillas. Pakistan's Inter-Services Intelligence Directorate (ISI) has been prominent in helping to sustain the Kashmiri resistance. In 1992, George Fernandes, the then Indian minister for Kashmir affairs, put Pakistan's role in its proper perspective: 'I do not believe any foreign hand created the Kashmir problem. The problem was created by us . . . and others decided to take advantage of it.'[16] This is a point as valid today as in 1992. Ten years later, Fernandes, the then Union minister of defence, did not indulge in any reiteration of this theme. There was, instead, intensity in his attacks on terrorism in both India and Pakistan, as well as their neighbours, and indeed in the world in general. It left little room for the balanced judgement he had showed in 1992.[17]

Improvements in mountain-climbing techniques have made it possible for both India and Pakistan to send their soldiers into the Siachen glacier region,[18] in a prolonged confrontation over the border in one of the most inaccessible parts of Kashmir, where the soldiers are more vulnerable to the bitter cold than to the weapons used by the opposing army.

None of the recent changes in the world around J&K have affected the public posture of the governments of India and Pakistan. The fact that Kashmir is an integral part of India is treated as something beyond debate by India. Any attempt by Pakistan to raise the issue at a diplomatic level is dismissed as an attempt to interfere in India's internal affairs. For Islamabad, Kashmir is an unresolved international dispute. The two principal protagonists remain inflexibly resistant to any change in their attitude.

Terrorism and Separatism in Sri Lanka

Sri Lanka provides an excellent case study in the emergence of a separatist movement and its transformation from a relatively peaceful agitation in the 1950s and 1960s to it becoming an extraordinarily violent struggle with regional ramifications. Although external forces were less important in precipitating the crisis in Sri Lanka than in J&K, the geographical proximity of the majority of Tamil population in India was conducive to the growth of separatist sentiment. There are cases when an ethnic (or religious) minority is concentrated in a region or regions of a country. In fact, it even constitutes the overwhelming majority of the population there, as is the case with the Tamils of the Jaffna peninsula and Jaffna district in the north of the Sri Lankan island (and to a lesser extent in the other component districts of the northern province). And where, in addition, there is a very large population of co-ethnics, in close proximity just across a narrow and shallow sea—in what was once the Madras Presidency of British India, and since the mid 1950s, the state of Tamil Nadu—geography and demography combined to provide an ideal breeding ground for a separatist movement. Ethnic cohesion and a heightened sense of ethnic identity, important ingredients for the emergence of a separatist sentiment, had existed in Jaffna and the Jaffna district since the mid 1950s. Some would argue that these had been in existence since the 1940s in the last decade of British rule.

However, the striking feature of the emergence of Tamil separatism in Sri Lanka—in contrast to contemporary separatist movements in Myanmar, Thailand and the Philippines—is its late development. It took twenty-five years or more for early manifestations of separatist sentiment (in the late 1940s and early 1950s) to develop into a full-fledged separatist movement. That transformation was the result of the operation of a number of factors. These included a sense of relative deprivation at the loss of, or the imminent loss of, the advantageous or privileged position the Tamil minority had enjoyed under British colonial rule. There was also a perceived threat to the ethnic identity of the Tamils from the political, economic and cultural policies introduced in the mid 1950s and thereafter. All of this resulted in perceived grievances of a political or economic nature or both. There were, in addition, episodes or incidents of ethnic violence in the mid 1950s—in 1956 and 1958.

The Tamil response went through several stages and phases. It began with exertion of peaceful political pressure in the mid 1950s, moving on to episodes of civil disobedience in the early 1960s, and then to incidents of violence in the 1970s. The violence then graduated from sporadic incidents to more systematic attacks directed against state property, the police and security forces. It culminated in a dangerous threat to the integrity of postcolonial Sri Lanka by the early 1980s. The avowed objective of the agitation in the earliest stages was greater autonomy for a region or a people within the Sri Lankan polity. This agitation moved on to pressure for conversion of the island's unitary structure into a federal or quasi-federal one, until it reached the most recent phase of an armed struggle for a separate state encompassing most or parts of the northern and eastern littoral regions, and their hinterlands.[19]

By the mid 1970s, radicalization of politics in Jaffna was an established fact. With radicalization came violence, including the beginnings of a terrorist campaign that was to last throughout the next two decades and more. In the beginning, that campaign was a bitter internecine struggle between competing separatist forces. The targets, in carefully chosen acts of political violence, were Tamils associated with the United Front (UF) government of that period, a coalition between the Sri Lanka Freedom Party (SLFP) and the Marxist parties. There was, for example, the attempted murder of a pro-government Tamil MP. It was followed by the murder in 1975 of the SLFP mayor of Jaffna, Alfred Durayappah, the most prominent of the Tamil supporters of the United Front government in the north. This takes on a special significance as the first political assassination associated with the future leader of the LTTE, Velupillai Prabhakaran, then a youth of seventeen. In an interview with the well-known Indian magazine *India Today*, he later claimed that it was his 'first military encounter'.[20] Thus began a familiar cycle of politically inspired violence. There was political rhetoric that espoused resort to violence, followed soon enough by attacks on the police or the killing of carefully chosen victims, generally supporters of the government in the Jaffna peninsula. These acts were aimed at conveying the chilling political message that opposition to and deviation from the Tamil United Front's (TUF)—the predecessor to the Tamil United Liberation Front (TULF)—programme carried fearful risks. A part of this programme included bank robberies, generally to finance the political activities of these groups but also to line the pockets of the leaders.

More ominously, by the mid and late 1970s, the increasingly turbulent politics of the Jaffna peninsula began to be treated in Tamil Nadu as an integral part of its own internal politics. The process of internationalization of Sri Lanka's ethnic conflict had begun. The Dravida Munnetra Kazhagam (DMK), effectively checked from pursuing its separatist goals in India, took vicarious pleasure in giving encouragement and support to separatist tendencies among the Tamils of Sri Lanka. To the latter, worsening relations with the UF government tended to make ties with Tamil Nadu more attractive than they had once been. Although the links were still fitful and tentative, Tamil politics in Sri Lanka came to have a regional rather than a purely local impact because of the Tamil Nadu connection.

These militant groups had begun as foot soldiers of the separatist struggle and had become a vital link between the established politicians of the TUF and, later, its successor the TULF. These groups, and the Tamil people in the north and the east of the country, were in no mood to let the TULF settle down to a more sedate role befitting its national position as an Opposition group within the Parliament. From 1977 to 1983, it was a TULF representative who occupied the influential position of leader of the Opposition. Soon enough—by late 1970s—these militant groups became much more than mere foot soldiers. They moved upwards to a subaltern status, and then to a position of alternative leadership. They stamped their influence on the ideology of separatism by giving it a more radical form through their emphasis on political violence. From that influential position, they proceeded to determine the strategy and the tactics for the campaign for separatism. They did it in association with the TULF whenever that was possible, and in opposition to them if they thought it necessary. By the early 1980s, the parliamentarians of the TULF were compelled to cede to them the primary leadership in the separatist struggle. In that position of leadership—and here again there was a remarkable similarity with a radical nationalist Marxist force in the Sinhalese areas of the country, the Janatha Vimukthi Peramuna (JVP)—they scorned parliamentary politics and proclaimed a preference for violent tactics and resort to terrorism.

A study of the LTTE's brief and tempestuous history[21] provides a classic example of two trends in separatist struggles in many parts of the world. Firstly, how the youthful cadres linked to conventional political parties for a common political struggle successfully undermine the leadership of the latter in situations of violent resistance to the state. And secondly, how a small, violent group among the separatist agitators and activists can establish their supremacy among conventional political practitioners through a ruthless and bloody internecine struggle. No similar group in other parts of South Asia and South East Asia illustrates the operation of these two trends better than the LTTE. In less than fifteen years of its establishment (in the 1970s), it succeeded in dominating regional politics in the Jaffna peninsula, and in the Tamil areas in the north and the east of the island. In the process, it systematically rendered its former mentors, as well as its rivals and opponents within the Tamil community, peripheral and dispensable. At the same time, it posed a serious threat to the integrity of the state. One by one its rivals and opponents among the Tamil separatist groups succumbed to the relentless violence of the LTTE. An essential feature of the process was the physical elimination of the leadership of several important Tamil separatist groups, including both its rivals and even one-time associates. Similar was the fate of hundreds of cadres of such groups. During its foundation and modest beginnings in 1972–76, to 1983, the LTTE was only one of several separatist groups operating in the Jaffna peninsula. As we have seen, the LTTE cadres were originally foot soldiers and, occasionally, shock troops in the TULF campaign of opposition to the United Front government in the 1970s. Both drew sustenance and nourishment from the association—the armed separatist groups gaining respectability among the Tamil electorate through their association with the TULF, and the latter, in turn, relying on the muscle power of the former to enforce a conformity to their separatist programme in the north and certain eastern parts of the country.

Between 1977 and 1986, the TULF consistently lost ground to the LTTE. The LTTE established dominance over the political life of Jaffna and the lives of the Tamils of the peninsula that it retained and consolidated since the mid 1980s.[22] Public support for the LTTE increased exponentially after the anti-Tamil riots of 1983, the most destructive post-Independence riot in terms of damage to property and lives lost. It became one of the most significant turning points in Sri Lanka's recent history for another reason as well when regional support from Tamil Nadu became more open than ever. The once covert support from the Indian government for Tamil militants in Sri Lanka became overt, helping transform Tamil separatism into a formidable force. The role Pakistan's ISI played in J&K was played by India's Research and Analysis Wing (RAW) with regard to the Tamil separatists in Sri Lanka.

The LTTE, who were not the favourites of the RAW, quickly seized the leadership of the movement. They were helped by the short-sighted decision of the TULF leadership to seek refuge in Madras after 1983. Actually, the threat to their lives came from the LTTE itself rather than from others, but it was more politic not to blame the former. The LTTE was soon strong enough to engage in a struggle on two fronts. Against the security forces of the Sri Lankan state and in internecine warfare in which it systematically eliminated all rival groups, culminating in the brutal massacre of the Tamil Eelam Liberation Organisation (TELO) group between 1 and 3 May 1986 in Jaffna and the killing of its leader Sri Sabaratnam.

In the early 1980s, there had been at least three prominent Tamil separatist groups and three contending leaders. By 1986, the LTTE under Velupillai Prabhakaran triumphed over them all. It established its position as the only significant Tamil political group and the undoubted heir to the separatist ideology originally propounded by the Federal Party (FP) and its descendent, the TULF, under the leadership of S.J.V. Chelvanayakam. From this point onwards, the LTTE had no real rivals among the Tamil political groups in the island. They set the pace and arranged the political agenda of Sri Lanka's Tamil minority. They also set about eliminating members of the TULF leadership living in Jaffna, killing them at regular intervals from 1989 onwards, including the TULF leader A. Amirthalingam himself that year. While it took the LTTE ten years to physically eliminate the bulk of the TULF leadership, it took them a mere five years to eliminate the leadership of yet another of their rivals, the Eelam People's Revolutionary Liberation Front (EPRLF).[23]

Among the distinguishing features of the LTTE cadres—especially those sent on missions in the Sinhalese areas of the country—was the cyanide capsule they carried, dangling from a gold (or gold-plated) chain. It was an evidence of the ultimate commitment to a cause. It indicated readiness to commit suicide on its behalf rather than surrender or be captured, and showed a level of commitment a more conventionally trained regular army could not match or could not be expected to match. The cyanide capsule, by its very nature, was a weapon of defence. But the underlying philosophy, a readiness to die for a cause, soon had another facet when it involved a conversion of politically inspired suicide into a deadly offensive weapon through the human bomb, male or female, wherein young persons were programmed to kill others in the process of sacrificing their own lives. The LTTE did not invent this macabre killing technique but learned it from others. Perhaps the role models were the two 'suicide bombers' who wrecked the US marines barracks in Beirut on 23 October 1983, killing 241 marines, thereby demonstrating the value of 'suicide bombing' as a technique of guerrilla warfare.[24] This was an incident that attracted enormous international publicity. The first LTTE suicide bomber attack came over three years later, on 5 July 1987, when an LTTE operative using the nom de guerre of 'Captain' Miller, drove a vehicle into a school in Jaffna housing Sri Lankan troops, killing eighteen of them, and killing himself in the process.[25] Once its effectiveness as an offensive weapon was demonstrated, the LTTE set about the business of perfecting the grisly technique of using suicide bombers for the purpose of killing chosen victims, quite often persons of importance in politics, but there would be others as well, less prominent. By carrying out over 200 suicide bomb attacks over thirty years, the LTTE became the most accomplished exponents of this form of terrorism in the world.

The meticulous planning that went into such attacks was demonstrated to the world in the killing of Rajiv Gandhi in May 1991 near Chennai in Tamil Nadu, while he was engaged in campaigning during the general election to the Lok Sabha. The suicide bomber in this instance was a Sri Lankan Tamil female. Two years later, on 1 May 1993, an LTTE male suicide bomber eliminated R. Premadasa, the Sri Lankan President, and a dozen or so of his security and personal entourage. No other guerrilla group in any part of the world could claim that it had killed a former prime minister and leader of a major political party of a large regional power, and followed it up by assassinating the executive President of the state against which it was in rebellion. In October 1994, another suicide bomber killed the presidential candidate of the United National Party (UNP), Gamini Dissanayake. On this occasion, over fifty persons in the gathering were killed, including several former and potential Cabinet ministers and the general secretary of the UNP. This was the largest number of persons killed by a suicide bomber in Sri Lanka up to that time.

The presidential election of December 1999 provided the LTTE with the opportunity to attack President Kumaratunga, this time through a woman, on the night of 18 December. She escaped with minor injuries. Once again, the security staff and bystanders were among those killed. On the same night, another LTTE suicide bomber, a man on this occasion, chose an election rally to kill a former army general expected to get a Cabinet position if the UNP had won. Twelve others were also killed on that occasion and nearly fifty wounded. The killing field was at Ja-ela, a township close to Colombo on the road to the national airport.

All this was apart from a staggeringly long hit-list of politicians and public figures, both Sinhalese and Tamil, blown to bits through time bombs or occasionally shot dead. Among those killed in the latter manner was Lalith Athulathmudali—in April 1993—who had masterminded the military campaign against the LTTE from 1984 to the end of 1988 as minister for national security. In March 1991 the target was Ranjan Wijeratne, who had played a similar role from 1989 to 1991 as deputy minister of defence, and foreign minister. Between 1991 and 1994, the LTTE had eliminated the core of UNP's political leadership of the 1990s.

The LTTE's treatment of minorities who lived in their midst in the Jaffna peninsula was also extraordinarily brutal. During the whole course of Sri Lanka's ethnic conflict, all the incidents of ethnic cleansing were organized solely by the LTTE. The Sinhalese population of the Jaffna peninsula were either killed or compelled to flee. The Sinhalese were a much smaller minority than the Muslims there. The LTTE attacked the Muslims of the northern and eastern provinces at regular intervals between 1984 and 1990, killing 300 of them. This included the massacre of 120 Muslims at an evening prayer gathering in August 1990 at a mosque in Kattankudy in Batticaloa in the eastern province.[26] These attacks culminated in the expulsion, en masse, of the whole Muslim population of the northern province (estimated at 80,000 persons), on 22 October 1990.[27] These victims of ethnic cleansing continued to live as refugees in the Sinhalese areas of the country, either in centres of Muslim habitation or among the Sinhalese.

The reference to the massacre of Muslims while at prayer in a mosque serves as an appropriate point of departure for an examination of another distinguishing feature of the LTTE's attitude: a total lack of concern for religious sentiments and sensitivities of those they regarded as their opponents or enemies. We need to begin with an incident of 14 May 1985 when LTTE guerrillas dressed in military uniforms attacked the ancient city of Anuradhapura—the capital of Sri Lanka for over 1000 years (to the tenth century CE)—and gunned down over 150 persons of all ages, all of them civilians.[28] They also attacked one of the two most sacred sites of Sri Lankan Buddhism, the precincts of the bo- (bodhi) tree, perhaps the oldest identifiable tree in the world, believed to be a sapling of the 'bo-tree' under which the Buddha had attained enlightenment at Gaya in India. This sapling had been brought to Sri Lanka in the time of the Mauryan Emperor, Asoka. The complicity of India's RAW in this attack was suspected from the outset and is now documented through reliable sources.[29] Two years later, on 27 July 1987, a group of LTTE operatives massacred thirty-two *sāmanēras* (young bhikkhus in training) at Arantalawa in the eastern province. Then on 25 January 1998, the LTTE blew up a large section of the Dalada Maligawa (Temple of Tooth) in Kandy, the most sacred site of Buddhist worship for the Sinhalese and for the Theravada Buddhist world. Fortunately, the tooth relic of the Buddha was not harmed, but there was extensive damage done to the building. In attacking the Dalada Maligawa, the LTTE was emulating the Portuguese, Dutch and British invaders of Kandy in the past except that there was no LTTE invasion as such but simply a case of operatives sneaking in to organize the bombing.

Separatist groups which indulge in acts of calculated violence are often accused of being terrorist organizations. But few separatist groups operating in South and South East Asia have deserved this epithet more than the LTTE. Generally, such groups have a terrorist section operating in association with it or as a peripheral unit. With the LTTE, terrorism was part of its core, and has been so from its inception. How much of this terrorism derives from the political culture of internecine warfare and of fratricidal violence in which the LTTE has had to operate, and how much has been due to the nature of its leadership and of its leader, Velupillai Prabhakaran, are matters for debate. There is no doubt, however, that the latter's—Prabhakaran's—personal attributes did have much to do with it. In a perceptive *New York Times* article, John Burns, the well-known Delhi correspondent (1995) of that newspaper, captured the essence of the problem thus:

> He has shown a bloodthirstiness in dealing with opponents that has been compared with some of the cruellest figures in recent Asian history, including Pol Pot of Cambodia.
>
> Prabhakaran who is 40, leads a movement whose deeds, in scale, pale alongside the genocide committed by Pol Pot's Khmer Rouge of the 1970s . . . But what they lack in scope, they make up in brutality . . .
>
> [He] has established a rule of terror in the city of Jaffna. According to scores of accounts from defectors and others who have escaped the Tiger tyranny, many of his own lieutenants have been murdered; Tamils who have criticised him, even mildly or in jest have been picked up, tortured, and executed; others have been held for years in dungeons, half-starved, hauled out periodically for a battering by their guards.[30]

Five years later, much the same assessment of him was made by a distinguished Indian political analyst.[31] It is, by far, the best assessment of the LTTE and its leader that we have had.

Conclusion

The brief studies on separatism in J&K as well as in Sri Lanka in this chapter illustrate some of the facets of terrorism in the politics of South Asia, and provide some clues on how terrorism establishes itself where a political system is under unusual and great stress. Once terrorism becomes a major factor in the political struggle, the prospects of negotiating a settlement become all the more difficult, as has been the case in J&K and Sri Lanka.

To a much greater extent than in Sri Lanka, the situation in J&K illustrates the importance of external factors as a stimulus of terrorism and in the triumph of those most prone to violence in the political contests. J&K is too close to some of the most disturbed parts of the Islamic world, to Afghanistan and to Pakistan, if not to Iran itself, to escape the pull of ideological forces at play there, and of the more violent techniques of political agitation. It is at once a domestic issue, a regional one and an international conflict.

Terrorism came to influence every one of these aspects in the Sri Lankan conflict—the internationalization was done largely by India—but in contrast to J&K, the terrorist features of the separatist struggle have been indigenous in inspiration, much more than through the pull of external factors. The Sri Lankan conflict has owed less to external factors in its origins than that in J&K. But once the conflict erupted and persisted, it was prolonged largely because of the Indian intervention. This Indian intervention—described in later chapters—made the Sri Lankan Tamil problem more complex and violent than it had been before. In his well-known study of the LTTE, M.R. Narayan Swamy, an Indian journalist, made this point very clearly:

> The lack of knowledge and reliable information on the covert role of India in Sri Lanka until the 1987 accord was one of the factors which precluded an intelligent analysis of the Indian involvement. Few Indians were aware of the kind of military muscle India was providing to Tamil groups to take on the government of a

neighbouring country. Most Indian commentators were taken in by New Delhi's repeated assertions that it was not involved in the arming and training of the Tamils. Many Indians genuinely believed that the Indian connection was confined to Tamil Nadu and MGR and that Rajiv Gandhi had probably reversed the clouded involvement begun during his mother's tenure.

No one asked questions when Tamil groups with Indian patronage massacred innocent Sinhalese—although the killings of innocent Tamils by Sri Lankan security forces was [sic] always denounced loudly. It would be pertinent for Indians today to look back and see how the average Sri Lankan must have felt over the brazen patronage extended to people dubbed 'terrorists' by Colombo. Tamil groups based in Tamil Nadu openly claimed credit for attacks on government/military targets in Sri Lanka—without inviting any criticism from the Indian government. Imagine the Punjab or Sind legislature in Pakistan announcing monetary aid to Kashmiri/Khalistani militants. Yet this is precisely what the Tamil Nadu legislature did in 1987.[32]

There is some similarity between the two conflicts in the marginalization of the so-called moderates. The Sri Lankan situation illustrated one unpalatable reality in such conflicts: the moderates propose a programme that is seemingly attractive. But with the passage of time, as events unfold, they lose control and are pushed to the periphery of the new political system. The Sri Lankan situation as regards Tamil politics illustrated this development with a clarity not always available in similar situations. Terrorism was a fact of life in every stage of the political struggle in Sri Lanka, and culminated in the marginalization of the moderates.

In J&K, as in Sri Lanka, those most prone to violence have inherited the system. Such a process has often led to violent conflicts between the separatist activists who triumphed over the moderates. The Kashmiri Muslims have succeeded in ensuring there is a multiplicity of separatist activists. The situation in Sri Lanka was fundamentally different. There the struggle for supremacy among the separatists culminated in the triumph of a single group, the sole 'leaders' of the Tamils. Every other group was crushed, and its leaders and other activists killed. Those who survived were reduced to servility, and they could remain in politics only if they served the needs of the winner. Worse still, not only did the struggle lead to the success of the most violent, it also led to a single individual occupying the top of the pile.

2

Sri Lanka's Prolonged Ethnic Conflict: Negotiating a Settlement

The earlier phases of the Sri Lankan conflict were much less violent than its later form. They also involved negotiations over a settlement. These negotiations were generally unsuccessful. The negotiations were of two types. First of all, they took place locally among the principals in the dispute, the successive governments of Sri Lanka and Tamil political parties. Secondly, they were in the nature of mediation by a regional power, India. (The long-drawn-out but eventually unsuccessful Indian mediation is discussed in considerable detail in a later chapter.) Later on, there was yet another external mediator or facilitator—a representative of the government of Norway. The Norwegian initiative was announced in 2000, and in its very early stage, discussions took place between the Norwegians and the principal Tamil separatist group, the LTTE, and between the Norwegians and the Sri Lankan government. However, this exercise proved to be as futile as the negotiations made by the Indians.

The first category of negotiations, i.e., locally among the disputants, took several forms. The early stages saw discussions and negotiations between the Sri Lankan government, and/or Opposition parties, with the principal Tamil party whose representatives could be described as politically moderate. Such discussions were held in 1956–57, 1960 and 1964–65. While these generally failed, the next set of negotiations in 1979–80 did achieve a measure of success.

With the anti-Tamil riots and disturbances of 1983, there was both a quantitative change in the negotiations and in the demands made by the Tamil representatives. There was also the emergence of an external factor, Indian mediation, which dominated the negotiation processes till 1990. Similarly, the traditionally powerful Tamil political parties were now being edged out by militant or activist separatist groups who entered the bargaining process on their own or were accommodated under Indian auspices. By 1986, the LTTE had secured the position of primacy among the Tamil separatist groups. Through a ruthless resort to force, the LTTE had virtually eliminated all their rivals among such groups, and had sent its mentor, the principal moderate Tamil party, the Tamil United Liberation Front, to the periphery of Tamil politics.[1] From 1986 onwards, the LTTE was a powerful influence in the negotiation processes whether with India or with the Sri Lankan (1986–87) government. After the failure of the Indian intervention, the LTTE became the principal, if not the sole representative, of the Tamils in direct negotiations with the Sri Lankan government (in 1989–90 and in 1995). Between 1991 and 1993, there was a third set of discussions between the government, the principal Opposition party, and the Tamil parties represented in the Parliament. These took the form of a parliamentary select committee. The LTTE, not represented in the Parliament, was not a party to the discussions. But its views could not be ignored by the government, the principal Opposition party or the Tamil groups in the Parliament.

The second category of negotiations, the external one, involved the Indian government in the role of regional hegemon. It covered the period 1983–91. Both the categories of negotiations, the local and the external, had to recognize the importance of a number of crucially important factors in the Sri Lankan political system. The first of these was the emergence and maturation of a separatist movement which in the 1980s enjoyed support from India and, in particular, the state of Tamil Nadu in the Indian Union. Like other Tamil separatist groups with whom they were to engage in a deadly and eventually successful power struggle, the LTTE owed a great deal to the shelter and arms provided by India. When Indira Gandhi returned to power in India in 1980, three years after being defeated in the 1977 Lok Sabha elections, the Sri Lankan Tamil political activists operating in India became beneficiaries of higher levels of support than before, and this naturally strengthened their morale. Though assistance from the Indian government stopped after 1987, the political parties in Tamil Nadu continued to support the LTTE and other Tamil political groups. In fact, the Indian government played a low-key role in Sri Lankan Tamil affairs in the 1990s, leading up to the year 2000. It was no longer the principal external influence in the negotiation process. Nevertheless, it remained a regional power whose views and interests could hardly be ignored, much less excluded, in the negotiations.

The separatist movement became much more complex and began to be viewed with greater hostility by the Sri Lankan government because of the movement's association with the concept of a Tamil homeland within Sri Lanka, a homeland whose territorial boundaries were seen to threaten the interests of the Sinhalese and the Muslims, as well as the country's territorial integrity.

Next, there was the rivalry among the island's minorities, the Tamils and Muslims in particular, with their conflicting political ambitions which had to be accommodated in the negotiations. Just as difficult, perhaps even more so, was the emergence in the 1980s and 1990s of a Tamil diaspora estimated to be between 5,00,000 and 8,50,000 people. All of them were located in western countries, with a very prominent concentration in Canada and in Toronto in particular. This diaspora is now among the most enthusiastic supporters of the LTTE and the establishment of Eelam, a separate Tamil state in Sri Lanka.

Power-sharing and Those Who Shared Power

The introduction of universal suffrage in 1931 in Sri Lanka—the first Crown Colony to enjoy that privilege—marked the beginnings of the democratization of the island's political structure.[2] The issue of power-sharing between the Sinhalese majority group in the island, and the country's minority groups, the Tamils, in particular, assumed importance almost immediately. The national debate on power sharing—such as it was—was conducted on purely political terms. It centred on the representation of the island's ethnic and religious diversity in its national legislature and especially in the Board of Ministers established in 1931, following the first general election conducted there under universal suffrage. That board represented a genuine sharing of power, first between the British and the Sri Lankan political elite with seven Sri Lankan ministers and three British officials, and then among the various ethnic groups' leaders in the island.

The underlying assumption was that the political dimension ought to take precedence over all others. There was very little discussion on concepts and on the prevailing forms of power-sharing arrangements among members of Sri Lanka's political elite, either in public life or in the national legislature or even in academic writings when the political debate began, with some rancour, in the late 1930s and early 1940s.[3] During the negotiations on the issue of transfer of power, the focus continued to be on the issue of representation in the national legislature. The rancour stemmed largely from the demands of

Tamil groups led by their principal political party of the 1940s and 1950s, the Tamil Congress (TC), which stated that seats in the national legislature be divided on a 'fifty-fifty' basis, with the Sinhalese majority (over 70 per cent of the population) entitled to just half the seats, while the minorities, just over 25 per cent of the population, entitled to the other half. Naturally, the Sinhalese refused to accept this, and they were supported in their opposition by the British. After Independence and the mid 1950s, the power-sharing issue was viewed largely in terms of devolution of power from the centre to the regions, with these claims and demands being advocated largely by the representatives of the Tamil minority.

The second distinguishing feature of these early years of democratic debate was the power-sharing arrangement that evolved in political practice from the early 1930s. Throughout the next eighty years or more, it is to political practice that we need to turn our attention in order to study the issue of power-sharing in the island's political and public life. The concern among the principal Sinhalese politicians has not been in expounding theories of power-sharing but in actually practising it in national politics.[4]

The country has a peculiar demographic profile with a concentration of Tamils in the north and to a lesser extent in the east. This has given Tamil parties, beginning with the Tamil Congress of the 1940s, a solid regional base which they have often succeeded in protecting against the efforts of national parties such as the United National Party (UNP), the Sri Lanka Freedom Party (SLFP) and left-wing parties, to field candidates of their own in those regions. The Federal Party (FP), the principal political party of the Tamils since the mid 1950s, and the TULF generally sought an independent role in national politics and in the national legislature, although the FP formed part of Dudley Senanayake's coalition government of 1965–70 led by the UNP during the tenure of which the FP was represented in the Cabinet for three years. In general, the FP and the TULF have succeeded in maintaining their identity as regional parties outside of the national political mainstream.

In contrast, the Muslims have generally been part of the principal political parties, represented at all levels in them, and so part of the national political process. Unlike the Tamils, the Muslims did not have a communal or an ethnic party with a regional base till the emergence of the Sri Lanka Muslim Congress (SLMC) in the 1980s. The SLMC, while drawing its electoral support mainly from the eastern province Muslims, (about a third of the entire Muslim population of the island), has always aspired to expand its support base to embrace all Muslims in the country. Its early promise of achieving such a national status was not fulfilled in the 1989 general election. It was not able to shake the traditional pattern of Muslim membership in the UNP and the SLFP. After the parliamentary election of 1994, however, the SLMC gained a significant presence in the legislature and was able to secure a Cabinet office for its leader as a component party of the governing coalition led by the SLFP. The association of the SLMC with that coalition continued even after the death of its dynamic leader M.H.M. Ashraff in September 2000. It was part of the coalition Cabinet formed in October 2000. Meanwhile, the two national parties, the UNP and SLFP, continue to retain a solid base among the Muslims.

The political behaviour of the Indian Tamils provides a strong contrast to that of the principal Tamil political parties. These parties have generally worked in association with the national parties, with the UNP from 1964 to 1994, and from 1994 onwards with the SLFP. From 1978 onwards, they started contesting as UNP members in seats to the national legislature to the provincial councils and to the local government bodies. All the while, they succeeded in maintaining their distinct identity within the UNP. Meanwhile, in 1999, with the death of S. Thondaman, the founder-leader of the Tamil political party the Ceylon Workers' Congress (CWC), the party split and its members joined either the UNP or the People's Alliance (PA).

In the search for explanations for the failure of the Sri Lankan Tamil leadership to bring the Indian Tamils together in order to form a pan-Tamil political force, the separate geographical location of the two groups is often suggested as the principal factor. This is only partly true. The main settlements of the Indian Tamils are in the central hills and in Colombo (where they now outnumber the Sri Lankan Tamils), and on the outskirts of that city. The more pertinent fact is that the two groups—the Sri Lankan Tamils and the Indian Tamils—do not have much in common except their language. Although both communities are mainly Hindu, the rigours of the Hindu caste system have served to keep them apart as effectively as the location of their settlements. The bulk of the plantation workers and other Indians belong to the scheduled castes in the Indian caste terminology and they are regarded as 'low-caste' Hindus by the Sri Lankan and Jaffna Tamil elite. While the LTTE with their more liberal attitudes to caste did not share this deeply set prejudice of the Sri Lankan Tamil elite, they were not able to make as much headway among the Indian Tamils as they would have liked to do.

There is finally the role of the CWC, the principal trade union of the plantation workers. Quite apart from being the largest trade union in the island, it is also the political party of the Indian Tamils. The leadership of the CWC has successfully protected its trade union membership base from encroachment by the Marxist trade unions, as also by the trade unions which the Tamil political parties, the FP and the TULF, sought to establish. While the CWC is ethnically distinct as a political party, as the authentic voice of the Indian Tamils, it is much less ethnically cohesive as a trade union. It has a significant Sinhalese membership (30 per cent of the plantation workers are Sinhalese). Nor is it exclusively a plantation trade union. It has branches in the industrial and commercial establishments in the city of Colombo and its suburbs, where naturally there is a large Sinhalese component in its membership.

Separatism

The first advocates of separatism among the Tamils were the dissident groups in the Tamil Congress, who broke away from that party when it decided to join the first post-Independence government in 1949. Separatism was thus the successor to the 'fifty-fifty' demand. That the advocates of Tamil separatism in Sri Lanka would seek to construct a case for it on the basis of the modern doctrine of self-determination was only to be expected. But the distinguishing feature of their campaign was the attempt to link it in time to the concept of 'traditional homelands' of the Tamils, 'homelands' that needed to be protected from 'outsiders', themselves citizens of the same country but hailing from other parts.[5] It is important to remember that at the time the concept of 'traditional homelands' of the Tamils of Sri Lanka was being adumbrated in the late 1940s and early 1950s, the first postcolonial government in Sri Lanka under D.S. Senanayake was taking great pains to foster a pluralist democracy under a Cabinet that was multi-ethnic and multi-religious.

From the outset, the concept of 'traditional homelands' of the Tamils was based on a fragile foundation of pseudo-historical data and a cavalier disregard to the composition of the demography of these 'homelands', past and present. In the late 1940s and early 1950s, the concept was inextricably linked with the political ideology of the Federal Party (FP), the progenitor of the Tamil United Front (TUF), 1972–76, and its successor the TULF, and was immanent in the principal political resolution adopted when the FP was established in 1949. At the first national convention of the FP in 1951, a claim was made that

> the Tamil-speaking people in Sri Lanka constituted a nation distinct from that of the Sinhalese in every fundamental test of nationhood . . . and, the 'separate historical past' of the Tamils was emphasised as an essential part of this.

Just five years later (January 1956), S.J.V. Chelvanayakam, the leader of the Federal Party,[6] and subsequently of the TULF, the father of Tamil separatism in Sri Lanka, accused the Sinhalese of proceeding to plunder Tamil lands after Independence

> by colonising the rich agricultural districts in Tamil provinces like Gal Oya and Kantalai . . . which even Sinhalese kings during the days of their most autocratic rule never dared to do . . . The Tamils held these provinces for the last three thousand years and now the Sinhalese, not satisfied with the seven provinces they occupy, are trying to usurp our land as well.

Every sentence in this extract is either historically inaccurate or pure invention. A pattern of distortion of historical facts and fanciful assertions was set for future discussions of separatist claims.

These were claims based on a hazy 'historical' memory of statehood in centuries past, then remembered and newly interpreted (and generally misinterpreted) as a continuous and continuing tradition of independent statehood and an unbroken national consciousness. In less than a decade of its first enunciation in 1949, this theory defined as the 'traditional homelands' of the Tamils, became an indispensable and integral part of the political ideology of the Tamil advocates of regional autonomy and separatism.[7] At this stage, there was very little by way of definition of the boundaries of these 'national areas' of the Tamils except for occasional references to Sri Lanka's northern and eastern provinces. The definition of the boundaries came in the mid 1950s and, amazingly, it was based on a single piece of 'historical' evidence. This evidence was in an introductory paragraph from an extensive document on the administration of justice and the revenue system under the government of the Dutch East India Company prepared by Hugh Cleghorn. Cleghorn was a Scottish academic who had come to the island in the earliest years of British rule in the late 1790s as a political troubleshooter, and later on served as the first colonial secretary. Cleghorn's memorandum had received a much cooler reception from the then governor Frederick North than from the Tamil politicians of the twentieth century.[8]

Tamil politicians and ideologues looking for historical data and evidence in support of their case for the 'traditional homelands' of the Tamils, seized upon one short extract from the document prepared by Hugh Cleghorn—the Cleghorn Minute as it has come to be called. It reads as follows:

> Two different nations, from a very ancient period, have divided between them the possession of the island. First the Cingalese [sic] inhabiting the interior of the country, in its southern and western parts, from the river Wallouve [Walawe] to that of Chilow [sic], and secondly the Malabars [Tamils], who possess the northern and eastern districts. These two nations differ entirely in their religion, language and manners. The former, who are allowed to be the earlier settlers, derive their origin from Siam, professing the ancient religion of that country.[9]

The second part of the last sentence, the Siamese or Thai origins of the Sinhalese, an egregious solecism, would have alerted readers to the limitations of this extract as historical source material. But most of the time ideologues of Tamil separatism carefully omitted this in their resolutions and documents on the theme of the 'traditional homelands'. They used the rest of this extract and ignored the fact that the overall material contained in Cleghorn's memorandum, mistakenly referred to as the Cleghorn Minute, did not support their claims.

One sees this first in claims advanced by the Federal Party, and then its successor the TULF, followed by other Tamil separatist activists—most prominently the LTTE—in defining the territorial limits of the 'traditional homelands' of the Tamils. In recent times, some Tamil scholars have followed the example of the politicians in this regard in quoting this extract without this last sentence, thus opening themselves to the charge of slipshod research in not reading the document in its entirety or indulging in political propaganda by deliberately misleading potential readers by not indicating that a sentence has been omitted.[10] This single extract from Cleghorn's memorandum used in support of their territorial claims has gained the status of scriptural sanctity among the advocates of a separate state for the Tamils of Sri Lanka. Its acceptance has almost become an act of faith, especially when confronted with proof of its unreliability as a historical source.[11]

From the outset, this 'homeland' concept sought to bring under its wings the Muslims too, who were Tamil speakers generally. The attempt was to bring the Muslims under the umbrella of Tamil politics, on the assumption that a common language linked them together, despite a fundamental difference in religion. It is a linkage that the Muslims have persistently rejected because of its assumption of Tamil tutelage over them. Nevertheless, this linkage constantly reappeared in Tamil agitational activity. Secondly, the 'homeland' concept was linked to the purposeful opposition of the Federal Party and its successors in the vanguard of Tamil politics, to the entry of Sinhalese into those parts of the country regarded as 'traditional' Tamil areas.[12] Thus, at the inaugural convention of the Federal Party (or Ilankai Thamil Arasi Kachchi (ITAK) in Tamil) in April 1951, a resolution urged:

> In as much as the Tamil-speaking people have an inalienable right to the territories which they have been traditionally occupying, the first national convention of the ITAK condemns the deliberately planned policy of action of the government in colonising the land under the Gal Oya reservoir and other such areas with purely Sinhalese people as an infringement of their fundamental rights and as a calculated blow aimed at the very existence of the Tamil-speaking nation in Ceylon.

The Sinhalese, the majority group in the island, and the Sri Lankan Tamils, the island's most significant minority, have sharply different perceptions about the nature of the Sri Lankan state. They have diametrically opposite attitudes to decentralization and devolution of power to regional units of administration. Although the early proponents of decentralization (from the 1920s onwards) were Sinhalese, the situation has changed since Independence. The main political parties of the Sri Lankan Tamils have become the principal, if not the sole advocates, of decentralization and devolution. These demands of the principal Tamil political parties have provoked strong opposition, partly at least because of a deliberate obfuscation of the issues by the FP as ideologues of Tamil separatism who spoke of a Tamil state or a kingdom when addressing their followers in the north of the island, and spoke of a federal state in their discussions in Colombo with the Sinhalese. Naturally, opposition to this has been strongest from the Sinhalese both in the mainstream political parties as well as in pressure groups representing Sinhalese-Buddhist opinion.

Many of these Sinhalese fear, if not believe, that the scheme of devolution of power to regional units are likely to lead to a political fragmentation of the island, and thus pose a potent threat to the country's territorial integrity. They nurse fears of a re-emergence of a separate Tamil state (thirteenth century to the early seventeenth century) and its possible linkage to Tamil Nadu in south India.

While the early years of independence were marked by sensible, pragmatic policies aimed at the maintenance of an equitable balance between the majority Sinhalese-Buddhists, and the minorities, the situation changed dramatically in 1954–55. There was the beginning of a campaign in the country for the elevation of Sinhala to the status of the national language. In the process, the language policy adopted in the early 1940s on the eve of transfer of power, whereby Sinhala and Tamil were to replace English as the official language, was unilaterally repudiated.[13] Similar pressures were at work in the rest of South Asia: in India where the boundaries of provinces and states were redrawn to reflect the linguistic profile of the people in those areas, and in East Pakistan where the attempt to impose Urdu as the national language drew impassioned opposition from the Bengali-speaking majority there, culminating in the rout of the state government in the 1954 elections.[14] Thus, in less than a decade after the transfer of power, linguistic nationalism was triumphant in South Asia in general, nowhere more than in Sri Lanka, where the landmark general election of 1956 marked the beginning of Sri Lanka's fall from grace. Ethnic harmony was replaced by ethnic conflict. The mid and late 1950s were marked by outbreaks of riots—in 1956 and 1958.

The change of political mood in the country, especially among the Sinhalese majority, should have given greater salience to the separatist sentiment among the Tamils. Surprisingly, the Tamils' advocacy of separatism did not move on from peaceful agitation to mass protest or sporadic violence till the 1970s. The political agenda of the Tamil leadership continued to emphasize regional autonomy, and the creation of a Tamil or a Tamil-dominated ethno-region, or regions, in the north and the east of the island, if not in the whole of the northern and the eastern provinces. The Tamil Congress which had been the principal political group among the Tamils since the 1940s was overtaken by the Federal Party after 1955–56. As we have seen, the objectives and the title of the Federal Party were ambiguous at best. In Tamil, the title of the party meant nothing less than the Tamil Kingdom Party or Tamil State Party. The Federal Party was deliberately vague about its political objectives. It would stress the case for a federal constitution in place of Sri Lanka's unitary structure. They would do this in all their negotiations and pronouncement in the Sinhalese areas of the island. In the Tamil-dominated Jaffna peninsula and other areas, the emphasis was less on regional autonomy, and more on the creation of a separate state.[15]

Within the Indian Union, the Madras Presidency, or Tamil Nadu as it became later, was one of the main centres of separatist tendencies in the years before Independence. The rise of the Dravida Kazhagam (DK) and later the Dravida Munnetra Kazhagam (DMK) in the early 1950s reflected the same powerful force of linguistic nationalism that was to transform the politics of Sri Lanka in the same period. By the early 1950s, the Congress Party in Madras had become more Tamil than it had been ever before, but this transformation did not prevent it from being supplanted by a more authentic instrument of Tamil regional sub-nationalism, the DK and later the DMK. Between 1952 and 1967, the DMK had risen from a challenger to the Congress to the ruling party there.[16]

The rise of Tamil separatism in southern India did not have as much of an impression and influence, immediately, on the thinking of the Tamil intelligentsia in Sri Lanka as one may have anticipated in a period of ethnic strife and the clash of linguistic nationalisms—Sinhalese and Tamil. Despite the tensions of the mid 1950s and early 1960s, there was no full-blooded separatist movement among the Sri Lankan Tamils in the 1970s. The situation changed decisively in the course of the years when a centre–left coalition of the SLFP and the Marxist Left, the United Front (UF), ruled the country from 1970–77. In its initial stages, it took the form of a reaction to the new policies introduced by the then government: one being the new republican Constitution of 1972, of which the mastermind was Colvin R. de Silva, a Marxist of the Trotskyist Lanka Sama Samaja Party (LSSP), and the other a short-sighted, unilateral change in the policy on admission of students to the island's universities.[17] There was, along with these, an external factor which was to affect the thinking of sections of the Tamil elite. It was the partition of Pakistan in 1971 and the emergence, with the help of India, of the state of Bangladesh, the one example till recent times of a successful separatist movement. The hope and assumption was that what India had done for the people of East Pakistan, it could be persuaded to do for the Tamils of Sri Lanka. Moreover, internal factors within the island provided the essential stimulus to the growth of Tamil separatism in the island. But its expansion and progress to its recent position would have been impossible without the support and encouragement from the political parties of Tamil Nadu and—as we shall see—the more calculating, self-serving and yet vital assistance of the Indian government to Tamil separatism in Sri Lanka in the 1980s.

Devolution of Power

From the mid 1950s to the present day, power-sharing has been linked with the political debate on devolution of power between the governments of the day, and the representatives of

Tamil opinion, especially the FP, and its later manifestation, the TULF. As a result, controversies over devolution of power to the regional bodies replaced other issues as the central theme in such negotiations and became in time the core of the current political crisis in Sri Lanka. Indeed it was the core of all the negotiations from the 1980s towards a political settlement of the island's ethnic conflicts.[18] One question that needs to be answered with regard to devolution is: why has there been so much opposition to it? The explanation should begin with the processes of centralization that had been vigorously pursued by the British during their rule in the island, partly if not entirely because of the centuries-long successful record of Sinhalese resistance to western colonial powers and the assumption that this centralization was necessary to consolidate the power of the colonial state. These processes have proved to be a formidably stable political legacy. Post-Independence regimes were both reluctant and unable to repudiate this legacy till the 1980s. Indeed, there is a striking contrast between the eager experimentation with electoral systems in Sri Lanka— the only country in South Asia to introduce proportional representation for seats in the national legislature as well as the local government bodies—and the hesitance in introducing a second tier of government between the national legislature and the local government bodies. A second tier of government had been recommended as early as 1928 by the Donoughmore Commissioners sent from Britain to review the constitutional structure of the island and to make recommendations for improvements in that structure. It took fifty-two years before such a scheme could be introduced (in 1980).

The first two episodes of negotiation on power-sharing on the basis of a second tier of government, one that would come between the Centre and the local government bodies, took place in 1957 and 1960.[19] The third set of negotiations came in 1964–65.[20] All these were discussions among politicians, representatives of the government (in 1957) and the FP. (With a hung Parliament in 1960, both the SLFP and the UNP negotiated with the TULF for parliamentary support to sustain a stable government. The FP chose to support the SLFP to form and maintain this government.) The discussions of 1956–57 collapsed in the face of an upsurge in the public's opposition to some of the proposals, especially devolution of power, and the creation of a second tier of government. Those of 1960 were less ambitious but not much more successful. The agreements reached were not put into practice by the SLFP when it won power in July 1960. In 1964–65, the negotiations between the Opposition UNP and the FP were conducted in secret. However, the agreement reached on this occasion was leaked to the press. Subsequently, faced with the threat of an extra-parliamentary agitation as had happened in 1957, the UNP-led coalition established in 1965 did not implement the agreement on the establishment of district councils as a second tier of government.

The negotiations between the UNP government that came to power in 1977, and the TULF were conducted at two levels: at the highest political level between J.R. Jayewardene as executive President and the leadership of the TULF, and through a commission of inquiry in 1979–80 consisting of public figures, including representatives of the UNP and FP. The recommendations of this commission, principally the establishment of district councils as the second tier of government, were accepted by the government and implemented in 1981.[21]

However, these district councils did not last very long. In the aftermath of the riots of 1983, the Indian government, entering the Sri Lankan political scene as a mediator with its own avowed political objectives, supported the TULF in insisting on abandoning these councils, and on the establishment of councils based on a larger administrative unit, the provinces. From this point onwards till 1990, the discussions and debates were tripartite, i.e., between the two governments and the Sri Lankan Tamil groups. When the state of Tamil Nadu insisted on its own role, the negotiations had four, not three, parties. We shall turn to India's role in this matter later in this monograph. Something significant needs to be pointed out at this stage. Under Indian pressure, efforts on the part of the Sri Lankan government in the 1980s to extend the scope of creative political initiatives on the devolution of power, hitherto been limited by a lack of political will, continued to face a major constraint in the form of conflicting perceptions within the country on the value of devolution of power as a political and administrative device. There was also another important consideration that the Sri Lankan government had to take note of in the context of the maturation of a separatist movement among the Tamils, and one that had support from all the Tamil political parties and groups: Would the granting of greater autonomy encourage the secessionist movement to go beyond autonomy to outright secession? These debates were apart from the parallel but subsidiary debate on the politically acceptable or viable size of the unit of devolution—whether it should be district or province. The pressures that emerged from these contentious issues stretched the limits of political action available to Sri Lankan politicians in power dangerously close to the breaking point. The alternatives were either their electoral defeat or major outbursts of violent opposition. The latter could be seen in the anti-government riots of late July and early August 1987 during the signing of an accord between the governments of India and Sri Lanka in which the issue of devolution of power in Sri Lanka was an important feature. The Indian intervention in Sri Lanka's ethnic conflict is examined in greater detail in a later chapter. Suffice it to say here that the popular opposition to the accord signed between the two governments continued when the agreement was implemented as the Provincial Councils Act 42 of 1987, and incorporated as the thirteenth amendment to Constitution of 1978. This opposition was both wider in its geographical spread, and infinitely more violent than in 1958.

The debate on devolution of power in Sri Lanka, and the passions that discussions on regionalism and regional autonomy arouse, illustrate two vital themes. The first concerns the dilemmas that confronted the political establishment in the recently independent nations in conceding legitimacy to regional loyalties. The political establishments in these nations, as legatees of departing imperial powers, passionately protected their territorial inheritance in the shape of the state bequeathed to them at the time of the transfer of power. They regarded centralized authority as an essential political and administrative instrument at their disposal. They often justified this by arguing that centralization was essential for the introduction and management of processes of social change designed to eliminate poverty. In such a situation, anything likely to encourage, if not lead to, communal or ethnic fragmentation was regarded with utmost suspicion. More importantly, once the threat of separatism appeared as an objective fact of political life, the choice was between the tolerance of those cultural traditions and ethnic identities that would fall well short of secession—in fact, permitting the full expression of such cultural traditions—and the suppression of secessionist demands by armed force, where necessary, if there were signs that secessionist aspirations were striving for fulfilment. On this matter, India's treatment of its variety of separatist struggles, in the north-west and the north-east of that country, and Sri Lanka's responses to Tamil separatist activity provide excellent examples. Devolution of power to the regions was recognized as having advantages, if not positive value, in generating political participation in decision-making at a provincial or district level. This principle was immanent in the two abortive attempts at establishing provincial and district-level councils, in 1957 and 1968 respectively, in Sri Lanka, and in the more productive exercise which led to the District Development Councils Act of 1980, and the more controversial Provincial Councils Act 42 of 1987 incorporated as the 13th amendment to the Constitution of 1978. Once the Provincial Councils bill and the thirteenth Amendment to the Constitution were approved by the Parliament on 12 November 1987, the moribund provincial structure bequeathed by the British got a fresh lease of life because of the insistence of the Tamils—a pressure that went back to the late 1950s—that a province rather than a district was the most appropriate unit of devolution.

The essential feature of the system of provincial councils introduced in 1987 was that they were modelled on the powers of the states of the Indian Union. But the difference was that the Sri Lankan provincial councils would operate within the framework of the country's constitutionally entrenched unitary system. The TULF and some of the Tamil separatist groups continued to press for a regional unit encompassing the northern and the eastern provinces as a Tamil-dominated ethno-region, a political manifestation of the concept of 'traditional homelands' of the Tamils in Sri Lanka, which the Federal Party and the TULF popularized in the politics of the Tamils and elevated to the status of a principal demand. But the UNP governments of the period 1977–94, held out against a permanent merger of these two provinces, as did the SLFP and representatives of Sinhalese-Buddhist opinion, and the Muslims too, including representatives of the Muslims residing in the eastern province.

Not surprisingly, differences of opinion over the administrative and spatial content of the devolution, between the Sri Lankan governments, and representatives of Tamil opinion, have proved to be virtually unbridgeable. A great deal of political adjustment of differences has nevertheless been achieved. This despite a general recognition among Sinhalese politicians that the capacity of devolution of authority to regional units, be they districts or provinces or something larger than provinces, to reduce ethnic conflict is more limited than the enthusiastic advocates of it—almost entirely Tamils—are willing to concede. That's because the principal and the most violent separatist group, the LTTE, has driven its forebears and rivals to the margins of Tamil politics, and would accept nothing less than a separate Tamil state.

When the district councils were established in 1980, the second tier of government came into existence fifty years after the proposals for such councils were first mooted, and forty years after the national legislature had approved such a scheme in principle. However, there was no longer a national consensus in support of them in the 1980s, unlike in the 1930s and 1940s. We need to examine the reasons for this. There is, first of all, the close proximity of the Jaffna region in the north of Sri Lanka to Tamil Nadu in southern India, a state given to frequent celebrations of Tamil cultural identity and which in the not-so-distant past, was a centre of separatist sentiment in India. Influential groups within the state government—and Opposition—there have encouraged, nurtured and protected Tamil separatist groups from Sri Lanka. Thus, devolution of greater power to provincial councils is problematic, even when it is conceded, because of fears that it could serve as a spur to separatist pressures rather than act as an effective check on these pressures in the north and the east of the island. Large sections of the Sinhalese view the Tamils' pressure for devolution of power as the first step in an inevitable progression towards the separation of the Tamil majority areas of the country from the Sri Lankan polity. Historical memories contribute greatly to the disquiet and apprehensions the Sinhalese feel about south India. There is a popular perception, fashioned by memories of events of centuries past, especially involving south India, that it is the single most powerful and persistent threat confronting Sri Lanka and the Sinhalese.

In the early years of independence, the Tamils of the north and the east of the island had showed little inclination to identify themselves with the Tamils of Tamil Nadu. Nevertheless, the Sinhalese had feared this possibility, and the campaign for a federal structure for the island served to aggravate these fears. Those in the forefront of the Tamils' agitation for devolution of power have always been vague, deliberately or unconsciously, in the terminology used in their arguments. Moreover, the distinction between provincial autonomy, states' rights in a federal union, and a separate state have been blurred by a fog of verbiage and obfuscation. The close links established in more recent times between the Tamil political groups ranging from the TULF to various separatist groups, with the government and the Opposition in Tamil Nadu, naturally aggravated the situation. It was made even worse by the establishment of training camps in the 1980s in Tamil Nadu for Sri Lankan Tamil separatist activists who made forays into the northern and the eastern coastal regions of Sri Lanka from these camps. The result has been that the matter of devolution of power, which was, and should be, a purely Sri Lankan matter has taken on a cross-national dimension. The most conspicuous features of this cross-national dimension have been India's role as mediator in the negotiations between the Sri Lankan government and the representatives of Tamil opinion in the 1980s, and the entry of the Indian Peace Keeping Force (IPKF) into the north and the east of the island in the period 1987–90.

Pressure for strengthening of the devolution concept is limited to the Tamils, and largely to the Tamils living in the north and the east of the island, where they are either a majority or form a substantial minority. There is no pressure—on the contrary, there's strong opposition—on this issue from other ethnic groups. Quite apart from the opposition of the Sinhalese majority to most schemes of devolution of power, the Muslim minority, especially those in the eastern province, have been deeply concerned about the dangers of their political marginalization in a decentralized political and administrative structure. The mass expulsion of the Muslims from the whole of the northern province by the LTTE on 22 October 1990, the sole example of ethnic cleansing in Sri Lanka, naturally strengthens these fears. Many, if not most of the expelled Muslims, live in refugee camps in the Sinhalese areas of the country.

The critical stumbling block in the negotiations on devolution in Sri Lanka, since the late 1980s, has been the demographic profile of the eastern province, where the Tamils are a minority, comprising only 40 per cent of the population, and perhaps even less than that today. The main Tamil separatist group, the LTTE, on its part, would accept nothing short of a separate Tamil state linking the northern and the eastern provinces. The linkage of these two provinces as a Tamil ethno-region was first advocated by the FP and the TULF. This has been taken over by the other Tamil groups, including the LTTE. The deadlock over the linking of the eastern province to the northern province continued till 2007. This devolution of power to units larger than a district or a province is perceived by the Sinhalese as threatening the territorial integrity of the island, while a smaller group, the Muslims, feel threatened by this in a more immediate way, since the Tamils are certain to dominate the affairs of this projected large territorial unit, a province or a regional unit linking the two provinces. A section of the Muslims led by the Sri Lanka Muslim Congress (SLMC) has responded by urging the creation of a separate administrative unit in the eastern province in which the Muslims would constitute a majority. A more elaborate version of this demand called for a Muslim province, with its main base in the eastern province but with enclaves or sub-units elsewhere such as in the Mannar district of the northern province.

Mediation and the Indian Intervention

Successive Sri Lankan governments resorted to a two-pronged policy in dealing with the threat posed by the Tamil separatist activists. A military response was often accompanied by political negotiations, while the priority given to one or the other of these depended on the success achieved or the political pressures exerted by and from India. The salient features of this two-pronged policy are summarized here. Throughout the period 1984 to 1986, negotiations for a political settlement continued sporadically against the background of regular outbursts of ethnic violence, especially in the north and the east of the island, and conflicts between the security forces and the Tamil guerrillas and terrorist groups. India was drawn into the conflict in the 1980s as a mediator but eventually became a combatant.[1] She had other roles as well, especially in internationalizing the conflict through the use of her diplomatic missions in the more important capital cities of the western world and in initiating or lending support to moves at the UN and in UN sub-committees to espouse the cause of Sri Lanka's Tamils.

India's support for the Tamil separatist cause was covert till 1983. But the official Indian policy never acknowledged the existence of bases, training camps and the provision of weapons. There was, above all, the Tamil Nadu factor. Seldom has a constituent unit (a province or a state) of one country influenced the relationship between it and a neighbouring country with the same intensity, persistence, and to the same extent that Tamil Nadu has been able to, as in the case of India's relations with Sri Lanka. The India–Tamil Nadu–Sri Lanka relationship is thus a unique one in international affairs. Admittedly, the Indian Central government's role with regard to the Tamil problem in Sri Lanka, from the 1980s to the present day, has been more complex than merely reacting to the pressures of domestic politics in Tamil Nadu. Nevertheless, concerns about the latter have always been an important consideration. The state governments in Tamil Nadu have provided Sri Lankan Tamil separatist activists with sanctuaries, training and bases. These have been apart from the financial and moral support—as well as the political pressure on behalf of Tamil separatists in Sri Lanka—that have been offered within the national political system in India. Not only did the Central government—under Indira Gandhi and then her son and successor Rajiv Gandhi—connive in the provision of such facilities by Tamil Nadu, it also tolerated the provision of training facilities and the existence of camps and bases in other parts of India. This began with Indira Gandhi in the early 1980s, that is to say, well before the riots of July 1983 in Sri Lanka. The extent of that support dropped sharply in the late 1980s when the Indian army moved to the Tamil areas in the north and the east of Sri Lanka in 1987–90 under the terms of the Indo-Sri Lanka Accord of 1987. However, as far as Tamil Nadu was concerned, the support did not disappear entirely.[2]

It took the assassination of Rajiv Gandhi in 1991 by the LTTE, on Indian soil, to force a noticeable change in the attitude of the Indian government towards the LTTE. Rajiv Gandhi's assassination by the LTTE was the direct result of the failure of India's role as mediator in Sri Lanka's ethnic conflict. The mediator's role had first been taken up under his mother's government as a calculated political response to the anti-Tamil riots of July 1983 in Sri Lanka. This role took on a more formal shape after 1987 under the leadership of Rajiv Gandhi himself. The mediatory process had three facets: it attempted to resolve, manage and settle Sri Lanka's ethnic conflict. In each of these functions, the Indian government had to respond to the demands and concerns of the LTTE. Throughout the period of 1983–90, India never abandoned her role of being a principal in the dispute, and the presumed protector of the interests of the Tamil minorities of the island. The result was that India was at once a negotiator and an advocate. After the signing of the Indo-Lanka Accord of 1987, the mediator found itself in the role of active participant and continued in that role to the middle of 1990, during which it fought the LTTE in the north-east of Sri Lanka. It was a unique example in the history of mediation in ethnic conflict where the mediator took on the role of combatant, and the presumed guardian of an ethnic minority waged an eventually unsuccessful military campaign against the principal political group of that minority as well as its military wing which India and Tamil Nadu had helped to build.

Between August 1983 and till the end of 1988—i.e., during most of the second-term of the presidency of J.R. Jayewardene—there was a series of high-level negotiations between the Indian prime minister (Indira Gandhi, up to 1984 and Rajiv Gandhi, thereafter) and President J.R. Jayewardene. There were either direct talks between them or between the Sri Lankan President, his colleagues and officials and the senior Indian officials designated for the purpose by the Indian government. From the Indian side, these talks were conducted either by a special official such as G. Parathasarathy (from 1983 to the end of 1984) or successive Secretaries of the ministry of external affairs.[3] G. Parathasarathy, for instance, was present in Sri Lanka during a major conference called by the Sri Lankan

President in 1984, between the government and a large number of Sri Lankan political groups, including representatives of Tamil parties. Occasionally, Indian ministers were also sent to Sri Lanka for talks with the Sri Lankan President, Cabinet ministers and others.

One initiative taken by the Indian government was to call a conference in Thimpu in Bhutan in July/August 1985 between representatives of the Sri Lankan government and the Tamil political parties, including the TULF, the LTTE and other Tamil separatist groups. After the failure of these talks, a more successful set of discussions was held in Delhi in August 1985 in an effort to resolve the Sri Lankan crisis. Thus, a draft accord, the Delhi Accord as it came to be called, was initialled on 30 August 1985.[4] Although the Tamil political parties under pressure from the LTTE refused to sign the Delhi Accord, it formed the basis of what later became the Indo-Sri Lanka Accord of July 1987.

In the meantime, in 1986, after the failure of the Thimpu talks, and the signing of the Delhi Accord, there was yet another set of discussions in Sri Lanka. Initiated by the Sri Lankan government, it brought together a large number of Sri Lankan political parties and groups. The TULF attended these talks. They were persuaded to do so by the Indian government. While these talks too ended in failure, they were not without influence on the Indo-Sri Lanka Accord of July 1987.

Just prior to the eventual signing of this accord by the President of Sri Lanka, and the Indian prime minister, there had been a few months of bad relations between the two governments when the Sri Lankan government engaged in an attempt to re-establish control over the Jaffna peninsula. The Sri Lankan army inflicted a number of defeats on the LTTE, and had them on the run—in the Vadamarachchi campaign under General Ranatunga. On that occasion, the Indian government threatened intervention in case the Sri Lankan forces entered Jaffna, the administrative capital of the northern province. The intervention included an 'invasion' of Sri Lankan air space by Indian aircraft which engaged in airdropping food in Jaffna town and its neighbourhood. The move had the desired effect of stopping the advance of the Sri Lankan army.[5] India thus saved the LTTE, and the latter lived to fight another twenty-three years or so—till 2009.

The Indo-Sri Lanka Accord of July 1987, like the other well-publicized accords negotiated by Rajiv Gandhi in India (in Punjab and Assam), failed in nearly all its objectives. Worse still were the consequences that flowed from it—apart from the failure to pacify Jaffna, it precipitated a serious political crisis in the Sinhalese areas of the country. The signing of the accord had led to violent protests in and around Colombo and parts of the south-west coast. It triggered some of the most serious anti-government riots since Independence. The government forces took three days to a week to quell the riots and they were able to do so only because of the rapid transport by air (by the Indian air force) of several thousand Sri Lankan troops from Jaffna. Although the IPKF (Indian Peace Keeping Force) was never seen outside the north and the east of the island (save perhaps in the north-central province on their way to the east coast), its shadow was cast across the country's political landscape. Its presence in the country was used as a political tool against the government, by a combination of the SLFP and the now-revived Janatha Vimukthi Peramuna (JVP)[6]—especially by the JVP, for whom opposition to the IPKF became the catalyst for violent political agitation, and for sporadic but calculated acts of violence in the Sinhalese areas of the country. The JVP is a left-wing nationalist group which has led two insurrections against Sri Lankan governments, the first in 1971 and the second in 1987–90.

With the signing of the Indo-Sri Lanka Accord on 29 July 1987, the IPKF arrived in the island. These peacekeepers soon became combatants against the LTTE forces and their allies. They grew from a small force of 5000–7000 men into an Indian army of around 1,00,000 men. They became almost as large as the Soviet army then in Afghanistan, and bigger than the British content of the Indian army of the Raj in its heyday in the late nineteenth and the early twentieth century. The Indian forces operated independent of the Sri Lankan forces. Despite assertions by the then Sri Lankan President that the IPKF was subject to his direction and authority, the ground reality was that the IPKF forces took their orders from the Indian government. Under pressure from India, President J.R. Jayewardene used his emergency powers to amalgamate the northern and the eastern provinces into one unit, an amalgamation that continued till 2007 when the Sri Lankan Supreme Court declared the whole process as unconstitutional.

The Indian army had intervened in the Bangladeshi independence struggle[7] in the late 1960s and early 1970s to secure the success of separatism. In the case of its intervention in Sri Lanka, the initial step was taken in 1987 in order to prevent the Sri Lankan armed forces from defeating the Tamil separatists—principally the LTTE—and regaining control of the disaffected areas in the north and the east of the island. The Sri Lankan armed forces had the LTTE on the run at that time. Having secured the objective of thwarting the Sri Lankan forces, the Indian army then fought the LTTE for a little over two years as part of the Indian government's own political agenda of opposition to the establishment of a separate Tamil state, for fear of its ripple effects in India itself where the government was engaged in quelling the separatist movements in Kashmir, Punjab and the north-east. Thwarting the Sri Lankan forces was achieved but not the third of its objectives, that of inflicting a telling defeat on the LTTE to make it more receptive and subservient to India's regional strategic objectives. The success with which the LTTE resisted the Indian army during the latter's intervention in Sri Lanka demonstrated the limitations inherent in external intervention in separatist struggles.

The IPKF's presence in the north and the east of the island was not without its advantages to the Sri Lankan government. Sri Lanka's expenditure on defence dropped noticeably after mid 1987. The Indian government bore the heavy expenditure involved in the pacification of the north and the east. However, this decline in defence spending on the part of Sri Lanka might have been more substantial if the threat posed by the JVP had not proved to be so serious. Under such circumstances, no reduction in the number of defence personnel was possible. On the contrary, because of the JVP threat, the army was expanded—by 1990, it had three divisions instead of the two that had been in existence—as was the police.

With R. Premadasa's election as President in December 1988, the IPKF's presence in the north and the east of the island became a point of contention between the Sri Lankan government and the Rajiv Gandhi government. Negotiations began almost immediately after the new Sri Lankan President assumed office for the removal of the IPKF from Sri Lanka. These proved to be both long-drawn-out and acrimonious. Eventually, the IPKF was withdrawn on a timetable determined by the new Indian government led by V.P. Singh. The process of withdrawal was completed by March 1990, thus bringing to an end an Indian intervention in Sri Lanka's ethnic conflict which had begun eight years earlier under Indira Gandhi.[8]

By the time the IPKF was withdrawn, there had been a surprising rapprochement between the Premadasa government and the LTTE, drawn together in a common opposition to the IPKF, and in the hope that the hostilities of a decade could be overcome by negotiations. A ceasefire was effected by the two sides, and the discussions began around May 1989 in Colombo. Senior Cabinet ministers led the government delegation, assisted by senior administrators and military officials. President Premadasa took the negotiations seriously enough to join in the discussions occasionally and to meet the LTTE delegates, most of whom were in the higher rungs of that party's leadership.

The period of peace (after May 1989) that followed the ceasefire in the north and the east, had one important consequence. It enabled the army to meet the ferocious challenge posed by the JVP. Thus it is grimly ironic but nevertheless true that the final phase of the IPKF presence in the island, and the negotiations between the government and the LTTE helped the Sri Lankan security forces—in particular the army—to meet and overcome the threat posed by the JVP.

In retrospect, the prolonged discussions between the government and the LTTE gave the latter most of the advantages that ensued. The Indian government had hoped and believed that the Sri Lankan armed forces would move in to occupy the camps vacated by the IPKF in the north and the east of the island. However, lulled into a false sense of security by the cordiality of the initial talks between the Premadasa government and the LTTE, the Sri Lankan troops did not move in. Even the large police force in parts of the east were withdrawn. Thus, the LTTE forces were permitted to establish themselves in the areas vacated by the IPKF in the north and the east of the island.

By the time the talks broke down—in June 1990—the LTTE seemed on the verge of winning at the bargaining table what they had not been able to win on the battlefield either from the Sri Lankan army or the IPKF. There had been little or no discussion on the mechanics of devolution of power, such as on whether any changes were required in the system established in 1987–88.

The LTTE broke the ceasefire agreement, and the renewed battle between it and the Sri Lankan forces continued till 2009–10 with the inevitable consequence that Sri Lanka's defence expenditure increased to meet the costs of the war. These costs involved expansion of the manpower resources of the security services, and purchase of military hardware.

After the failure of the talks between the LTTE and the government, the latter turned to another set of negotiations, this time in the form of a parliamentary select committee. All the political parties represented in the national legislature met in this select committee chaired by a senior Opposition (SLFP) MP. The discussions on the select committee related entirely to the devolutionary process. The government and the SLFP were then able to agree—for the first time—on a system of devolution but were unable to convince the Tamil parties that the sophisticated constitutional system devised to coordinate activities in the northern and the eastern provinces was the only politically viable mechanism. The Tamil parties kept insisting on the merger of the two provinces (Parliamentary Series, Select Committee, No. 47, November 1993).

The People's Alliance and the LTTE

The left-of-centre People's Alliance (PA) coalition which won the parliamentary elections of August 1994, inherited these problems. Its immediate response was to accord high priority to the issue of restoring peace in the country. Its leader, Chandrika Kumaratunga, projected herself as a peace candidate at the parliamentary and presidential election campaigns of August and November 1994. After a narrow victory in the parliamentary election held in August 1994, she went on to secure an overwhelming one in November that year in the presidential election. Among the principal features of this latter victory was the massive vote she received from the Tamil minority, including the Indian Tamils, wherever it was possible for the Tamils to vote (i.e., outside the Jaffna peninsula of the northern province).

With this solid mandate, the PA immediately invited the LTTE for negotiations. The talks began in October 1994 in the wake of its parliamentary victory . They were briefly interrupted by the assassination (by the LTTE) of Gamini Dissanayake, Kumaratunga's UNP opponent in the presidential election—on 23 October—but were resumed with the objective of exploiting the PA's electoral triumph in November 1994 in order to negotiate a political settlement. As a gesture of conciliation to the LTTE, the government decided that the talks should be held in Jaffna, in LTTE-held territory. Thus, the second set of direct negotiations with the LTTE by a Sri Lankan government took place (less than five years after the first), wherein two sets of talks were held in 1994–95. While the LTTE was represented by senior personnel in its political hierarchy, the government's nominees were senior officials and others. Surprisingly, there were no politicians in the Sri Lankan government's delegation. While the negotiations with the Premadasa government had lasted for over a year before they broke down, the LTTE's talks with the new government collapsed within a few weeks, by 19 April 1995 to be exact.[9] Needless to say, the two parties blamed each other for the collapse of the talks but the available evidence would justify the conclusion that, as in 1990, the intransigence of the LTTE was the principal factor. The LTTE attacked Sri Lankan security forces notwithstanding the formal ceasefire. Shortly afterwards, the violence was directed at the Sinhalese living in the eastern province.

Eventually, the government decided on a more vigorous course of action: a military campaign in the Jaffna peninsula, the LTTE's stronghold. The campaign began in early July 1995 and despite some setbacks in the initial stages, it culminated later in the year in the capture of Jaffna town and parts of the Jaffna peninsula with a surprisingly small number of civilian casualties. The next stage began in May 1996 when the army drove the LTTE out of the entire Jaffna peninsula. This was the second time in the space of ten years that the Sri Lankan army was engaged in a military campaign in the Jaffna peninsula. In July 1986–87 when the first attack was launched, it was stopped in its tracks, after some early success, by the threat of Indian intervention. On the second occasion, India maintained a studied silence, evidence that it had no intention of intervening. The third phase began in May 1997, in an attempt to establish control over the A9—the road from Vavuniya to Jaffna—the main supply route as it was called. After some initial success in this campaign—named Operation Jayasikuru—there emerged stiff resistance from the LTTE. As a result, it had to be terminated later in 1998.

As they had done in 1987–90 when the Indian army brought the Jaffna peninsula under its control, the LTTE moved their operations headquarters to the areas just south of the peninsula, Kilinochchi and Mullaitivu, and retained control over them. In September 1996, the Sri Lankan army captured Kilinochchi town after a long battle with the LTTE (but lost control of it again by mid 1998). The Mullaitivu district then served as the last LTTE stronghold and its *soi-disant* administrative capital. Over ten years earlier, the LTTE cadres had survived in the forests of Kilinochchi and Mullaitivu districts for over two years withstanding the efforts of the IPKF to dislodge them. The low-intensity conflict in the country's north-east continued into the last quarter of 2000. In a brief and brisk campaign in November 1999, the LTTE recaptured townships and villages that they had lost to the army eighteen months earlier. The campaign culminated in the capture of the army base of Elephant

Pass, in April 2000, and the LTTE seemed poised to expel the government forces from Jaffna and the Jaffna peninsula. But the Sri Lankan army fought back and within a month the LTTE advance lost its early momentum, and by mid June 2000, the LTTE's threat to the government's control over Jaffna town and the Jaffna peninsula had clearly receded.

The PA's military campaign was based on the assumption that the LTTE could be defeated militarily or at least weakened to a point wherein it would settle for something much less than the separate state for which it had fought for so long. Certainly, the fall of Jaffna town and the loss of control over the Jaffna peninsula was a significant reverse for the LTTE, a reverse which could have meant a decisive defeat if they were unable to prevent the Sri Lankan armed forces from consolidating their hold on that densely populated region.

The other facet of the PA's programme was more ambiguous and had less to show for it. This was the attempt to draft a new Constitution for the country, incorporating a stronger commitment to the issue of devolution of power to the provinces, and so a more quasi-federal Constitution. The hope was that devolution on such a scale would form a politically viable alternative to separatism, and that it could form the basis of a new set of talks for the resolution of the conflict. When the proposals were first published in 1995, they attracted considerable criticism in the Sinhalese areas on the grounds that they went too far in the direction of federalism. In response to this criticism, the proposals were amended in 1996 and 1997. A belated attempt was made to reach a consensus with the UNP on these proposals in the hope that a two-third majority of parliamentarians could be secured to introduce the new Constitution. By early August 2000, the attempt to secure such a majority in the Parliament had clearly failed. So rather than facing defeat, the proposals were withdrawn. The attempt to introduce this new Constitution attracted wide public protests, not on the scale of July 1987 against the Indo-Sri Lanka Accord but wide enough to make it clear to the government that there was no consensus possible in the Sinhalese areas of the country for such a constitutional reform. Once the PA failed to secure a majority in the parliamentary elections of October 2000 (the PA received 45 per cent of the national vote), the prospects for the introduction of a new Constitution became bleaker.

The survival of the LTTE against the IPKF and the Sri Lankan armed forces could be explained partly by the LTTE's skills in guerrilla tactics, partly by divided counsels within the Indian government and its bureaucratic machinery, and partly by other factors as well. Among these other factors, the most important was the inestimable advantage of easy access to the sea, something that few other separatist groups in South and South East Asia possess. The indented coast of the Jaffna peninsula with its isolated coves provides both access and security, access to men and arms from abroad—India and South East Asia, in particular—and security because the state's, whether Sri Lankan or Indian, large naval craft are much less effective in such waters than the small boats and catamarans used by the smugglers. The fact is that throughout the period of its confrontation with the IPKF, the LTTE was still able to send its wounded cadres across to the Tamil Nadu coast for medical attention, while smuggling of arms from Tamil Nadu and elsewhere continued but on a more modest scale than earlier.

From the very outset, the LTTE made optimum use of its access to the sea. First of all, this helped in transporting narcotics arriving from the Golden Crescent and the Golden Triangle, to the West, particularly to Europe. This had begun as early as 1984.[10] Narcotics provided the LTTE with its principal source of income till very recently when the smuggling of people—generally Tamils from Sri Lanka—to western Europe and Canada became as lucrative, if not more so.[11] Access to both sides of the Indian Ocean made it easy to smuggle weapons, originally from India, but later from sources in South East Asia—Myanmar, Thailand and Cambodia—weapons ranging from small arms to heavy artillery. Access to the seas also gave the LTTE the means of transporting its seriously wounded cadres across to medical centres in Tamil Nadu for treatment. The LTTE was perhaps unique among separatist groups in developing its own fleet of merchant ships which combined clandestine movement of weapons and narcotics with the more humdrum business of commercial transport of goods. This grew to a fleet of about twenty freighters, generally heavily armed and flying flags of convenience—of Panama, Honduras and Liberia. While the Indian government internationalized the Sri Lankan conflict in the 1980s, the LTTE took the process of internationalization several notches higher, both through the virtually global reach of its merchant fleet, and its exploitation of the support it received from the Tamil diaspora.

The Moros of Philippines have a similar advantage of access to the sea, and like the Sri Lankan Tamils, they have access to parts of neighbouring states with friendly co-ethnics who, in this instance, share a common religion—with the Malays of South East Asia. The substantial difference is that they have not had the advantage of direct intervention by a regional power on their behalf as was the case with India and Tamil separatism in Sri Lanka. The most significant difference between the LTTE and the Moros, however, is the LTTE's large support base among the expanding and influential Tamil diaspora communities in Europe and in North America and Australia. The origins of that diaspora go back to the 1960s with the migration of Tamils of the professional classes. The numbers increased in the 1970s but not as much as they did in the 1980s and 1990s.

The principal presence of this diaspora is in Canada. The

Canadian city of Toronto houses a Sri Lankan Tamil population of over 1,50,000, making it the city with the largest concentration of Sri Lankan Tamils in any part of the world. Emigration to Canada began in the 1970s and increased in numbers after the riots of 1983 when the Canadian government opened the doors to Tamil asylum seekers. While professionals were especially welcome, the overwhelming majority who came to Canada were people without any skills, generally young men from the Jaffna peninsula. It is estimated that about 5,00,000 to 8,50,000 Sri Lankan Tamils are living in North America (Canada, in particular) and in Western Europe.[12] The importance of this diaspora to the LTTE as a source of funds and as support bases for lobbying could not be overestimated. As a US State Department publication, *Patterns of Global Terrorism*, put it in 1995, this diaspora is

> a significant overseas support structure for fundraising, weapons procurement and propaganda activities ... [Its] overt organisations support Tamil separatism by lobbying foreign governments and the United Nations. The LTTE also uses its international contacts to procure weapons, communications, and bomb-making equipment ... [exploiting the] Tamil communities in North America, Europe and Asia to obtain funds and supplies for its fighters in Sri Lanka.[13]

Subsequent annual issues of this official review have repeated this point.

Apart from Toronto in Canada, the LTTE had two principal propaganda centres and offices, both in Europe—London, where its showpiece Eelam House is located, and Paris. In addition to its own network of supporters, the LTTE had the support of several front organizations:[14] the World Tamil Association (WTA), World Tamil Movement (WTM), the Federation of Associations of Canadian Tamils (FACT) and the Ellalan Force.

The last of these operated in Sri Lanka and overseas. Others not identified in this report (the state department's 'Patterns of Global Terrorism') included the International Federation of Tamils (IFT) in the UK, the Swiss Federation of Tamil Associations and the Tamil Co-ordinating Committee in Norway, as well as the Illankai Tamil Sangam in the USA.

Apart from the fact that no other separatist group in South and South East Asia had the support of a diaspora as large as this, there is the advantage that large numbers of these groups are highly trained and highly competent professionals. They have provided the LTTE with a propaganda machine which the Sri Lanka government is not able to match.

One of the principal setbacks that the LTTE suffered in recent times had to do with the ban imposed on it by the US in 1997, calling it a terrorist group. The LTTE failed in its efforts to get this decision revoked. The Canadian government, too, became much more wary of Tamil asylum seekers than they were in the past.[15] In addition, there was the issue of the assassination of Rajiv Gandhi for which Prabhakaran was wanted in India. As late as November–December 2000, there were requests for his extradition to India to be tried for masterminding that assassination.

When the Sri Lankan government resumed talks with the LTTE in 2005, this time with a Norwegian facilitator, there was little room for optimism that there would be an easy, much less early, resolution of the conflict. The negotiations were as nasty and short as they had been previously. Both sides would have hoped to enter the negotiations from a position of strength relative to the other. But neither had a decisive advantage. Certainly, had the LTTE succeeded in its efforts to capture Jaffna in May 2000, and expel the Sri Lankan army from the Jaffna peninsula, it would have negotiated from an obvious position of strength. But that did not take place. So it returned to its propaganda campaign by publishing its own version of why the talks with the Kumaratunga government in 1995 had failed—this viewpoint was presented in their ideologue, A. Balasingham's *The Politics of Duplicity: Re-visiting the Jaffna Talks*,[16] a slick volume published in London in mid 2000. The volume contains correspondence between the government of Sri Lanka and the LTTE during the period of 1994–95.

There was also a more chilling message—not contained in Balasingham's volume. For the Sri Lankan political leadership, at its highest level, negotiations with the LTTE carried a lethal danger, the prospect of assassination. Three years after the failure of his talks with the LTTE, R. Premadasa was assassinated in Colombo on 1 May 1993. Just over five years after the failure of her talks with the LTTE, Chandrika Kumaratunga narrowly escaped death on 18 December 1999 in a botched LTTE assassination attempt which left her blind in one eye. No head of state/head of government negotiating the resolution of a deep-rooted conflict in any part of the world would have faced such personal dangers.

SOWING THE WIND

Part two of this monograph examines some of the policies that are believed to have sown the seeds that later members of the Sri Lankan political class reaped in the form of a whirlwind. Together, the chapters that form part two of this volume show that except with regard to the policy on university admissions, there was little evidence of a systematic scheme of preferential policies. Above all, these chapters deal with the efforts made to modify these policies when the political elite was confronted with criticisms. These chapters also show how rivalries between Sri Lanka's ethnic groups affected both the formulation and the modification of those policies.

4

Sri Lanka: From Demilitarization to Militarization

Post-Independence Sri Lanka provides an interesting case study in the expansion, indeed, virtual creation, of combat-oriented security services and a defence establishment, in response to the rise of the LTTE, the early stages of which we have reviewed in the previous chapters. Much of that expansion of the security forces took place over twelve years or so beginning in 1985–86. While other chapters will deal principally with the period after 1985–86, a review of important issues and developments in the armed services prior to 1985–86 is presented here as an essential prelude to the analysis of the process of militarization from 1985–2011.

We begin with the practice and tradition of British rule in South Asia, and the clear subordination of military to civilian authority. Despite its geographical location in close proximity to the British Raj—the territories presently constituting India, Pakistan, Bangladesh and Myanmar—Sri Lanka was never a part of the Raj. It was a crown colony, and as a crown colony it inherited a more civilian-oriented administration than the countries which emerged from the Raj. In the Raj, while civilian control over the military was a central feature of administration, as it was in a colony such as Sri Lanka, the military was a much more powerful presence there than it was in colonial Sri Lanka.

The successor states that emerged from the British rule in South Asia provide evidence of an amazing variety of policies and experiences in civil–military relations. Sri Lanka and India, the two countries with close to an unbroken tradition of democratic rule since Independence, have also had an unbroken record of subordination of the military to civilian authority. Pakistan and Bangladesh have had long periods of military rule. Despite a brief period of ten years or so since 1987–88 when civilian authority was restored through the electoral process, the military has remained a powerful influence in public life in Pakistan, a point illustrated by the ease with which General Pervez Musharraf toppled the Nawaz Sharif government in 1999. In Bangladesh, on the other hand, the armed services—and especially the army—has kept a low profile with the restoration of civilian rule in the 1990s. But the subordination of the armed services to the civilian authority has yet to be securely established.

Sri Lanka, traditionally, has taken pride in its welfare-state model developed since the mid 1930s.[1] The price it paid for this was the neglect of its security services. Figure I shows the low priority attached to defence in the period up to 1960, in a continuation of pre-Independence patterns of allocation of resources through the national budget. This was despite Sri Lanka's role in the Second World War as a major base of operations in the allied campaign against Japan. In April 1944, the headquarters of the South East Asia Command (SEAC) moved to Sri Lanka, and the town of Kandy in particular.[2] The expenditure incurred on these ventures came mostly from the allied powers and very little of the local budgetary resources were used for this purpose. While the large number of allied

military and naval personnel (largely British and American) in
the island created opportunities for civilian employment in the
bases and camps, there was no substantial Sri Lankan presence in
these forces and, as a result, the absence of a military tradition,
one of the notable features of life in the late nineteenth and
the early and mid twentieth century Sri Lanka, continued
without a change.

**Figure I: Expenditure on Defence and External Affairs,
1951–60**

		Year									
		1951	1952	1953	1954	1955	1956	1957	1958	1959	1960
Rs (millions)	Total defence and external affairs expenditure	13.4	14.9	17.1	19.7	25.2	30.5	47.1	48.8	53.8	78.1
	Percentage of total government expenditure	1.07	1.18	1.71	1.84	1.99	2.06	3.13	2.75	2.91	3.95

Source: *Review of the Economy*, Central Bank of Sri Lanka

At Independence, in February 1948, there was, of course, a
police force but it was not till 10 October 1949 that the first of
the armed services was formally established. This was the army.
The establishment of the navy and the air force followed shortly
thereafter. The first commanders of the Sri Lankan army, navy
and air force were seconded British officers.[3] The nucleus of
the officer corps of the army consisted of men who had been

Figure II: Expenditure on Defence & External Affairs, 1951–60

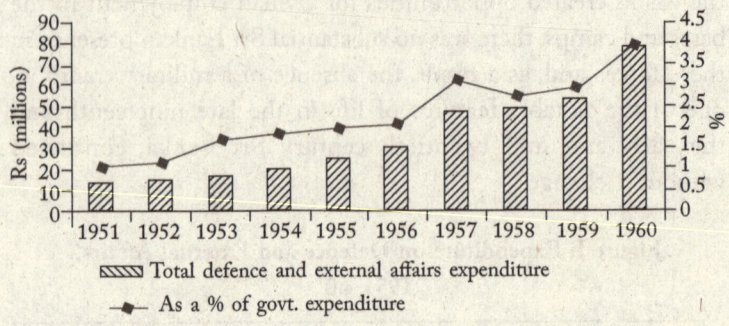

commissioned in the late 1930s or early 1940s, and had served during World War II. Most of the officers of the new regular army had served in the old volunteer units. Once the regular army was established, the former Ceylon Defence Force reverted to its earlier designation of Volunteer Force, and each regular army unit had a parallel unit of volunteers. As early as 1953, volunteers were called in to reinforce the regulars in dealing with such minor disturbances as there were. These duties came at irregular intervals. Generally, the army was a parade ground force wheeled out on ceremonial occasions. At this stage, the esprit de corps of the armed forces and the police had not been damaged by the divisive forces of ethnicity and religion as they were after the mid 1950s.

The most striking feature of the ethnic and religious composition of the officer corps of the army—the largest of the armed services—in the early and mid 1950s, was the over-representation in it of Tamils and Burghers (a minuscule community of Dutch and Portuguese extraction), the Burghers far out of proportion to their numbers in the population. More significantly in relation to the problems of the next decade, Sinhalese-Buddhists, who constituted above two-third of the population, formed only two-fifth of the officer corps in the pre-1956 period. On the other hand, Christians, less than a tenth of the population, were over-represented by a factor of six. The rank and file of the army reflected much more accurately the demographic profile of the country, with the Sinhalese forming about 70 per cent of these ranks. In less than ten years after the establishment of the army, however, the Sinhalese began to be over-represented in the officer corps as well.[4]

Political Changes and their Impact on the Security Services

The principal factor in this over-representation was undoubtedly the change of government in 1956, marking the beginnings of a period of ethnic confrontation interspersed by outbreaks of violence till 1958.[5] The background to this confrontation, and its principal features and events have been reviewed in a number of articles and monographs.[6] It is not intended to deal with these in any great detail here, except for the consequences relevant to the issues discussed in this chapter. These outbreaks gave greater salience to the armed services than in the first decade of the postcolonial era.

Here the principal concern is with the impact of the political changes that followed the election of 1956 on the officer corps of the police and of the armed services. Perceptible changes with regard to the criteria used in appointments to the higher bureaucracy—the elite Ceylon Civil Service—could be seen very early during S.W.R.D. Bandaranaike's tenure as prime minister (1956–59), wherein neither seniority nor proven ability received as much attention as they did in the past. However, similar changes in the equivalent grades in the police and armed services came much more slowly. The first of the changes came in the police force late in 1958 when the post of Inspector

General of Police (IGP) became vacant, and the prime minister, overlooking the claims of the three deputies to the IGP, reached out to the public service to find a man whom he regarded as a suitable IGP. The three deputies were all Christians, one a Roman Catholic and the other two brothers from a Protestant Christian family. The newly appointed IGP was a Buddhist. The message was clear: religious affiliation would be an important consideration in appointments to politically sensitive posts such as that of the IGP.

The armed services were spared such changes till the early 1960s, i.e., till after Bandaranaike's assassination and the succession of his widow Sirimavo Bandaranaike as prime minister in July 1960. But the army officer corps had cause for concern as early as May 1956, in the first weeks of Bandaranaike's administration, when he made a singularly ill-considered intervention in matters of discipline in the army. Eighteen men of the Ceylon Garrison Artillery unit stationed at Mannar in the north-west of the island went on a hunger-strike to ventilate a grievance and make a demand for redress. Instead of leaving the military authorities to handle this on their own, Bandaranaike chose to fly to Mannar to engage these men in negotiations.[7] While he succeeded in persuading them to call off their strike, he had overtly undermined the authority of the army's officer corps and the discipline of the armed forces.

Very soon, he had to rely on the armed services to put down the anti-Tamil riots that erupted in Colombo and elsewhere in the wake of the changes introduced in the language policy in 1956. While the situation was quickly brought under control by the army acting in support of the police, and through a resort to the Public Security Act, the continuing political crisis resulting from the debates and negotiations on the changes in the language policy left little room for any active interference in appointments to the armed services. In May–June 1958, there was a much longer period under emergency regulations as the armed services brought the second of the ethnic riots of this period under control. On this occasion, it was the head of state (the Governor General) rather than the prime minister who took charge during the crisis, giving political direction to the armed forces and the police[8] in a blatant contravention of the conventional relationship that existed between the head of state and head of government in a parliamentary democracy modelled on Westminster.

The political instability of the last two years of Bandaranaike's tenure of office as prime minister reached its denouement with his assassination in 1959. After a brief period of intrigue and regrouping, the SLFP desperately sought a new leader, and found one in his widow. She led the party to another decisive electoral victory in July 1960, and it was during her first period as prime minister, in 1960–65, that the hitherto untroubled relationship of subordination of the armed services to civilian authority first came under great strain. These strains appeared when she sought to increase the number of Sinhalese-Buddhists in the officer corps of the armed services and the police, and to give greater influence to them in the running of the armed services and the police. At the time she came to power, fewer than half the officers commissioned in the army line units were Sinhalese. Major shifts in the ethnic and religious composition of the police and army officer corps became evident almost as soon as she came to power. These were accelerated after an abortive coup d'état in 1962.[9] As the coup leaders saw it, discipline was being eroded and the esprit de corps of the forces was being undermined by the deliberate intrusion of the political and religious conflicts of the wider society. The emergence of a Buddhist association within the regular army greatly perturbed the officers, including some Buddhist officers, who felt that such segmental organizations were simply out of place in the armed services.[10] Political divisions were less sharply focused but were growing in prominence.

Not surprisingly, one consequence of the failure of the coup was a purge of the officer corps, since the coup leaders were senior officers in the army, the police and the navy, almost all of them Christians—Roman Catholics or Protestants. The guiding spirit in this drastic process of reconstitution of the officer corps of the armed services and the police was religion, not ethnic identity, an important aspect of the long conflict between Buddhists and Christians in Sri Lankan society which was reaching its climax at this time.[11]

When a United National Party-led coalition was in power (1965–70), there was yet another abortive coup attempt in 1966. This time the conspirators—with one exception—were subalterns and non-commissioned officers, Buddhists to a man, and intent on protecting the Sinhalese-Buddhist identity of the armed services from any possible dilution by the new government. Two of the men prosecuted for being part of the conspiracy were General Richard Udugama, the army's commanding officer who had enjoyed the confidence and support of Mrs Bandaranaike when she was prime minister, and a powerful bhikkhu (a member of the Buddhist order) well-known for his political sympathies (which were pro-SLFP) and political activities.[12] After a long trial, the prosecution failed to establish its case and the accused were discharged by the courts.

Another phase in the changing composition of the officer corps of the armed services came in 1970 when Sirimavo Bandaranaike was back in power as the head of the United Front coalition between her party and two Marxist groups. The commissions of a number of officers were withdrawn. This time the guiding principle was not religious identity but political conviction if not affiliation. Anyone suspected of not toeing the political line of the left-of-centre coalition that Mrs Bandaranaike led was removed, and for the first time men with political influence were appointed in the army, at least one of whom—a kinsman of the prime minister—was an active politician and continued to be one during his brief and not very distinguished career in the regular army. (This individual, Anuruddha Ratwatte, Mrs Bandaranaike's cousin, became the deputy minister of defence in Chandrika Kumaratunga's PA government of 1994–2005.) The rank and file, both of the armed services and the police, were by now overwhelmingly Sinhalese and Buddhist.

One of the paradoxes of civil–military relations in Sri Lanka is that the two coup attempts of the 1960s came at a time when there were no significant episodes of civil commotion in the form of anti-government political agitation or instances of ethnic tension taking on a violent form. Moreover, these coup attempts were made when the armed services were so much smaller unlike what they became in the 1980s and 1990s. In contrast to the 1960s, the tradition of subordination of the military to civilian authority prevailed throughout the much more turbulent times of the 1980s, 1990s and thereafter, even when the Sri Lankan state faced a severe threat from the LTTE and the JVP, and when—as in 1988–90—its very survival was at stake. Apart from the abortive coup attempts of 1962 and 1966, there has been no attempt by the military to play a role in Sri Lankan politics, much less to subordinate the civil power to its authority.

In seeking to explain how this could have happened, one can only make some tentative hypotheses. The 1960s were a time when military regimes still had the reputation of being more efficient and less corrupt than civilian authorities. Pakistan under Ayub Khan seemed to be doing much better at holding the country together and at stimulating economic growth than what it did under civilian politicians. Some of the leaders of the abortive coup of 1962 in Sri Lanka regarded Ayub Khan and his experiment in 'indirect democracy' as a model to be emulated in Sri Lanka[13], then in the throes of its first phase of the Sinhala–Tamil ethnic conflict, and in the penultimate phase of the conflict between the Buddhists and the Roman Catholics. All the coup leaders blamed the governing party for the ill-effects of its populist policies: turmoil in the form of riots, economic stagnation if not decline, and political instability. They believed they had a remedy for all this, in the installation of a Sri Lankan form of 'indirect democracy' under the rule of a junta of ex prime ministers.

Fortunately for Sri Lankan democracy, the coup never got off to a start. One of the plotters developed cold feet and leaked the information to his father-in-law, an MP of the ruling party. Had the coup succeeded, Sri Lanka's subsequent political evolution would have followed the Pakistani or Bangladeshi pattern, not the Indian one. Its failure strengthened Sri Lankan democracy but not without adverse effects on the country. Since the bulk of the leaders from the armed services and the police belonged to the country's religious and ethnic minorities, the purge of the officer corps—of the armed services and the police—that followed transformed the armed services and the police into overwhelmingly Sinhalese-Buddhist entities. The second abortive coup, in 1966, can only be understood in the context of this radical change in the ethnic and the religious composition of the armed services and to a lesser extent the police force. The fragmentary evidence available about the motives of those engaged in this futile enterprise would appear to suggest that they hoped to ensure that this process—of changing the ethnic and religious composition of the armed forces—would not be reversed through the change of government that had taken place in 1965.

At a different level, there is little doubt that the failure of these two attempted coups helped to strengthen the tradition of civilian control over the armed forces. At no stage in the 1980s, 1990s and later on was the principle of the subordination of the armed forces to the civilian authorities ever challenged. While they may not match the Indian, Pakistani or Bangladeshi forces in numbers, possession of expensive military hardware, or length of military tradition, the armed services have a presence in the Sri Lankan polity today which they did not have in the 1960s. Since the 1990s, the Sri Lankan army, for instance, has been a large, professional fighting force of more than 1,50,000 men (and a small number of women). In terms of the population ratios, and given that India has fifty times of Sri Lanka's population, Sri Lanka has had more active servicemen per million people than in the case of India and other South Asian countries, including Pakistan.[14] And the recruits have been volunteers, not conscripts.

Figure III: Number in the Armed Forces as a Percentage of Population, 1995

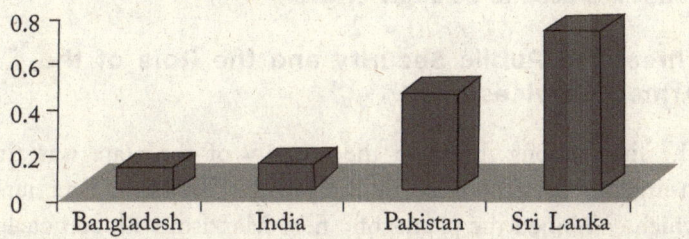

The armed services have never had much difficulty in attracting recruits especially during the times when the services were successful in the struggle against the Tamil separatist forces. The high level of unemployment in the country—generally over 10 per cent—may explain this phenomenon. But given the risks that service in the armed forces carry in a situation of violent confrontations with well-entrenched separatist forces, unemployment is not the sole explanation for the attraction the services hold for the country's Sinhalese youth. The fact of the matter is that the army is a genuinely popular national institution. While there has been no threat to the principle of subordination of the armed services to civilian authority since the 1960s, the popular support these services have in the country (understandably, the police force does not enjoy a similar popularity) does act as a constraint on the freedom with which a government could move regarding issues on which the electorate, in general, or large sections of it, hold strong views. There is always the nagging fear that the armed services themselves would be affected by such views and strong expressions of opinion or by the ebb and flow of debates. This is not to suggest, however, that the principle of the subordination of the armed services to civilian authority or leadership is in any serious danger but merely that an army as large as the one Sri Lanka has had in recent times is something new, and politicians need to be aware of this.

Threats to Public Security and the Role of the Armed Services

The first serious threat to the security of the state was the insurgency of 1971,[15] led by the Janatha Vimukthi Peramuna which combined the planks of a fiery Marxism with an equally fiery Sinhalese nationalism. On this occasion, it required the intervention of the three services, the army, the navy and the air force, to repel the threat to national security. The JVP attacks were concentrated on the ill-equipped police force and the principal targets were police stations. Although the security forces quelled this insurgency with ease, they were seen to be both undermanned and grossly ill-equipped in terms of materiel when they confronted this unexpected upsurge of politically motivated violence. During this time, at the request of Mrs Bandaranaike's coalition government, the United Front, Indian troops were rushed to the island to defend Colombo's international airport, while the Indian navy patrolled the seas to prevent ingress of materiel that could help the insurgents.[16]

In the wake of the JVP attacks, there were some efforts, in 1971–74, to provide the armed services and the police with more modern equipment. However, the additional expenditure incurred did not amount to an increase of more than 2 to 3 per cent in the defence expenditure allotted in the annual budget. Even this increase was not sustained into the mid- and late 1970s despite the perceptible change in the politics of the north of the island and the threat from the Tamil separatist forces operating from there, a threat that had a transnational aspect because of the support these separatist activists enjoyed from their co-ethnics in the Indian state of Tamil Nadu.

Figure IV: Expenditure on Defence and External Affairs, 1968–72

Year	Total defence and external affairs expenditure (Rs/millions)	As % of total government expenditure	US$ equivalent (million)
1968–69	155	4.0	26.7
1969–70	164	4.0	27.5
1970–71	284	7.0	47.8
1971–72[1]	295	7.0	49.1
1971–72[2]	369	7.0	61.5

[1] A period of 12 months (from 1 Oct. 1971- 30 Sept. 1972)
[2] A period of 15 months (from 1 Oct. 1971- 31 Dec. 1972)

Source: Central Bank of Sri Lanka, *Annual Reports*

Note: During the period 1947 to 1977, the prime minister of the day served as minister of defence and external affairs. Thus the budgetary allocation did not distinguish between defence and external affairs. In general, it would be correct to say that the bulk of the expenditure was on defence rather than on external affairs.

Figure V: Expenditure on Defence and External Affairs, 1968–72

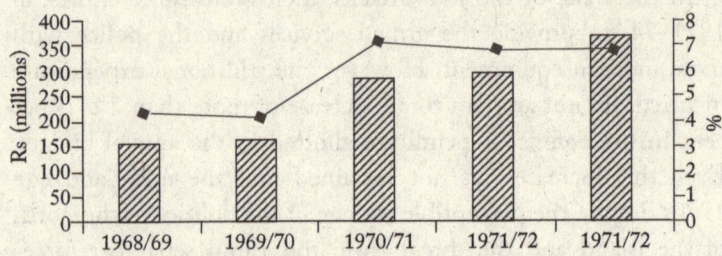

🔲 Total defence and external affairs expenditure
🔺 As a % of govt. expenditure

The point to be emphasized here is that it was the JVP, a Sinhalese group, which first resorted to violence against the Sri Lankan state. The armed attacks on the police and security services by the Tamil separatist groups came a few years later. To what extent they were emulating the example set by the JVP is not clear. From the outset, however, there was an external or regional aspect to Tamil separatism in Sri Lanka. Equally important was the role of the Indian government.

In the mid and late 1950s, India had treated the episodes of ethnic violence in the island as a matter of Sri Lanka's domestic politics, one which did not call for any Indian diplomatic or political intervention. The situation changed in the 1970s, after India's successful intervention in East Pakistan and the creation of Bangladesh. The other factor which influenced the relationship between the two countries was the Tamil Nadu connection and its impact on the Sri Lankan situation. The rise of the Dravida Kazhagam and later the Dravida Munetra Kazhagam in Tamil Nadu in the early 1950s, two powerful political parties representing Tamil ethnic interests, embodied the same powerful force of linguistic nationalism that transformed the politics of Sri Lanka in the same period. Tamil Nadu was a great reservoir of Tamil identity just across the narrow and shallow seas that separate the Jaffna peninsula, in the north of the island, the principal centre of Tamil habitation in Sri Lanka. Once a separatist movement emerged among the Tamils of Sri Lanka, it began to be fostered, nurtured and protected by Tamil Nadu.

5

Appraisals of the Conflict

S ri Lanka's ethnic conflict which erupted dramatically with the general election of 1956, and indeed in the two years before 1956 (i.e., in 1954 and 1955) when the campaign for the election had begun, attracted the attention of scholars and journalists. Many of them sought to understand and explain how a country known for ethnic harmony suddenly became known for ethnic conflict. In the 1930s and 1940s, this harmony had remained a feature of political life even when there was a spirited contest for advantages in fashioning the transfer of power from the British to the Sri Lankans. This ethnic harmony and the skill with which the transfer of power was negotiated earned for Sri Lanka (or Ceylon as it was called before 1972) the title of 'model colony'. It was a colony which had been absorbing the challenges of universal suffrage since 1931 and which had begun the task of establishing a 'mini-welfare' state with commendable skill, even as it sought dominion status and responsible governance. The negotiations on the transfer of power impressed the mandarins of Whitehall and the politicians in charge of the colonies because of the mastery of the processes of government which the Sri Lankan politicians had demonstrated.

Scholars and journalists sought to understand the change of mood among Sri Lankan politicians and the political class once the earliest of the tensions erupted in 1956–58. Among the first of the scholars to provide a comprehensive explanation was an American, W. Howard Wriggins, who had been in the island as a graduate student for three years or so during the emergence of the ethnic conflict and the holding of the election campaign of 1956. He had travelled extensively in many parts of the island during the campaign and was known to have predicted that the government of the day—the well-entrenched United National Party—would be routed by the Sri Lanka Freedom Party-led coalition, the Mahajana Eksath Peramuna (MEP) or the People's United Front. He added that the UNP would get just eight seats in the Parliament, losing over forty seats it held. The election campaign was notable for the entry of an organization of bhikkhus, the Eksath Bhikkhu Peramuna (EBP), which converted the campaign into a moral crusade against the UNP, while also supporting the dramatic change in the language policy. What they sought was the abandonment of the language settlement negotiated in the 1940s as part of the transfer of power arrangements. This settlement envisaged the replacement of English as the official language by Sinhala and Tamil over a ten-to-fifteen-year period. The EBP, during the campaign, came up with a 'Sinhala-only' demand. This proposed change in the language policy attracted enthusiastic support and even compelled the UNP itself to abruptly change its policy of supporting the language settlement of the 1940s in favour of 'Sinhala only'. In short, this was a classic case of a triumph of linguistic nationalism. Howard Wriggins not only understood this but was also able to explain its ramifications in his book, *Ceylon: Dilemmas of a New Nation*, published by the Princeton University Press in 1960. This masterly volume captured the essence of the 'Sinhala only' agitation and of its perils in a multi-ethnic society and political system as no other monograph had done regarding the Sri Lankan situation till then. Not only had he travelled to most parts of the island gathering data for the volume, he had also met most of the prominent politicians and public figures in the island and discussed the issues involved in the election campaign. His monograph became the model by which the works of later American and European scholars would be judged. We turn now to three of these scholars of the 1980s and 1990s.

In a well-known book, *Preferential Policies: An International Perspective*,[1] published in 1990, Thomas Sowell, of the Hoover Institution in Stanford, an Afro-American scholar and a strong critic of affirmative action policies, treated Sri Lanka as a prominent example of the damaging impact of the introduction of preferential policies on a multi-ethnic society and polity. He identified the language policy changes effected in the years 1956–58 as heralding the introduction of such policies into Sri Lanka. He treated the controversial university admissions policies of the 1970s as the second phase in the growth of affirmative action policies in Sri Lanka.

Professor Robert Oberst, a political scientist at Nebraska Wesleyan University, who has a much longer acquaintance with Sri Lanka studies—about twenty-five years or more—than Sowell, went further back than the mid 1950s to trace the genesis of the introduction of affirmative action policies in Sri Lanka. That was in state-sector employment. He first made this point in a wide-ranging, if tendentious, chapter, 'Policies of Ethnic Preference in Sri Lanka', in a book called *Ethnic Preference and Public Policy in Developing States*, published in 1986.[2] In it he dealt with issues such as language policy and university admissions as well. He returned to these themes in 1996, very briefly, in the course of an article called 'Tigers and the Lion: The Evolution of Sri Lanka's Civil War'.[3] In contrast to Thomas Sowell's observations on Sri Lanka, Robert Oberst's oft-quoted article published in 1986 is an inadequately researched essay in which conclusions have been reached on the back of very flimsy evidence. It lacks a historical perspective and is very selective in its use of sources. For someone who regarded himself as an expert on Sri Lankan affairs, and was treated as such in the US, his essay, 'Policies of Ethnic Preference in Sri Lanka', falls far short of the exacting standards of scholarship that should generally go with expertise.

His comments on such policies in the article 'Tigers and the Lion: The Evolution of Sri Lanka's Civil War', extracts of which are quoted below, are even more tendentious than his longer article published ten years earlier.

> Without anti-majoritarian safeguards, the Sri Lankan government had taken a number of actions which benefitted only the majority community. Most significant of these is the Sinhala Only policy in 1956 which required the government to operate only in the Sinhala language. In the 1970s the government created a quota system to increase the number of Sinhalese to a level equivalent to their percentage in the population. This policy simultaneously reduced the number of Tamils admitted to the universities, and the issue of university admissions issue [*sic*] became a focal point.
>
> Even more insidious was the exclusion of Tamils from public sector employment. At the time of independence, Tamils were over-represented in the public service, creating a sense of resentment among many Sinhalese. The government moved to address the imbalances, and by the late 1970s very few Tamils were being allowed into public service jobs, the most desirable positions in Sri Lanka.[4]

These two paragraphs may have been excusable in the case of a journalist—on a hurried visit—trying to explain to a not very well-informed readership, at home, the essence of the problem in Sri Lanka, as he saw it. But in the case of a man who claimed expertise in the affairs of Sri Lanka, they are a deplorable mixture of half-truths, inaccuracies and distortion of facts. The short cuts he indulges in, as for example the reference to 'the Sri Lankan government', are inexcusable, because Sri Lanka has been well-known for changing its government through the ballot—on six occasions from 1956 to 1977, the incumbent government was defeated at the polls. A scholar of Oberst's standing should have indicated *which* government introduced the policies he refers to and, more to the point, should have shown that these policies were often changed. Instead, his comments convey the mistaken impression that a policy was converted into a legal enactment or an administrative regulation, and implemented in that form, without subsequent modification.

The second of the paragraphs quoted here is a collection of distortions of the truth. The fact of the matter is that there was no policy of *excluding Tamils from public sector employment*. Nor is it correct to say that by 'the late 1970s very few Tamils were *being allowed* [emphasis mine] into public service jobs'.

Thomas Sowell who makes no claim to expertise on Sri Lankan affairs, provides a refreshing contrast to Oberst in his approach to affirmative action policies in Sri Lanka. Even where one has reason to fault Sowell's judgement on some issues or disagree with his interpretations, one has to concede that he reaches his conclusions on the basis of a careful examination of the data he had gathered. His conclusions are judicious, and his assessments are always fair. Above all, an examination of his endnotes in the references to Sri Lanka will show that his reading has been much wider than Oberst's and that there has been much greater care in the search for evidence, and far greater discernment in the assessment of that evidence.

The third scholar who has commented on Sri Lanka's ethnic conflict is the Cornell-based political scientist Milton J. Esman, a distinguished student of ethnicity and ethnic conflict. In his *An Introduction to Ethnic Conflict,* published in 2004, he has made a number of references to the situation in Sri Lanka, some of which deal with language policy and university admissions policy as factors in precipitating the ethnic conflict or in aggravating it.

On page 80,[5] he writes as follows:

Access to higher education as the pathway to more prestigious and lucrative careers is a common source of ethnic conflict. Governments as in Malaysia and Sri Lanka, arrange for their ethnic constituents to gain preferential admission to universities, often at the expense of better qualified (by scores at entrance examinations or secondary school performance) applicants from other backgrounds. This pattern of discrimination is deeply resented, since it is perceived as penalizing and blocking the legitimate aspirations of deserving youngsters, precisely those who are most likely to provide the corps of activists for ethnic protest movements. Much of the leadership of the Tamil Tigers were drawn from young men whose university admission was blocked by the requirement that entrance exams be administered only in the Sinhalese language.

On page 72, he claims:

When the Sinhalese-dominated government of Sri Lanka decreed that henceforth all tests for university entrance and exams for civil service position were to be in the Sinhalese language, members of the Tamil ministry interpreted this not only as an assault on their employment opportunities, but also as a sign that their culture would be received with no respect by a government committed by Sinhalese nationalism. This proved to be the policy that triggered the Tamil demand for a separate state and the ensuing civil war.

As we shall see in chapter 7, the Tamils were guaranteed the right to educate their children in the Tamil language and to sit in public examinations at all levels in the same language, a right that was never in jeopardy despite the changes attempted in the language policy. Esman is right in arguing that changes in the language policy helped trigger the ethnic conflict between the Tamils and the Sinhalese in Sri Lanka. It is not correct, however, to argue that '[m]uch of the leadership of the Tamil Tigers were drawn from young men whose university admission was blocked by the requirement that entrance exams be administered only in the Sinhalese language'.

The purpose of chapters 6 to 8 is to examine the scope and impact of affirmative action policies on Sri Lanka, and to do so through an examination of three themes—university admission policies, language policy and employment in the state sector, in that order. It will be shown how affirmative action policies first came to Sri Lanka as late as 1970, with the left-of-centre United Front coalition that won power at the general election of that year; and how from the outset, these policies were limited to university admissions alone. Owing to the worldwide attention that Sri Lanka's ethnic conflict has received, analyses of the causes of the spread and growth in intensity of this conflict often treated the changes in university admission policy introduced in the early 1970s as the crucial factor in the intensification of this conflict.

As we shall see in chapter 6, affirmative action policies in Sri Lanka are confined to university admissions alone, and even in that regard, only in the undergraduate section. They do not operate in the postgraduate sphere. Nor are they in place when it comes to staff appointments and promotions.

Introduced as a temporary measure, this very limited exercise in affirmative action has survived for over thirty years now.

Language policy and university admissions policy or policies are two of the most complex issues in a study of how Sri Lankans sowed the wind in what turned out to be a prolonged period of ethnic conflict. These policies require an understanding of the history of the country and, of course, an understanding of the demands and claims of the various groups in conflict. More especially, an understanding is required of the evolution of the policy and its modifications over the years. In the specific case of the university admissions policies, what is also required is an understanding of the details of a particular policy and its modifications in response to pressures.

Finally, it has to be noted here that in their attempt to explain how the Sri Lankans mishandled the evolving contest for advantage among the ethnic groups, none of the three scholars—Sowell, Oberst and Esman—show Howard Wriggins's familiarity with the complexity of the problem or the command of data in setting out a case in their writings. If anything, Sowell does better than Oberst.

6

University Admissions Policy

At the very outset of this chapter, I need to make two points. First of all, I have had considerable personal knowledge of the university admissions policy of Sri Lanka, first as a critic of the policies introduced in 1970 and then as a policymaker at the official non-political level as a member of the University Grants Commission (UGC) and its vice chairman. In this latter capacity, I chaired an official committee in 1987 which investigated the impact of these policies on the Sri Lankan university system. Moreover, in 1993, after I had left the UGC (I left in 1989), I chaired another official committee appointed for the same purpose.[1] On both occasions, the committees recommended a radical reform of the system and the gradual elimination of preferential policies. The recommendations of these committees, especially those of 1987, are reviewed later in this chapter.

The second point is that an examination of the introduction and implementation of preferential policies in Sri Lanka's university system, and the impassioned resistance to modifying them, not to speak of reversing them, provide an excellent introduction to the complex nature of Sri Lanka's ethnic conflict, and the political ramifications of the rivalries between Sri Lanka's minorities—Muslims against Tamils, divisions among Tamils, quite apart, of course, from the wider theme of the rivalries between the Sinhalese and the Tamils. It is not without significance that a Muslim minister of education, Badi-ud-din Mahmud of the SLFP, was one of the prime movers in the introduction of these policies, and that another Muslim minister, A.C.S. Hameed of the UNP, successfully prevented the implementation of the reform of these policies in 1987 at the tail end of J.R. Jayewardene's second term as executive President.

Sri Lanka's politicians had long regarded university admissions as too important a matter to be left to university administrators and teachers to handle on their own. Since the mid 1960s, university seats, i.e., the number of students to be admitted, and the basis of admission, have been settled at the highest political level—the Cabinet, no less. It was in the 1960s, when Sinhala and Tamil replaced English as the medium of instruction in the higher classes of the secondary schools, that political and ethnic pressures on the universities began to build up. The rapid growth of secondary education resulted in intensified competition for entry into the universities, especially to the most esteemed of them, the University of Ceylon at Peradeniya (now the University of Peradeniya). Such political pressure as there was in the 1960s had been for the expansion of the universities to accommodate the ever-increasing numbers of students. The procedure for admission became a political issue from 1970 onwards with the victory of the United Front coalition. It then led to an acrimonious struggle among the main ethnic groups. The crux of the problem was that the indigenous Tamils who constituted about 11.1 per cent of the population—as distinct from the Indian Tamils of the plantation areas—had for years enjoyed a predominant position in the faculties of science, engineering and medicine of the University of Ceylon at Peradeniya and Colombo. This was partly a result of their higher rate of literacy in English and partly because of the excellent facilities for education in science in the schools of the Jaffna district from which many of them entered the universities. In 1970, for instance, the Tamils bagged just over 35 per cent of the admissions to the faculty of science. In engineering and medicine, this figure was as high as 45 per cent. With the changeover to *swabasha*—the indigenous languages, Sinhala and Tamil—there were, in effect, two distinct streams of students seeking admission to the university, one educated in Sinhala and the other in Tamil. In addition, a small group of students of almost all ethnic groups continued to be taught in English in the secondary schools and took the university examinations in that language. They were mainly of British, Dutch or Portuguese extraction or the offspring of mixed marriages between Sinhalese and Tamils. Muslim students were also entitled to enrol in the English medium classes. Since the examiners graded answer scripts in one language stream only, it was a matter of time before the superior performance of the Tamils was attributed to deliberate favouritism and grade inflation on the part of the Tamil examiners. Late in 1970, the government introduced a lower qualifying mark for students who took the examinations in Sinhala, in order that a politically acceptable ratio of Tamil to Sinhalese students could be admitted to the science, engineering and medical faculties of the University of Ceylon at Peradeniya and Colombo. (Admissions to the humanities and social sciences courses did not present any great difficulty.)

This fundamental and unilateral change in the university admission policy heralded the abandonment of the merit principle and the introduction of a system of affirmative action. Entrance to universities had hitherto been on the basis of academic achievement tested through rigorous competitive examinations.[2] When Badi-ud-din Mahmud[3] committed the UF government to a fundamental change in policy, to a system of standardization by language media in which students sat for the university entrance examination, he was setting in motion a train of events which contributed to exacerbating Sri Lanka's ethnic conflict.

All marks were reduced to a uniform scale so that the number of students qualifying in each language became proportionate to the number appearing for the examination in that medium. It was a device to neutralize the superior performance—purely based on marks obtained—of the Tamil medium students in the science subjects. The result was that Tamil students had to obtain higher aggregate marks than their Sinhalese counterparts to gain admission to the science, engineering and medical faculties of the University of Ceylon. Not only was this system maintained for a few years after 1970 but other changes were also introduced. All these changes departed from the practice of selecting students on the basis of marks obtained in an open competitive examination. Among the changes was the district quota system, ostensibly involving a balance in favour of rural areas and backward communities. In fact, it gave a decided advantage to the Sinhalese and—as we shall see—the Muslims.

Those who suffered most from the change were undoubtedly the Tamils of the north, although the Sinhalese in the city of Colombo and the crowded Colombo district fared badly too. The new university entrance policy of the 1970s made entry into the scientific and technical education streams more difficult for the Tamils than before. Thus, this new policy played an important role in the deterioration of ethnic relations in the island in the 1970s because it contributed to the alienation of Tamil youth of the north and the east of the island. The new scheme of admissions was seen as a grossly unfair system, deliberately devised to place the Tamils at a disadvantage in the increased competition for admission to science-based faculties.

Although the then Tamil political leadership protested strongly against the differential 'qualifying marks' for Sinhalese and Tamil candidates, the immediate effect of the change in terms of the number of Tamil students admitted to the science-based faculties was merely marginal:

> . . . a drop from 35.3 per cent to 33.6 per cent, and an actual increase in the aggregate from 337 to 359 . . . [The] real significance of the change in 1971 [did] not lie in these figures. It marked the ascendancy of a group of Sinhalese [officials and advisers] in the Ministry of Education, a group which firmly believed that some adjusting mechanism was necessary to give Sinhalese students a chance in competing for the coveted places in science-based courses at the University. It was this group which came up with the suggestion for media-wise standardisation for [the 1973 admission].[4]

'Media-wise standardization', to use the jargon of these administrators, was a device to weigh the marks of the candidates so that those qualifying for admission from each language group would be proportionate to the number who sat for the examination through that language. The proponents of the measure argued that the difference in performance between Sinhalese and Tamil students must be attributed to the qualitative differences in facilities, teaching or marking, and that 'standardization' was merely a way to mitigate the effect of such inequality. This was a baseless argument since there were as many such inequalities within each linguistic or ethnic group as there were between them.

However, as we have seen, the immediate effect on the numbers of Tamils entering the university was marginal. It was also far less damaging to Tamil interests than the acrimony caused by the suggested change. Professor C.R. de Silva, a leading expert on the subject of the political agitation about the university admission policy in Sri Lanka, has pointed out:

'The Sri Lankan Tamils, though they constituted just 11.1 per cent of the population, provided about 30 per cent of the science students in the secondary schools and the scheme of [media-wise] standardization ensured that this proportion of places in the university accrued to them.'[5]

In the next year 1974 a modification of the scheme was introduced: the 'district quota' system. Clearly it was intended to satisfy two interest groups, the rural Sinhalese in general and those in the Kandyan areas in particular—i.e., areas which formed part of the Kandyan Kingdom—and the Moor-Malay group. Both groups regarded themselves as 'educationally backward'. Neither was content with the changes in admission policy after 1970. Both had powerful sources of influence within the principal party in the UF coalition, the Sri Lanka Freedom Party. Since the Moor-Malay group gained their education mainly through Tamil, the scheme of 'standardization' pitted them against the Tamils in the intense competition for places in that medium of instruction. And they saw the contest as an intrinsically unequal one. Mahmud, leader of the Islamic Socialist Front within the Sri Lanka Freedom Party, was always mindful of the Moor-Malay group's interests. The 'district quota' system was designed to allocate university places in proportion to the total population resident in each district. The scheme benefited the Kandyan region, and the rural areas generally, as well as the Moors-Malays. A refinement of the system was then devised to benefit this latter group. The criterion generally used in determining a student's district for purposes of this quota, in the case of Sinhalese and Tamil students, was the location of the school or schools from which they sat for the examination. In the case of Moors-Malays, it was the district of birth. Thus, a Sinhalese or a Tamil student from an educationally backward district who had won a scholarship to a Colombo secondary school and sat for the examination from Colombo, would be treated, for the purpose of admission to the university, as a student from the Colombo district. In contrast, a Moor-Malay in the same circumstances would qualify for admission through his home district where the qualifying mark was substantially lower than for the Colombo schools.

For the Tamils, this district quota system was a heavy blow: the percentage of university seats they held in the science-based disciplines fell from 35.3 in 1970 to 20.9 in 1974, and 19 in 1975. In 1974, for the first time, there was a substantial fall in the absolute number of Tamils entering the science courses, despite a continued expansion in the total intake of those courses.

The Sinhalese, on the other hand, gained substantially, although those resident in Colombo—and to a lesser extent in other urban areas—also suffered a drop in admissions. In the science courses, the Sinhalese constituted 75.5 per cent in 1974, while this figure rose to 78 per cent in 1975. Since the Sinhalese students occupied over 86 per cent of the seats in the humanities and social sciences streams, they were, by this time, in the same privileged position in the universities as were their politicians in the national legislature in terms of seats—an accurate measure of how the universities reflected the thrust of Sinhalese national politics. The Moors-Malays saw their number of admissions to the science courses double between 1970 and 1975, even though they were still well below the ethnic proportion of 6 to 7 per cent of the total population, which some of their political leaders advocated as their due.

Opposition to these changes came swiftly and strongly. It came from the Tamils naturally enough and, more effectively, from the Sinhalese of the urban areas of the south-west coast, especially Colombo and its suburbs. The question came before a Cabinet sub-committee—the sectoral committee on social overheads, mass media and transport of the National Planning Council.

This sub-committee, in a report submitted early in October 1973, recommended the abolition of 'media-wise standardization' and commented adversely on the district quota system and the rationale behind it. Nevertheless, the committee did not carry its criticisms to their logical conclusion and recommend the abandonment of the district quota system. Eventually, it did recommend a complicated modification of the admissions system: 70 per cent on 'raw marks' and 30 per cent on a district basis, of which half or 15 per cent was to be reserved for what were termed educationally backward areas. When these proposals were submitted to the Cabinet, only a modified district quota system was adopted—while district quota seats were granted to Jaffna and Colombo along with other districts, the 'standardization' scheme was retained.

Figure I: University Admissions Policy

Prior to 1965
Universities conducted their own entrance examinations.
1966–70
Admissions were centrally controlled through the National Council of Higher Education (NCHE). They were based on aggregates of marks from four subjects at the GCE (A/L) examination. The criterion was the order of merit only.
1970
Standardization by media introduced. Students to science-based courses were admitted on the basis of separate pre-determined minimum mark levels applicable to each of the three language media.
1971
The principle of standardization of marks was extended from language medium to subjects as well.

1974

The principle of district quotas introduced. Eligible students were classified according to the administrative districts from which they had taken the GCE (A/L) examination. Students were selected in the order of merit of standardized marks. The number of places available for each course of study was allocated to the districts in proportion to their general population.

1976

70 per cent of the places in each course were filled according to the order of merit on an all-island basis as determined by the standardized marks obtained at the GCE (A/L) examination. The remaining 30 per cent were filled on a district basis.

The concept of 'educationally underprivileged districts' was introduced in this year and one-half of the places were filled on the district quota basis, i.e., 15 per cent of the total number of places was reserved for students from ten districts classified as being 'educationally underprivileged'.

These districts were:

1. Ampara
2. Anuradhapura
3. Badulla
4. Hambantota
5. Mannar
6. Monaragala
7. Nuwara Eliya
8. Polonnaruwa
9. Trincomalee
10. Vavuniya

A Three-tier Admissions Policy, 1977 and After

The reversal of the controversial university admissions policy of the UF government was announced on 4 August 1977 by a new government, just after it had taken office. Given all that had happened with regard to the admissions policy between 1970 and 1977, this was a bold decision, even for a government that had inflicted an overwhelming defeat on its opponents and now commanded an overwhelming majority in the Parliament.[6] It took several months, however, to reach even an untidy compromise, a matter of makeshift and expedience rather than of strict adherence to abstract principles. However, before the government could go about this complicated and time-consuming business, it had to cope with the communal riots that erupted unexpectedly in August 1977, a few weeks after it came to power. So, while the admissions to the universities for the year 1977 were being dealt with, the country had hardly recovered from the impact of the communal riots.

It was necessary therefore to step warily through the minefields of the issue of university admissions. Professor C.R. de Silva summarized the main features of the problem confronting the government:

> When the marks were processed it became clear that if district quotas and standardisation were not applied, the Tamils would considerably outnumber the Sinhalese in the much sought after faculties of Medicine and Engineering. Some inkling of this situation reached the members of Sinhalese nationalist groups. Assertions were made by them that Tamil examiners had inflated [the] marks. A one-day strike by all Sinhalese secondary school children in protest against [the] government policy was planned [in February 1978] and indeed, this was only averted by the closure of all government schools for the day and by taking into custody several of the alleged organisers.[7]

Among the latter were a few of the leading lights of the Sinhala Tharuna Sanvidhanaya (literally, the Sinhala Youth Organization), a politically influential activist group which had agitated for the change in admissions policy in 1970 and succeeded in their agitation. It had also helped organize opposition to the UF government's decision to move away from the rigid district quota scheme that prevailed from 1975.

The new government honoured its mandate by abandoning 'standardization' on the basis of the language in which students sat for the examination for entry into the university. But it decided nevertheless that all students who would have gained admission had there been such a standardization should be admitted. The 3700 students originally admitted on the basis of 'raw marks' were now joined by nearly 900 others, many of them Sinhalese. Subsequently, a third set of over 250 students, from what were called educationally underprivileged districts, were admitted to the universities.

This awkward but perhaps more prudent decision brought advantages to everyone. The Tamil political leadership tacitly accepted the compromise. They had good reason for satisfaction, for the number of Tamil entrants into the medical and engineering faculties rose by over 250 per cent compared to the previous year. On the basis of this change, the proportion of Tamil students who entered the science courses equalled or exceeded the 35 to 40 per cent proportion under the system of open competition in 1969–70 and 1970–71.[8] Those who had been agitating for an increase in the total number of admissions to the universities had reason to be satisfied: admissions were up by 25 per cent. The number of Sinhalese entering the universities also increased, especially from the rural areas.

From this stage onwards, Sri Lanka's university admissions policy changed from one of ethnic preferences to one of regional preferences in favour of rural areas—without regard to ethnicity or religion. A modification of the scheme of district preferences first introduced in the early 1970s was now elevated to the position of the central feature of the university admissions policy, a position it retained in the 1980s.

By mid 1978, the whole question of university admissions became once more a matter of acute political controversy because many Sinhalese supporters of the standardization scheme, distinctly unhappy with the compromise of early 1978, were intent on upsetting it. They repeated the contention that the Sri

Lankan Tamil minority of 11 per cent could consistently obtain such good results—constituting about 35 to 40 per cent of the medical and engineering entrants into the universities—only by resorting to unfair means. They alleged that examiners in the Tamil medium were being partial in their grading of scripts at the national examination through which entrance into the universities was determined.

In persisting with these criticisms, the proponents of the standardization scheme were bent on persuading the government to reconsider the recent change in policy. Soon, they found a champion for their cause within the Cabinet itself, the minister for industries and scientific affairs, Cyril Mathew, then beginning his controversial role as the outspoken champion of Sinhalese-Buddhist interests, and the most vociferous critic of the Tamil United Liberation Front, the principal Tamil political party at that time. At an acrimonious parliamentary session, he produced answer scripts submitted in one of the science subjects at the General Certificate of Education (Advanced Level) (GCE (A/L) examination of 1977, and used them as evidence that Tamil examiners were prone to deliberately and consistently give Tamil students higher marks than they were entitled to. In making these accusations, Mathew touched a raw nerve. The evidence he produced was inadequate to substantiate his charge of widespread partiality in the grading of examination scripts but enough to confirm the suspicions of those already inclined to doubt the impartiality of the Tamil examiners.

The arguments of the proponents of 'standardization' were in fact a part of a larger drive on behalf of a new and allegedly foolproof mechanism for university admissions: namely, quotas for ethnic groups in proportion to their percentage in the population. There was no support for this policy from the government as a whole, but many politically active Sinhalese-Buddhists urged its adoption, and so did representatives of the Indian Tamils. It was also taken up enthusiastically and persistently by the Moor-Malay group which would benefit the most if such quotas were introduced.

The new institutional framework for higher education adopted in 1979–80 helped to stabilize the formula introduced in 1978, which was a combination of a new 'national merit quota', 'regional merit quotas' and a special allocation for eleven educationally backward districts. These quotas were all based on aggregates of marks, referred to in technical language as 'raw marks'. (The concept of educationally backward districts had been introduced in 1976 with ten such districts being identified.) It was, in short, a three-tier admissions policy. With the establishment of the University Grants Commission in 1978 and the creation of a ministry of higher education and, above all, in placing these directly under the President of the republic, the university admissions policy was protected from the worst of political pressures.

From 1979 onwards, changes in the admissions policy were much less frequent than in the early 1970s. There was also relative stability in terms of ethnic proportion in university admissions, with the 'Sri Lankan' Tamils' share remaining consistently higher than their proportion in the population, and much higher than that in the science disciplines, especially medicine and engineering. They were seldom lower than 35 per cent in these disciplines since 1978, and this percentage was maintained for ten years or more. As for the 'Indian' Tamils in Sri Lanka, they had yet to gain their 'ethnic quota' in university admissions. However, there was a distinct improvement in the position of the Moor-Malay group.

The compromise of 1978 was kept under constant review. Once more a committee was appointed for this purpose. Among the problems attracting attention was the special allocation of 15 per cent of places to eleven 'educationally disadvantaged districts'. Under pressure from parliamentarians, the number of such districts was increased to twelve in 1979. With the addition of Puttalam to this list, in 1980, more than half of the country's twenty-four administrative districts at the time—the number of districts was raised to twenty-five later on—became beneficiaries of this special allocation of seats.[9] Of these districts, Batticaloa, Mullaitivu and Vavuniya were Tamil majority areas. Indian Tamils were a significant minority in Badulla and Nuwara Eliya, while Muslims were, similarly, a significant minority in Batticaloa, Trincomalee, Ampara, Mannar and Puttalam. In most of these districts, the minimum marks required for university admission was lower than those for students from Colombo and Jaffna, where the competition was the keenest, by as much as 100 out of a total of 400 marks. In a situation where a single mark could make a crucial difference between admission to the medicine and engineering streams—for which competition was the keenest and performance levels the highest—and admission to the agriculture or science streams for example, this practice was grossly unfair. There were additional disadvantages, especially reflected in the growing clamour from politicians in other rural districts to share the benefits conferred on the fortunate 'disadvantaged' districts. It was an agitation based on the argument that by any standard of assessment, their districts were only slightly better off in terms of schools, equipment and teachers than those that were benefiting from the prevailing policy.

In late 1981, a new formula was announced for the academic year 1982–83. The principle recommended was a two-tier system in which 40 per cent of all students were chosen on the basis of the highest aggregate marks attained at the examination on a country-wide basis. A second tier was to be chosen on the highest aggregate marks achieved at the district level. The 60 per cent of students chosen in the latter way would come in at a lower level than the 40 per cent who were on the wider 'merit list', with the aggregate marks of the former category of students varying greatly from district to district. The 15 per cent special allocation for educationally backward areas was thus to be eliminated. The proposal to abolish this allocation was received with relief by critics of the system who argued that the pendulum had swung too far towards the 'underprivileged' districts. However, ministers and MPs representing these 'underprivileged' districts put up a spirited defence and succeeded in preventing the introduction of the new scheme.

In the election years of 1982 and 1983, the government preferred to let the existing system continue rather than pursuing a change in policy. In defence of the 15 per cent allocation, an extraordinary coalition of forces had been forged. Naturally, the Sinhalese from the rural areas led the campaign, but they had also the support of the Tamils from the districts of Mannar, Mullaitivu, Vavuniya, Batticaloa, Trincomalee and Ampara—in short, all Tamils except those from the Jaffna district—as well as the Muslims as a whole. Thus the system of district preferences, introduced originally as a temporary device, survived into the late 1980s and even later.

The next attempt to grasp the nettle of university admissions came in 1984 when a committee of university academics, educationists and public figures interested in education, headed by the chairman of the UGC, made an analysis of the problems involved in university admissions. The committee concentrated on the least troublesome nettle, and succeeded in eliminating most of its sting—the nettle of educationally underprivileged districts. It proposed these districts be reduced in number from thirteen to five, and that the number of places available to them be reduced from 15 per cent to 5 per cent. The more formidable nettle of district preferences or quotas was not touched at all. The committee recommended that the percentage of places in the district quota be increased to 65, while the merit quota would remain at 30 per cent. There was still some resistance to this attempt to modify the formula devised in the late 1970s, but the political pressures were less effective than in 1982. The new formula came into operation from the academic session of 1986–87. It represented a minor victory for academic considerations over political pressures, but it was not a lasting victory.

These continuing controversies over the formula on university seats took place against the background of an expansion in the number of universities—the number increased by two, and the Open University was founded.

Figure II: University Admissions Policy

1978

Standardization was abandoned and the new government decided that admission would be on the basis of raw marks as was the practice prior to 1970. At the same time, it also decided that a student who would have gained admission to a university had there been a standardization of marks should not be deprived of such admission owing to the abolition of standardization. The number of underprivileged districts was increased to eleven with the inclusion of the Batticaloa district to the category.

1979

The government decided that admission should be made only on the basis of raw marks and that the seats available in 1979 should be filled according to the following formula:

(a) 30 per cent of the seats in each course of study were to be filled on an all-island merit basis.
(b) 55 per cent of the seats in each course of study were to be allocated to the twenty-four administrative districts in

proportion to their respective populations, and filled on the basis of a district mérit list.

(c) The remaining 15 per cent of the seats in each course of study were to be allocated, in proportion to their respective populations, to twelve administrative districts deemed to be 'educationally underprivileged'. The students from these districts were also to be chosen on the basis of a district merit list.

These districts were:

1. Ampara	5. Hambantota	9. Nuwara Eliya
2. Anuradhapura	6. Mannar	10. Polonnaruwa
3. Badulla	7. Monaragala	11. Trincomalee
4. Batticaloa	8. Mullaitivu	12. Vavuniya

1980

The number of underprivileged districts was increased to thirteen with the inclusion of the Puttalam district.

1985

The government decided to change the district and underprivileged district quota as follows:

(a) the national merit quota to remain at 30 per cent

(b) increase in the district quota from 55 per cent to 65 per cent, and

(c) reduction in the underprivileged district quota to 5 per cent from 15 per cent; also, reduction in the number of such districts to five from thirteen.

These underprivileged districts were:

1. Ampara	4. Mannar
2. Badulla	5. Mullaitivu
3. Hambantota	

The seats available in the universities, especially in the medicine and engineering streams for which the demand was the greatest, also increased, as did those in other higher educational institutions under the ministry of education. The number of students admitted annually to undergraduate courses increased steadily—from 3500 in 1976 to nearly 6000 in 1985–86. The two main areas in which pressure from the better students was the greatest, medicine and engineering, saw a substantial expansion in the number of seats available. In medicine, two new faculties were established in this period—in Jaffna and Ruhuna—while the two older faculties at Colombo and Peradeniya universities admitted a much larger number of students than in the sessions of 1970–71. While the number of seats available in the medical faculties nearly doubled between 1971 and 1985, seats in the faculty of engineering at Peradeniya University and the University of Moratuwa—a technological and engineering institution—trebled during the same period. The expansion was most rapid since 1979–80. The Open University, on its part, was soon admitting large numbers of students. By 1985, the numbers enrolled there reached 10,000.

Admissions Policy: An Abortive Attempt at Change

In 1987, the UGC appointed a review committee, with this writer as its chairman, to investigate and report on possible changes in the university admissions policy. The report of this review committee was published in December 1987. By this time, the Parliament itself had appointed a select committee[10] on the situation in the universities. That select committee also examined the problems relating to the admissions policy. The publication of the select committee's report preceded the publication of the UGC review committee's report by a few days. The 'principal recommendation' of the UGC committee was that the merit element in the admissions formula should be given greater emphasis than . . . at present and that a corresponding and progressive reduction be made in the district quotas as well as in the quotas for educationally-underprivileged districts till they were eliminated over a six or seven years period beginning [at the end of 1987].

The quota for 'underprivileged' districts was to be abolished by the end of 1991 and the 'district quotas' themselves by the end of 1995. There was to be an immediate increase in the merit quota to 40 per cent by the end of 1987, and a progressive increase in that quota, 10 per cent at a time, till the elimination of the 'district quotas' by the academic year 1994–95. The committee reported that the time span of six to seven years for the elimination of these district-level quotas had been deliberately chosen. These district quotas, originally introduced as a temporary measure, would then have survived for a quarter of a century, time enough and more for the elimination of the imbalances in educational resources—especially in the rural districts and more isolated areas in the country—the prevalence of which provided the justification originally for the introduction of the system and subsequently for its continuation. There was evidence from authoritative sources that these imbalances had been reduced to a large extent. It was felt that an additional six to seven years would be quite adequate to complete the process of reducing such disparities as existed in 1987.

The special quota for 'educationally underprivileged' districts found little support in the memoranda received by the committee or in the oral evidence given by delegations or individuals. Only two delegations, one representing Muslim interests, and a delegation representing the views of the Indian Tamil community, advocated the continuation of this special quota system. Quite clearly, they believed that it helped students from their communities enter the university system in larger numbers than they would if such a quota did not exist. It was their contention that this quota had been in existence only since 1985–86 and that it was too early to eliminate it. There was little merit in this argument, for the principle of a special quota for 'educationally underprivileged' districts had been in existence since 1976 and what had happened in 1985–86 was that it was narrowed down to five districts and 5 per cent of the seats. The committee felt that this quota could and should be eliminated three years from the end of 1987 without any serious harm being done to the educational interests of the districts concerned or to those of the ethnic and religious minorities who advocated its continuation.

The committee's proposals were adopted by the University Grants Commission, with just one change. The commission recommended that a further review be made in 1992 to consider the impact of the proposed changes. In recommending the adoption of the report, the commission was encouraged by the brief comment in paragraph 16 of the parliamentary select committee's report, which appeared to suggest that the committee shared the concerns of the academic community about the 'scheme of selection to the universities [compounding] the problem . . . [of the] wide gap between the standards of secondary education and the standards of university education.'

The review committee on admissions had strongly urged an increase in the minimum mark a candidate needed to apply for admission to the universities. It recommended that the minimum mark be raised to 200, out of a total of 400, from 180, out of a total of 400, with effect from the academic year 1988–89. The minimum mark had been increased steadily from 140 to 180 over the period 1978 to 1984, in keeping with the general improvement in performance standards at the General Certificate Examination (Advanced Level) over the years. Research conducted by the UGC and in the universities had shown very clearly that students who entered the universities with less than 200 marks generally performed very poorly in the examinations. In addition, the improvement in the levels of performance had been very substantial since 1984. It was felt this should be reflected by raising the minimum mark to 200.

Figure III: Minimum Requirement for Admission

1965–79

Candidates should have sat for exams in four approved subjects and passed in at least *three* of them with not less than 25 per cent marks in the fourth subject. *The minimum aggregate required was 145 marks* out of 400.

In addition to the above, an applicant should have completed the prescribed (faculty or course) requirements at the GCE (A/L) examination.

1980

Candidates should have passed in at least three approved subjects and obtained a mark of not less than 25 per cent in a fourth approved subject *at one and the same occasion at the GCE (A/L) examination.*

They should also have obtained an aggregate of not less than 160 marks out of 400 for the four subjects.

1982

Minimum mark requirement was increased to 165 out of 400.

1983

Minimum mark requirement was increased to 170 out of 400.

1984

Minimum mark requirement was increased to 175 out of 400.

1985

Minimum mark requirement was increased to 180 out of 400.

Above all, it was found that by 1987 some students securing an average of A-minus in their examinations and scoring an aggregate of 260–279 marks were being rejected by the engineering and medicine faculties under the existing three-tier system. These students came not only from the so-called privileged districts of Colombo and Jaffna but also from other areas such as Galle and Matara in the south, Kandy in the central region, Kalutara in the western region, and Kurunegala and Puttalam in the north-west. Puttalam had been classed as an educationally underprivileged district until 1985–86. The gap between the highest mark achieved by a student not securing admission to a particular faculty, and the lowest marks at which a student was admitted, had widened by 1987. The gap was as high as 191 marks in engineering, 154 in medicine and 135 in physical sciences, out of a total of 400 in each case.

The decision to raise the minimum mark for admission to 200 with immediate effect attracted sharp criticism, some of which came from the radical students within the universities. Much of the criticism stemmed from confusion between the minimum mark at which students were entitled to apply for admission, and the actual marks at which they were admitted. In most cases, there was a large gap between the two. Thus, if this minimum mark of 200 had been adopted in 1986 for those seeking admission to the universities in 1987, less than 3 per cent of the 6143 students actually admitted that year would have been left out. Only one student out of 493 who secured admission in the medicine stream would have been excluded, a mere eight out of 465 in engineering, one in law and none at all in the arts, commerce and management faculties. The percentage excluded would be relatively higher in the biological and physical sciences. But that would be because the policy of the UGC was to take into the universities as many students as were necessary to fill the places available in the laboratories in these disciplines.

The opposition to this increase in the minimum mark was seized upon by the left-wing and nationalist Janatha Vimukthi Peramuna, as a means of linking the radical students in the universities with the radical students in the secondary schools whom they were actively encouraging at this time. They contended that raising the minimum mark was evidence of the government's deliberate reduction of the opportunities for students from the rural areas to enter the universities. Very soon, opposition also emerged from other sources, especially from the Muslim educationists who felt that their students would be affected.[11]

This opposition notwithstanding, the UGC set in motion the legal procedure for securing the approval of the ministry of higher education for the execution of the decision. University admissions policy was one of the three main areas in which the minister of education was empowered to issue written directives to the commission. A letter from President Jayewardene to the chairman of the UGC on 27 January 1988, informed the commission that they could proceed to give effect to the changes outlined in the report of the committee reviewing university admissions. The vice-chancellors and deans of faculties welcomed the changes outlined. There was satisfaction that, at last, a start was being made in halting the deterioration of academic standards at the stage of admissions to the universities. A meeting of all non-academic members of the university councils, together with vice-chancellors, was called by the UGC on 26 March 1988, to discuss the situation in the universities, and in particular to see how some of those which were closed because of student agitation could be reopened. The new university admissions policy was one of the main themes under discussion. There was overwhelming support for it from the nearly 100 persons present.

There was a single dissentient voice, a Muslim educationist who strongly opposed the decision to raise the minimum mark and drew attention to the criticism it had evoked from many sections of the population. He argued in favour of retaining the three-tier system of admissions unchanged, and urged that the principle of 'district quotas' and quotas for 'educationally backward' districts be retained. He received no support from anyone present.[12]

However, within four days of this meeting, the government reversed its position on the changes to the admissions policy approved in President Jayewardene's letter of 27 January. A terse communiqué issued by the Cabinet office announced that the new policy and the recommendations of the UGC's admissions review committee had been discussed at a meeting of the Cabinet on 30 March through the initiative of Minister Hameed and that it had been decided to return to the status quo ante.[13] No reasons were given. This sudden reversal of a change announced in January 1988, a few weeks earlier, provides further evidence of the operation of a sort of Gresham's Law with regard to the university admissions policy in Sri Lanka. At every critical moment, political considerations would drive out arguments based on proven academic needs. In this instance, a Muslim Cabinet minister's perception of potential damage to the interests of his community with regard to university admissions took precedence over the general academic good of all the ethnic/religious groups in the country.

The rest of the story shall be briefly told. Another review committee on university admissions was appointed in 1993. Its report endorsed the conclusions reached by the review committee of 1987. But on this occasion, the report was not published—the change of government in 1994 accounts for that—and it is very likely, gathering dust at the UGC. The system that had evolved in the 1980s remained: a three-tier system of a national merit quota, a district quota and a quota for educationally backward districts.

A refinement of this came in 1996–97 when the Tamils from the Jaffna peninsula, hitherto the most vocal critics of the system, joined in asking for the status of a disadvantaged district for Jaffna itself. This claim was first made before the UGC review committee of 1993. On that occasion, it was rejected by the committee. With the change of government, they succeeded in securing the status of a disadvantaged district. This reversal of the position taken by Jaffna politicians from being the most vigorous advocates of a merit system to being somewhat low-key claimants for the benefits of district quotas was not a temporary one. More importantly, this illustrates the significance of the change that had occurred in the university admissions policy. It had ceased to be an affirmative action based on ethnicity in support of the Sinhalese majority, and even politicians from the Jaffna district were comfortable with it as a form of regional, i.e., district, preference.

Figure IV: University Admissions Policy

1990	
In 1990, the number of 'educationally underprivileged' districts was increased to twelve:	
1. Ampara	7. Monaragala
2. Anuradhapura	8. Mullaitivu
3. Badulla	9. Nuwara Eliya
4. Hambantota	10. Polonnaruwa
5. Kilinochchi	11. Trincomalee
6. Mannar	12. Vavuniya
1996–97	
Jaffna was added to the list of underprivileged districts.	

Figure V: Educationally Underprivileged Districts

Ampara	Since 1976
Anuradhapura	1976–85; 1990–
Badulla	Since 1976
Batticaloa	1978–85
Hambantota	Since 1976
Jaffna	Since 1996–97
Kilinochchi	Since 1990
Mannar	Since 1976
Monaragala	1976–85; 1990–
Mullaitivu	Since 1979
Nuwara Eliya	1976–85; 1990–
Polonnaruwa	1976–85; 1990-
Puttalam	1980-85
Trincomalee	1976–85; 1990-
Vavuniya	1976–85; 1990-

From 1996–97 to the present day (2012) the administrative structure of the government's university admissions policy remained unchanged except for the introduction of a mathematical formula based on the performance of students at the General Certificate of Education (G.C.E. Advanced Level (A/L) which determined the fare of students seeking admission to the universities. This formula, properly known as the 'Z score', gained acceptance when it was introduced after 1998. Its substance was challenged in an appeal to the Supreme Court. The 'Z score' is likely to become a matter of public discussion now (2012) and will be so in the years to come. Whether it will be a matter of a return to the drawing boards, which we have outlined in this chapter, only time will tell. One policy change worth considering is a return to the system of permitting the universities to conduct their own entrance examinations as it was before 1965.

7

Language Policy

In this chapter we examine the views advanced by analysts such as Thomas Sowell and political scientists such as Robert Oberst that the change in language policy introduced in Sri Lanka in the mid and late 1950s could be treated as part of a policy of affirmative action in favour of the Sinhalese majority. However, neither Sowell nor Oberst provide any evidence to substantiate this contention.

A review of the debate on language policy in the national press and in pamphlets, in the early 1950s, immediately preceding the abandonment of the consensus on the policy reached in the national legislature in 1943–44, four years prior to the transfer of power, would appear to provide evidence to suggest that some of the proponents of the unilateral change in the language policy in 1956 did think of the change in terms of an ethnic preference.[1] But from the moment the policy change was given legislative form, efforts were made to modify it in favour of recognizing the language rights of the minority Tamils in many key areas of state policy. The modification of the National Language Act No. 33 of 1956 began in earnest in 1958 with the result that in its implementation, the language reform introduced in 1956 had very few elements—indeed if any at all—of a policy of affirmative action. The modifications introduced in 1958 survived the rapid political changes of the period 1958–66: three changes of government after three general elections. These were the UNP's very brief minority government of March–July 1960, the SLFP government of 1960–64 and the short-lived SLFP–LSSP coalition of 1964–65.

More importantly, despite the sanguine expectations of the 'Sinhala Only' activists of the mid-1950s, Sri Lanka remained very much a bilingual state (or a trilingual one if English were to be added, as it must be, to Sinhala and Tamil) and as much of a multicultural country as it was before the 'Sinhala Only' agitation began. Many, if not most, of the advocates of the 'Sinhala Only' policy—Professor G.P. Malalasekera for one—also argued the case for assimilation of the minorities of Sri Lanka into the dominant Sinhalese-Buddhist culture.[2] But no government sought to adopt such a policy on any systematic basis, and no major politician in power advocated that as a national objective to be imposed on the minorities. This at a time when assimilationist policies did not have the sinister connotations they have today. The minorities—the Tamils especially—were sensitive with regard to language and education policies, and viewed these developments with deep suspicion on account of the potential such changes had for assimilationist ends.[3]

The principle of bilingualism had been at its strongest in the most sensitive area of ethnic relations—education. The education reforms of the 1930s and the 1940s had, as one of their vitally important features, the use of the 'mother tongue' of the students in the learning process. One result of this policy was the evolution of two-language streams, beginning with the primary schools, extending into secondary education in the 1940s and culminating, in the 1960s, in university education. Tamil parents were guaranteed the right to educate their children through the medium of the Tamil language. This right was not restricted geographically to predominantly Tamil-speaking areas—it applied to all parts of the island.

The right stemmed from the education reforms of the 1930s and 1940s, and was well entrenched by the mid-1950s. More to the point, the 'Sinhala Only' Act of 1956 did not imperil this right. Indeed, the education of Tamil children through the Tamil language proceeded apace over the decade of 1956–66. Linked to it was the right that those educated in Tamil could appear for public examinations—ranging from general education certificate examinations and university entrance examinations, to examinations for entry into public sector employment—in that language.

The right to education through the Sinhala or the Tamil language was treated, from the very inception, as a group right rather than as an individual right.[4] Both Sinhalese and Tamil politicians were agreed on this, and were insistent about it—the Sinhalese for fear that if the wishes of individual parents were conceded it would help perpetuate the primacy of English education, and the Tamils for fear that some parents would opt to educate their children through Sinhala, and thus begin a process of assimilation. Children of mixed marriages were in a more advantageous position: their parents could choose the language medium in which such children were to be educated—Sinhala, Tamil or English. (English as a medium of education continued in schools till the 1970s.) Over the years, the resistance to permitting individual parents to decide on the medium of instruction of their children has persisted, especially on the part of the Tamils. The Sinhalese are much less opposed to such a change in policy, but no attempt was made by successive governments to make such a change.

A special provision, however, was made for the Muslims. There has been a noticeable sensitivity to the special needs of the Muslims, themselves a Tamil-speaking group although quite distinct from the Tamils in ethnic identity. This policy of acknowledgement of the special needs of the Muslims originated in the 1940s, and was continued in the years after Independence. It received a great impetus with the appointment of a Muslim, Badi-ud-din Mahmud, as minister of education by Mrs Bandaranaike on two occasions, 1960–63 and 1970–77.

Muslim children had the right (till 1974) to pursue their studies in any one of the three language media—Sinhala, Tamil or English—a privilege no other group in the country enjoyed. Special government-funded training colleges were also set up for the Muslims for training teachers. Moreover, Arabic is taught in government schools as an optional language for Muslim pupils. The *maulavis*, appointed by the ministry of education and paid by the state, are the ones teaching this language. More importantly, in recognition of the cultural individuality of Muslims as distinct from Tamils whose language is the home language of large numbers of Muslims, a new category of government schools was established for them. The usual practice was to categorize schools on the basis of the language of instruction and thus the Muslims formed part of the Tamil-speaking school population. In the 'Muslim' schools, the sessions and vacations are determined by the special requirements of the Muslim population, in particular the annual Ramadan fast. The establishment and expansion of these schools, it must be emphasized, vitiates the principle of non-sectarian state education which has been the declared policy of all governments since 1960.

Although the rhetoric of the language policy did not conform to the reality, that rhetoric had a life of its own. There was, for instance, the virulent campaign waged by a combination of the SLFP and the Marxist parties against the regulations under the Tamil Language (Special Provisions) Act of 1958, introduced in the the Parliament by the UNP-led coalition in January 1966. The Opposition unleashed a sustained barrage of racialist propaganda in which the SLFP, the traditional advocates for the Sinhalese-Buddhist domination of the Sri

Lanka polity, was joined by the Lanka Sama Samaja Party and
the Communist Party, the latter recent but enthusiastic converts
to a cause it had once despised. The massive demonstrations
organized by these parties on this occasion marked the triumph
of the rhetoric of the language policy over the hard reality of
its practical application. This attitude had lasting effects as
was seen in 1972 when these parties established a coalition
government—the United Front—and were in the throes of
introducing a new Constitution. The Constitution of 1972
unequivocally consolidated the 'Sinhala Only' policy of the
1950s and emphasized the essentially subordinate role of the
Tamil language. Thus, while the use of the Tamil language
was recognized and permitted within the limits set out in the
Tamil Language (Special Provisions) Act No. 28 of 1958, the
regulations drafted under the provisions of the Act were deemed
'subordinate legislation'. The reference was quite deliberately
directed at the Tamil Language (Special Provisions) Regulations
adopted by the the Parliament in 1966. The rhetoric, not the
actual policy, had become—to the constituent parties of the
governing coalition—the political reality. This was much more so
in the case of the Tamils who often, if not generally, preferred
to judge the government by what it said, and not by what it
actually did. The tragedy was that this ostentatious elevation of
rhetoric to the realm of political reality confused the situation,
perhaps deliberately, concealing the fact that these changes had
made no difference as regards the language policy in education,
public administration or public life. In practice, the language
policy in these spheres did not change in any significant way from
what it was prior to 1972. Actually, there was no change at all.

In contrast, the framers of the 1978 Constitution deliberately
sought a more conciliatory language policy and gave this objective
very high priority. The terms of that accommodation incorporated
in that Constitution were, at the least, a consolidation of the

modus vivendi on language rights that had emerged after two decades of strife. They were, in fact, much more than that, as would be clear by comparing the provisions of the Constitution of 1978 relating to language rights with those of its immediate predecessor.

We have seen how the Constitution of 1972 unequivocally consolidated the 'Sinhala Only' policy of the 1950s and emphasized the essentially subordinate role of the Tamil language. In contrast, Chapter IV of the 1978 Constitution, while maintaining the status of Sinhala as *the* official language (Article 18), recognized Tamil as a national language[5] (Article 19), a significant modification of the 'Sinhala Only' policy.[6] Chapter IV of the 1978 Constitution is an elaboration of Articles 14(1)(f) and 27(6), which, respectively, guaranteed an individual the freedom to use his or her own language, and laid down as a principle of state policy, that 'no citizen shall suffer any disability by reason of language'. Moreover, all the rights enjoyed by the Tamil-speaking people of the island under the Tamil Language (Special Provisions) Act No. 28 of 1958 were incorporated in the Constitution and could not be changed except by way of a constitutional amendment.

Most language rights set out in Chapter IV of the 1978 Constitution had been in existence in the past, derived from the language legislation of the 1950s and regulations connected with it such as those approved by the the Parliament in 1966, or from legislation relating to education, public administration and justice, to mention only the most important areas of public interest relevant to the use of the Tamil language. Yet in theory, if not in practice, ordinary legislation could override these rights. Although this had seldom happened, the more important point was that no real remedy was available against their denial through regulations or even administrative decisions. The language provisions of the 1978 Constitution changed all that.

Ten years later the thirteenth amendment to the Constitution, certified on 14 November 1987, raised Tamil to the level of an official language, with English given the position of a link language. Although there was some ambiguity about the position of English, its legal status was equal to that of Sinhala and Tamil. The provisions of the thirteenth amendment were clarified and consolidated by the sixteenth amendment (certified on 17 December 1988). Article 25A introduced on that occasion stated that in the event of any inconsistency between the provisions of any law and the provisions of Chapter IV of the 1978 Constitution, the latter shall prevail.

With the introduction of a new Constitution in 1978, and a new language policy, the Official Languages Department was re-established after the language reforms of the 1950s, this time to implement a policy of bilingualism (if not trilingualism) instead of the 'Sinhala Only' policy. That department had lost much of its importance and influence in the early 1970s. In 1973, its obligations and responsibilities had been dispersed among other ministries and departments on a directive of the then minister of public administration, local government and home affairs. The department itself had been reduced in status to a mere division in the ministry of public administration.

Its revival on 1 January 1979 marked a new phase in the implementation of the language policy in Sri Lanka. That policy had come full circle: from 'English Only' under colonial rule, to Sinhala and Tamil from 1944 to 1956, to 'Sinhala Only' from 1956 to 1978, and on to Sinhala and Tamil along with English from 1978 onwards. Much of the ambiguity in the language law, and hence in the official language policy, had been settled with the Constitution of 1978 despite the lack of precision in terms such as 'official', 'national language' and 'link language'.

In 1989–90 under President R. Premadasa, the UNP government took the important policy decision to establish an

Official Languages Commission with wide powers to oversee the implementation of the official language policy. The proposal for the establishment of such a commission had been made as early as 1945–46 by the Select Committee on Official Language Policy of the State Council under the chairmanship of J.R. Jayewardene, then a backbencher in the national legislature. Such a commission had been established in 1951 and its initiatives in language planning and implementation in the years 1951 to 1953 had been one of the major creative phases in the history of Sri Lanka's experimentation in changes in the language policy. The Official Language Commission appointed on 21 December 1991 with the passage of the Official Language Commission Act No. 18 of 1991 enjoyed wider powers than the commission of 1951–53, with regard to the implementation of the language policy since the 1951 commission was the creation of the administration and not a legal entity. Based on a Canadian model, the Act of 1991 provided a legal framework to monitor and supervise the implementation of the country's official language policy.

The establishment of Sri Lanka's Official Language Commission in this form was a manifestation of a contemporary phenomenon, the transfer of institutions from one political culture and one political environment to a totally different one in the hope that they would take root and even flourish there. The institution was new even in Canada. The chances of successful transplantation seemed difficult enough at first glance: the Canadian situation involved a conflict between two international languages which share a common script. In Sri Lanka, the conflict was between a purely Sri Lankan language, and a regional one which has two centres, one in Sri Lanka and the other in Tamil Nadu. To complicate matters even further, there was the 'link' language, English. There were thus three scripts, and those who sought bilingual proficiency in Sinhala and Tamil needed to master two scripts, and a third as well in the form of English. But the willingness to import an institution from one troubled environment to another was evidence of a strong political will to seek accommodation on an issue which had destroyed civil peace when it first erupted four decades ago. After a long period during which its opinions were virtually neglected, it was revived with much publicity in 2011.

Bilingualism (or indeed trilingualism) was seen in the use of the Tamil language in the national insignia, coins and currency, postage stamps, in road signs and in all official and semi-official documents at every level—many if not most of these documents were in both Sinhala and Tamil or in Sinhala, Tamil and English versions. Tamil was also a medium used in the national radio, and then in television when it was introduced to the island in the 1980s. The right of Tamil-speaking citizens to correspond in Tamil with state officials, and with employees of state-owned corporations and public sector autonomous bodies, was protected. But the snag was that quite often their right to receive a reply in Tamil was observed in the breach. Even when the government has shown the political will to implement this policy—and governments since 1977 have been consistent in showing that political will—the lethargy of lower-level bureaucrats in combination with a shortage of bilingual officials have proved to be formidable obstacles in giving the Tamil minority satisfaction on this sensitive issue. A sense of grievance has continued with regard to the language policy, one that focuses on this gap in the system while ignoring the reversion to a policy of parity of status for Tamil and disregarding the advantages that Sri Lanka's Tamil minority have had in the field of education.

A Comparison with Switzerland's Language Policy

The language rights of Sri Lanka's Tamil minority are on a par with those of the French in Canada, substantially better than those of the English-speaking minority in Quebec, and immeasurably superior to those of the Tamils of Malaysia who form an overwhelming majority of the Indian community in that country. Sri Lanka, by a curious irony, is the only sovereign state in which Tamil is recognized as an official language. The unusual and somewhat unreal situation, of course exists in Singapore where Tamil is recognized as one of the four official languages, the other three being Mandarin Chinese, English and Malay. In reality Tamil has a distinctly subordinate position there to the others, especially if compared to Mandarin Chinese and English. A more appropriate comparison is with the language rights of the minorities in the cantons of Switzerland. The comparison is appropriate because Switzerland is often cited by Tamil critics of Sri Lanka's language policy as the most important success story of modern pluralist democracy. They identify Switzerland's language policy as one of the keys to this success.[7] Such critics focus attention on Article 116 of the Swiss Constitution which lays down that

[i]n direct dealings between the citizen and the confederation, and *vice versa*, the federal government must adapt to the language of the individual within the limits of the official language.[8]

There are two principles in operation in the Swiss language policy: the principle of personality at the federal level, and the principle of territoriality at the cantonal level.

As Christopher Hughes points out in his book *Switzerland*:

[T]he Territorial Principle . . . regards the map of the Country as divided into French, German, Italian areas, the boundaries of which are unalterable. [Under] . . . the Personal Principle, . . . everyone can speak 'his' language in communicating with emanations of the state. The territorial principle takes precedence over the personal one in most cases of conflict.[9]

It is at the cantonal level that the more relevant comparison with the Sri Lankan situation lies. These cantons are not only remarkably homogenous but more or less unilingual, and persons 'moving to a new canton are obliged to use its local languages for the transaction of official business'.[10]

> [T]he canton (in accordance with the principle of territoriality) determines the official cantonal language (or in a few cases, languages). The cantonal language is the medium of instruction in the public schools. In addition, all cantonal laws and regulations are issued only in the official language(s).

While compromises are made in practice, the cantons have no legal obligation to provide translations or deal with citizens in languages other than their own.[11]

Hughes also refers to:

> The crisis of the territorial system which comes over the question of the school: it is here that official recognition has to be made when the actual boundary of the spoken language has shifted . . . The burden of political decisions usually falls upon the canton, and in particular the all important decision as to which is the official language of the lowest unit of local government. The power to determine this last point is called the *Sprachenhoteit*, language-sovereignty, of the canton, and federal authorities acknowledge the cantonal decision here.[12]

Thus the practical realities of the Swiss language policy show the language policy of Sri Lanka in a more favourable light than its critics would have it, and the comparison would be even more favourable if one were to focus attention on education. Sri Lanka's Tamil minorities—indigenous and Indian—have always enjoyed the right to an education through the medium of the Tamil language in whatever part of the country they live in.[13] This right is valid in the case of university and technical education as well. Apart from the University of Jaffna—in the Tamil-speaking northern province—which teaches in Tamil and English, and the Eastern University of Sri Lanka, located in the largely Tamil-speaking eastern province (with its Tamil and Muslim majority) which also teaches in Tamil and English, the University of Peradeniya provides instruction through three languages—Sinhala, Tamil and English. The University of Colombo provides instruction in Tamil in some of its departments of study, in addition to instruction in Sinhala and English. So far as education is concerned, the Tamil minorities of Sri Lanka have enjoyed advantages which minorities in the Swiss cantons have not or have seldom enjoyed, not to mention a similar situation with the Tamil minority in Singapore and Malaysia.

Again, because the language rights guaranteed to the Tamils are operative in all parts of the island, and not merely in the north and the east, their practical value is at least on a par with, if not superior to, the language rights available to the minority population groups in the cantons of Switzerland. The great majority of such cantons are 'officially unilingual'.[14] Although Switzerland maintains more than one official language, the languages are spoken in clearly defined territorial areas.[15]

Looking back on these controversies, one feels that the price Sri Lanka has paid in terms of the breakdown of its ethnic harmony, and in the distortion of its national priorities, outweigh the undeniable benefits the emphasis on indigenous languages has brought to the people at large. Had the Sinhalese political leadership that succeeded the first post-Independence prime minister D.S. Senanayake not forced the pace of language change by seeking to give Sinhala the pride of place through an abrogation of the settlement on language reached in 1943–44, and had they been more patient and eschewed the path of unilateral change, they may well have ensured the primacy of their language on a much more solid basis. There would have been none of the rancour and bitterness that has been the price paid for the 'Sinhala Only' policy. Quite apart from the natural advantages accruing to Sinhala as the language of nearly three-fourth of the population, there was the powerful attraction of economic necessity—the Sinhalese areas offered by far the greatest opportunities in employment and trade. But as things turned out, the objective of 'Sinhala Only' was pursued, and the Tamils were able to take all the advantages of proclaiming to a sympathetic world that they, as a minority, have suffered greatly in the change in the language policy imposed on them by an unsympathetic majority. But the reality has been that the 'Sinhala Only' policy, in its starkest form, has proved to be an elusive objective. At the same time, adjustments and accommodations on language rights were made through political necessity and as part of a realistic adjustment to life in a plural society and a democratic state from as early as 1958. These had all but granted parity of status to the Tamil language by 1978.

A de facto status was elevated to a de jure fact by 1987–88. Yet the political benefits the Sinhalese majority were supposed to enjoy because of these working arrangements have proved to be just as elusive as the quest for the 'Sinhala Only' policy as the main representatives of Tamil political opinion in the country have never publicly or officially acknowledged that the reality of the language policy had deviated from its rhetoric over the years.

8

State Sector Employment

If an examination of the realities of Sri Lanka's language policy since the mid 1950s shows there is little justification in regarding the policy as part of a system of affirmative action, there is even less reason for accepting Robert Oberst's view that the recent and current dominance of the Sinhalese in Sri Lanka's public sector employment is the result of a deliberately introduced system of affirmative action policies. An examination of the record will show that this is not supported by evidence.

Much of the bitterness underlying the controversies on employment is explained in part by the conflict between the Tamils' traditional anxiety to maintain levels of employment in the state services they had grown accustomed to under British rule and the attempt on the part of the Sinhalese to insist on what they regard as their legitimate share of it. The economic resources of the northern province are severely limited. As early as the last quarter of the nineteenth century, it was evident that with an increase in the population of the region, many could not be accommodated in the traditional occupations based on land. The Tamils turned to state employment and the professions much more than to plantation agriculture and trade, as their avenues of employment.

The schools system that had developed under the British rule was concentrated, not diffused. The region in and around

Colombo served as the principal location, along with some main towns. One area surprisingly became a schooling centre—the Jaffna peninsula, the northern part of the island, with its hard, dry climate and lack of natural resources. Missionary enterprise found a very receptive people there. In that region alone, American missionaries (headquartered in Boston) were permitted to operate, though this was not restricted to just American missionaries. The historical legacy of the missionaries' endeavours was the creation of a superb network of schools and the production of generations of educated Tamils equipped for service in the lower rungs of the British administrative system. But Jaffna did not have the economic resources to support this increasingly educated population. So it began to export this 'labour' in the form of literate and educated youth to the more prosperous southern parts of the island, to establish a secure position in the clerical grades of the bureaucracy. Parodying Dr Samuel Johnson's observation that the most pleasing prospect in the Scotland of his day was the road that led to London, it could be truly said about much of the nineteenth century and early and mid twentieth century Jaffna that its most pleasing prospect was the road that led to Colombo.

These Tamils did not face much Sinhalese competition till the 1930s at least when the advantageous position enjoyed by the Tamils in the state services first became a point of bitter division in politics. Earlier, the more enterprising among them had left for other British colonies, principally to what is now Malaysia and in much smaller numbers to East Africa. This emigration to Malaya—as it was then known—came to a stop in the 1930s, and the movement to Colombo and the Sinhalese areas was strengthened. An official report written in 1946 explained that

> The acute shortage of trained staff for administrative and clerical functions caused the government of Malaya to appeal to the

Government of Ceylon to send Ceylonese [Sri Lankans] for service to Malaya, and from the year 1867, at the invitation and encouragement of the Malayan Government, large numbers of Ceylonese subordinates practically all of whom were Ceylon Tamils from Jaffna, secured employment in building roads, in surveying lands and doing the work of clerks, dressers [sic] etc. About 25 years ago [that is, about 1921] more than 50 per cent of the Junior Officers in the Government Services, General Clerical, Railway, Posts and Telegraphs, Medical, Public Works etc. were Ceylon Tamils.[1]

By the early years of the twentieth century, the Tamils had come to be singularly dependent on government service. Precisely because they had no deep roots in the island's plantation economy or trade for that matter, they were compelled to defend their position in public service all the more zealously. By the 1930s, Tamils dominated the public sector as clerks, teachers and technicians, and were also well established in the professional services as doctors and engineers. More significantly, they now faced Sinhalese competition, and their advantageous position in government employment became a point of contention and division in politics. The Soulbury Commissioners appointed in 1944 to report on the constitutional changes needed in Sri Lanka in preparation for independence, reported in 1945 that appointment to the public services

provides a common source of dissension between majority and minority communities . . . [The] Ceylon Tamils appear, at any rate as late as 1938, to have occupied a disproportionate number of posts in Public Services . . . That they have won for themselves a much larger share is a consequence of the higher standard of literacy and education which this community has so long enjoyed, and of its energy and efficiency. For similar reasons the Burghers have achieved an even more remarkable position.[2]

The commissioners viewed

the Sinhalese challenge to the predominant position of the Tamils in public appointments . . . [as] the natural effect of the spread of education and of the efforts being made to bring other portions of the island up to the intellectual level of one portion of it[3].

Having identified the problem, they turned to the British experience to reassure the Tamils:

In this connection, we cannot help recalling a period in our own history when, as the result of the superior educational facilities and better teaching prevalent in Scotland, a minority was enabled to secure a larger share of administrative and executive posts in the United Kingdom than could have been justified on any proportional allocation. Since then the English have made strenuous and not altogether unsuccessful endeavours to redress the deficiencies of their past.[4]

At the time of the transfer of power, the Tamil minority was warned in the clearest possible terms—even though the style chosen for the warning was understatement rather than exaggeration—that hard times lay ahead of them as educational standards improved among the Sinhalese. Unlike some achievement-oriented minorities in other parts of the world—the Chinese in Malaysia and other parts of South East Asia, for instance—the Sri Lankan Tamils grew accustomed to state employment. Their position in commerce and industry and plantation agriculture did not match their stake in their chosen field of concentration. The determining factor was a quest—almost a passion—for security and a steady income, a reflection of their awareness of the limited opportunities of employment available to them in the Jaffna peninsula. This made them exceptionally vulnerable and exceptionally sensitive to changes—changes in the language policy, changes by way of educational reform and changes in the mechanisms for determining admission to tertiary education in a country in which expansion in university education lagged far behind the expansion of secondary and primary education.

After Independence, competition increased, especially with the rapid expansion of educational opportunities in the Sinhalese areas. This greatly reduced the prospects of the Tamils in their search for positions in government service. Over the next twenty-five years, they would be overtaken in almost every sector of state employment and in the professions by the Sinhalese, overtaken but far from being overwhelmed. For a while, they retained their advantageous position in some of the professions—medicine, law and engineering—but lost it by the early 1980s. This represented the intellectual capital of the past, carefully gathered, protected and augmented but in their eyes, not expanding rapidly enough to overcome what they saw as the disadvantages that would face the next generation of Tamils. They preferred to believe that it was a matter of discrimination. In fact, it was the natural result of an expansion of secondary-level education in the Sinhalese areas.

The drop in the numbers of Tamils in the state service was marked after 1956. While representatives of Tamil opinion often argue this was the inevitable result of the change in the language policy adopted that year, there were other powerful forces of change at work. Given the demographic structure of the country, the Tamils could have hardly maintained the percentage of posts they held up to the 1930s.

In an assessment made in 1984 of this complex situation, S.W.R. de A. Samarasinghe points out:

The Tamils have already lost the relative position in central government employment that was enjoyed in the past. Apart from the obvious economic loss this entails, there is the psychological adjustment that many Jaffna (Tamil) families must make in the wake of this change. There is the fact that government jobs are no longer as easily obtained as they were a generation or two ago. The Sinhalese, on the other hand, are bound to view the change as a natural and inevitable adjustment that bestows on them their 'due' share. Clearly there are two different perceptions of the same phenomenon. The result is the Tamils have begun to feel they are 'discriminated' against and the Sinhalese feel recent changes have simply reversed the 'discrimination' they had been subjected to in the past.[5]

Samarasinghe's assessment holds true for the last thirty years as well, i.e., for the post-1984 period. If one excludes the state-owned plantation sector where the vast majority of the employees are Indian Tamils, the number of Tamils in *all* grades of state employment has declined to 10 per cent or less. This is about a third or a fourth of what it was in the early 1940s.

Many factors have contributed to this sharp decline in numbers after 1984. Firstly, there is the issue of large-scale emigration of Tamil youth from all strata of society to western countries such as Canada,[6] and Britain principally, and to Australia, and to the Scandinavian states (largely to Norway and Sweden). This migration took place in the wake of Sri Lanka's ethnic conflict, more particularly because of the disturbed political situation in the Jaffna peninsula, wherein the youth fled the rigours of life under the LTTE regime, thereby also escaping the harsh reality of compulsory military service in the LTTE's army. Secondly, there has also been a steady stream of 'economic refugees' to Denmark, Germany, France and Switzerland[7] in western Europe, and to Canada. There is, next, the collapse of the civil administration of the north of the island and in parts of the east for thirty years or so—until the defeat of the LTTE in 2009. This greatly reduced state employment opportunities for the Tamils who lived there. In addition, there is another factor: the expansion of the private sector for the first time since the mid 1950s. Since the late 1970s, the private sector (including import–export trade) has been providing opportunities for employment, outside the control of the government and the political processes, without the system of patronage that often govern admission to state employment. The expansion of the private sector has been on a scale that would have seemed impossible in the early 1970s. Among the principal beneficiaries of this expansion are the minorities, Tamils and Muslims. More to the point, state employment is no longer as attractive as it once was, pitted as it is against the private sector's greater flexibility in terms of wages, promotions and greater recognition given to merit and personal initiative. Above all, the private sector has been relatively free from political interference. Nevertheless, remedial measures—perhaps a form or forms of affirmative action—are required to get the country's public services to reflect more accurately than it does today the country's ethnic profile in the composition of its staff.

THE DEFEAT OF THE LTTE

The emergence of the Liberation Tigers of Tamil Eelam to the position of leadership of Tamil opinion in Sri Lanka and their elimination of rival Tamil parties, including the principal parties of the Tamil moderates, has been dealt with in part one of this monograph. Four chapters of part three, namely chapters 9, 10, 11 and 12 deal with both the recovery and fall of the LTTE against the background of parliamentary politics in Sri Lanka. Chapters 12 and 13 deal with the bolstering of the security forces which then went on to defeat the LTTE in 2009. The contests between the principal Sri Lankan political parties form the context to the various phases in the evolution of the LTTE, an organization that during its last phase became an important player in Sri Lankan politics.

The Indian Central government saved the LTTE from the impending assault on Jaffna and the LTTE positions there and in the northern province that General Ranatunga had planned in 1987. However, the LTTE chose to confront the challenges of the Indian intervention in Sri Lanka in 1987–90. At the outset, the LTTE gave a lukewarm response to the Indian Peace Keeping Force and then proceeded to fight it but was defeated after a prolonged series of military encounters.

Once the IPKF left Sri Lanka in 1990, the LTTE was able to make a recovery largely because President R. Premadasa did not take over the areas controlled by the LTTE—and held by the IPKF—as the Indians had expected him to do.

Instead, Premadasa attempted a rapprochement with the LTTE. He conducted negotiations with it and permitted it to occupy the areas earlier held by the IPKF. Thus the LTTE was saved, this time by the Premadasa government who provided it with money and even weapons, and then permitted it to occupy the areas vacated by the IPKF. Eventually, however, Premadasa's negotiations with the LTTE failed, and in 1993 he was assassinated by the LTTE.

With the change of government in Sri Lanka in 1994–95, President Chandrika Kumaratunga initially—rather exuberantly—followed Premadasa's policy of seeking a peaceful settlement to the Sri Lankan conflict. She went to the extent of conducting negotiations with the LTTE in Jaffna itself, the LTTE headquarters at that time. However, the talks failed and in the ensuing violence, Kumaratunga was compelled to call on her army to eliminate the LTTE in Jaffna and the northern province. She succeeded in this enterprise to a large extent. But by 1996–97, the LTTE had staged a recovery and very soon drove the Sri Lankan army out of many of the territories it had won from the LTTE in 1995–96. Kumaratunga also expanded the army and re-equipped it. The LTTE attempted to assassinate Kumaratunga in 1998 when she vied for a second term as executive President. The attempt failed, but she was injured.

Kumaratunga's successor Mahinda Rajapaksa inherited these problems. The situation became complicated when the UNP under Ranil Wickramesinghe won the parliamentary elections in 2001 and in 2002. As prime minister, Wickremasinghe too chose to negotiate with the LTTE. In 2002, the two parties—the prime minister and the LTTE—signed a Cease Fire Agreement (CFA) and began negotiations for a settlement. Once again, however, the negotiations failed.

When Mahinda Rajapaksa won a narrow victory at the presidential election of 2005, his early response to the problem of dealing with the LTTE was to continue with the policies of Wickremasinghe. But his attitude changed within a year and by

2006, he sought to engage the LTTE in conflict. As we will see in later chapters of part three of this monograph, he eventually abandoned the Sri Lankan government's commitment to the Cease Fire Agreement.

By 2006–07, the LTTE had been weakened by the defection of its eastern province cadres. Meanwhile in 2007, the Supreme Court endorsed a challenge—by a section of the Sri Lankan Opposition—to the amalgamation of the northern and the eastern provinces, saying that it was a constitutionally flawed process (this amalgamation process had been initiated by President Jayewardene in 1988). With that—as we shall see—the LTTE lost control of the eastern province.

Over the years 2007–09, the Sri Lankan army, under Lieutenant General Sarath Fonseka, inflicted a succession of defeats on the LTTE forces and drove them to seek refuge in the coasts of the Mullaitivu district.

President Rajapaksa assiduously celebrated the victories of the army, and more to the point, claimed them as his own. The army's victories naturally became part of the political process in Sri Lanka. Mahinda Rajapaksa cashed in on these victories to strengthen his government electorally, in anticipation of the next presidential election scheduled for 2010.

A Weak Government and a Resurgent LTTE

Sri Lanka's fourth presidential election was held on 21 December 1999, about eleven months ahead of schedule. For the second time in succession, the results of a Sri Lankan presidential election were affected by the actions of the LTTE. On this occasion, the LTTE inflicted a series of defeats on the Sri Lankan army in the north of the country, in October and November, during a brief and very successful campaign, as a result of which the government forces lost control of large areas of territory they had secured between 1995 and 1997. These demoralizing defeats (amidst reports of large-scale desertions and mutiny in the ranks of the army) embarrassed the government of President Kumaratunga and gave the prospects of her principal opponent, Ranil Wickremasinghe of the UNP, an unexpected boost. As a result, the latter's electoral campaign gained in credibility, and by the end of November, he seemed a potential victor in the contest. Wickremasinghe retained this favourable position until a failed assassination attempt by an LTTE suicide bomber on 18 December, the last day of campaigning, left the terrorists' target, Chandrika Kumaratunga, slightly injured. This helped reverse the emerging pro-UNP trend in the election process. The shock of the failed assassination attempt (which killed more than twenty people) was cleverly exploited by the government. This was done through the use of the state-controlled electronic media, particularly television broadcasts, and through hastily organized small public meetings held across the country, in direct violation of the ban imposed by electoral laws on any form of electioneering two days prior to the holding of an election. The principal theme of the government's last-minute campaign was that the LTTE had planned the assassination to help Wickremasinghe's cause. The scale of Kumaratunga's victory, on this occasion, by 51 per cent of the total votes compared with 43 per cent for Wickremasinghe, was substantially below that attained by her in the campaign of 1994. The JVP candidate's relatively poor performance in this election (which was contested by thirteen candidates and attracted a 73 per cent electoral turn-out) also benefited the incumbent President. Had the JVP garnered more support, Kumaratunga's margin of victory would have been even smaller. With allegations made by neutral observers, as well as by the defeated UNP candidate, of widespread electoral violence, blatant malpractices and vote-rigging, the flawed presidential election cost the new government heavily in terms of integrity. In addition, it faced the prospect of a serious legal challenge to the validity of the election, a challenge which did not come.

Political and Military Challenges

The dawn of the new century brought forth more LTTE suicide-bomber attacks. In early January 2000, despite tightened security in the capital, another suspected LTTE suicide bomber killed herself and twelve other people outside the office of Prime Minister Sirimavo Bandaranaike in Colombo in what police described as a failed assassination attempt. Then in June, an LTTE suicide bomber killed at least twenty people, including a prominent Cabinet minister, the minister of industrial development, Clement V. Gunaratna, and his wife, at a parade in the capital marking the country's first War Heroes' Day.

Once President Kumaratunga had recovered sufficiently from the trauma of the pre-election attempt on her life (in which she had sustained wounds to her right eye), she applied herself once more to the process of constitutional reform, and by mid February 2000, she had succeeded in persuading Wickremasinghe and the UNP to send a delegation to participate in the preparation of a new Constitution (based on the proposals regarding devolution presented by the Kumaratunga government in 1997). The first such meeting took place in March. Meanwhile, in mid February 2000, Norwegian Minister of Foreign Affairs Knut Vollebæk, during a visit to Colombo announced that the Norwegian government had accepted a request from the Sri Lankan President as well as the LTTE to serve as a mediator to bring the two parties together for discussions. Although the previous year, Norway had been posited to play the role of such a facilitator, it had little effect in checking the LTTE's military operations, which had continued throughout November and December 1999. It is clear that the successes achieved by the LTTE in the last weeks of 1999 were a prelude to a determined bid to capture the large army base at Elephant Pass, on the strategically important isthmus that links the Jaffna peninsula to the rest of the island. The garrison there (under government control since the IPKF's withdrawal in 1990) was seized by the LTTE in late April 2000, in the group's most comprehensive military victory since the 1990s. In response, a panic-stricken Sri Lankan government appealed for assistance both from regional powers and elsewhere to deal with the rapidly advancing LTTE forces. The response from the regional powers was ambivalent at best. Adopting a more circumspect policy than its predecessor had done in the 1980s, the BJP-led Indian Central government decided that it would not interfere directly in the Sri Lankan conflict. All requests from the Sri Lankan government for military assistance in the form of weaponry were turned down. All that was on offer from India was 'humanitarian assistance', a pronouncement interpreted in Colombo as including the transfer of Sri Lankan troops out of the Jaffna peninsula presumably by Indian ships, should the need for such an evacuation arise. India also announced, however, that it was extending its ban on the LTTE by two more years. The ban had first come into place in the wake of the assassination of Rajiv Gandhi in 1991. A more fruitful initiative by the Sri Lankan authorities was the restoration of diplomatic ties with Israel and successful negotiations with that country for the supply of sophisticated weaponry and military aircraft. Other countries too responded with the supply of arms: namely, Russia, Pakistan and, more importantly, China. On 3 May, President Kumaratunga put Sri Lanka on what was called a 'war footing' by invoking the Public Security Ordinance. This constituted the first use of the measure, which gave the police extensive powers of arrest and confiscation, since the time when the country became independent in 1948. At the same time, the President imposed a ban on strikes and political rallies, and stricter censorship on all forms of media reporting.

The resurgence of the LTTE in 1999–2000 had a noticeable effect on Tamil Nadu politicians in the form of a revival of pro-LTTE sentiment, which had largely been dormant since the assassination of Rajiv Gandhi in 1991. In early June 2000, the then chief minister of Tamil Nadu, Muthuvel Karunanidhi, called for a partition of Sri Lanka, allegedly on the model of the former Czechoslovakia, into two states, one of which would be a Tamil state. There was immediate opposition to this proposal both within Tamil Nadu and in other parts of India. (This was quite apart from the opposition from a wide range of parties in Sri Lanka.) Karunanidhi's proposition and the outpouring of pro-LTTE sentiment among other Indian politicians belonging to parties of the then BIP-led governing coalition in New Delhi were acutely embarrassing to the Indian government. The administration of Atal Bihari Vajpayee responded, clearly enough and repeatedly, by asserting that it would not countenance the establishment of a separate Tamil state in Sri Lanka, and indicated a preference for the allocation of greater autonomy to the Tamil areas of the island.

Meanwhile, in response to the escalating military crisis, the Sri Lankan government imposed draconian security measures, banning all those activities perceived as a threat to national security and giving sweeping powers to the armed forces and the police. It also renewed the censorship law on the foreign media. By early May 2000, LTTE forces, buoyed by their recent military gains, were close enough to Jaffna town to suggest they were poised to drive the Sri Lankan army away from Jaffna and the peninsula and to compel the government forces to abandon the airport at Pallali and the naval base at Karainagar, which the LTTE had never been able to control previously. Within a month, however, the LTTE advance had lost its earlier momentum. This was because of a change of leadership in the Sri Lankan army in the Jaffna peninsula, which saw two experienced generals with exemplary records as field commanders—one of whom was General Sarath Fonseka, later the head of the army—being posted there. It was also because of the recent provision of high-tech weaponry, which the army had lacked at the time of the fall of Elephant Pass. These moves enabled the Sri Lankan security forces to regain the initiative and by mid June 2000, the threat posed by the LTTE to the government's control over Jaffna town and the peninsula had clearly receded. By early September, the army was making efforts to compel the LTTE to move out of some of the towns in the vicinity of Jaffna. Despite early setbacks, these attempts began to prove successful by mid September.

In any event, the successful holding operation by the army in Jaffna gave the government the opportunity to return to its preparation of a new Constitution through discussions with the UNP. The government's avowed objective was to have a new Constitution presented to and approved by the Parliament in July or August 2000, all the time bearing in mind the fact that the national legislature's term of office expired on 24 August 2000 (unless it was to be dissolved earlier). The discussions with the UNP leadership on the draft of the new Constitution proceeded smoothly enough until early July, when complications arose in the form of sharp disagreements over the role of President Kumaratunga in a new parliamentary system. While the government insisted that Kumaratunga should have a dual role as the new prime minister after the parliamentary elections should the elections be won by the PA, and as executive President until the expiry of her current six-year term, the UNP argued that her tenure of presidency should come to an end within a short time of the promulgation of any new Constitution. For the new Constitution to gain approval, it required a two-third parliamentary majority, not achievable once the UNP leadership had declared its opposition to the draft Constitution. Meanwhile, the Tamil parliamentary parties—the EPDP, the Democratic People's Liberation Front and the TULF—also rejected the proposals regarding the new Constitution on the ground that they gave inadequate autonomy to the Tamil regions of the country. The government sought to overcome this by attempting to persuade the UNP MPs to support the new Constitution in the Parliament. In the event, a number of UNP MPs did cross over to the government's side during the debate on the proposed Constitution in early August. However, the number of members who did so fell far short of the government's targeted number. When this situation became clear, the draft Constitution was not presented for a vote (voting on the controversial bill was postponed indefinitely). Instead, after an inconclusive and acrimonious debate, with large and vociferous crowds expressing their opposition to the draft Constitution, the Parliament was dissolved on 18 August, and new parliamentary elections were scheduled for October.

Meanwhile, on 10 August 2000, Sirimavo Bandaranaike resigned as prime minister and retired from political life at the age of eighty-four. The veteran politician was replaced in the premiership by the erstwhile minister of public administration, home affairs and plantation industries, Ratnasiri Wickremanayake, who was regarded as a Sinhalese hardliner close to the Buddhist sangha (the Buddhist order). Later, in mid September, the minister of shipping and shipping development and president of the SLMC, Mohamed H.M. Ashraff, was killed in a helicopter crash in the Kegalle district. A high-level investigation was immediately ordered into the incident amidst speculation that the aircraft may have been shot down by LTTE guerrillas.

The results of the parliamentary election of 10 October 2000 were a disappointment to both the PA and the UNP. The election, which according to official figures attracted a 75 per cent turn-out, was marred by widespread malpractices and systematic violence and intimidation (particularly on the part of the incumbent PA). The PA secured only 45 per cent of the votes cast, while the UNP received 40 per cent. The JVP gained ten seats (having secured 6 per cent of the vote), and from the beginning, considered itself a possible balancing force in a Parliament in which neither the PA nor the UNP had won an absolute majority (with 107 and 89 out of the 225 seats, respectively). After much bargaining by the two main parties, the PA, having gained the support of the EPDP, and the National

Unity Alliance (NUA), a remnant of the SLMC itself, was able to form a coalition with a very narrow majority. It was evident that the government would be vulnerable to shifts of opinion within the Parliament, as well as throughout the country.

The death of Sirimavo Bandaranaike, on the day of the election, deprived the SLFP of a leader who had served it for forty years, as well as of a respected stabilizing influence. The election of Anura Bandaranaike, the President's estranged brother and now a member of the UNP, as parliamentary speaker by a unanimous vote was seen, in the early stages at least, as heralding the beginning of a period of greater cooperation between the PA and the UNP. However, in fact, the establishment of a forty-four-member Cabinet, with thirty-eight deputy ministers, underlined the inherent instability of the government, and its potential vulnerability in the face of a challenge by the UNP. Every group in the coalition was represented in the Cabinet, including the SLMC and its affiliate, the NUA. It was evident very soon that President Kumaratunga's principal concern was to ensure the survival of the government in a situation where, under the terms of the Constitution, the Parliament could not be dissolved for at least one year after an election, in this instance until 10 October 2001.

The priority for the new government was set by the LTTE, which declared unilaterally that it would begin a period of ceasefire from 24 December 2000 as a prelude to talks with the government. The LTTE also proposed that the talks be facilitated in the early stages by a Norwegian representative. Although the government readily accepted the principle of a Norwegian facilitator, it refused to accept the LTTE offer of talks. The government also refused to lift the proscription on the LTTE. It insisted on a set of conditions as a prelude to accepting a unilateral cessation of hostilities. The LTTE, nevertheless, implemented its ceasefire declaration and regularly renewed it until the end of April 2001, ignoring the conditions set by the government. The government suspected the LTTE of seeking a period of time during which it could rebuild its forces and its equipment. However, a low-intensity conflict continued in the north and the east.

By June 2001, the government's priorities shifted more emphatically to its political survival, as a result of a serious miscalculation on the part of the President. Kumaratunga had dismissed the new leader of the SLMC, Rauf Hakeem, from his position as minister of internal and international trade, commerce, Muslim religious affairs and shipping development, in the belief that the latter's party would not stand by him. However, as a result, six other members of the SLMC withdrew their support from the PA, thereby reducing the coalition government to a minority in the Parliament. The UNP was subsequently able to claim that the anti-PA groups had a parliamentary majority, with 115 of the 225 seats. It challenged the government with a 'no-confidence' motion. It proposed a parliamentary debate on this motion to be held in mid July. However, as the national census of 2001 was scheduled to take place at this time, the government suggested mid August as a more appropriate time for the debate.

That said, in early July 2001, the President unexpectedly prorogued the Parliament for two months to forestall the attempt to defeat the government on a no-confidence motion. Kumaratunga then ordered a referendum to be held on 21 August in order to seek a mandate for a new Constitution. The decision to prorogue the Parliament breached a settled principle of democratic governance, that the Parliament must not be prorogued when the government faces a vote of no-confidence, especially when it has lost its majority. The second ruling regarding referendum was unconstitutional. It deliberately ignored the special provisions in the Constitution that dictate the procedures for constitutional reform.

President Kumaratunga's decisions, taken without prior consultation with the Cabinet, plunged the country into a constitutional crisis. The UNP-led Opposition embarked on a campaign of peaceful popular resistance, marred by occasional violence, demanding a revocation of the prorogation of the Parliament. There was also opposition within the Cabinet, especially to the referendum. As a result, in early August, the President considered it expedient to postpone the referendum to mid October. The announcement was made two weeks after the LTTE, using its miniature air force, made an attack on Colombo's international airport, and adjacent air base, towards the end of July. This attack exposed serious flaws in the security system of the Sri Lankan air force and the airport. It also resulted in an embarrassing damage to the country's economy and the tourist industry. Incidents of violence between the Tamil guerrillas and the government escalated following the attack. Earlier that month, the President had circumvented the Parliament and reimposed a state of emergency invoking the anti-terrorism laws. The President had also passed an order to reimpose the ban on the LTTE. Unsurprisingly, those events led to the further erosion of the government's political credibility.

In an attempt to resolve the crisis, the prime minister and some senior Cabinet members began conducting negotiations with the UNP on a possible coalition government. Although the UNP showed some interest in this, it eventually decided to join other Opposition parties with the objective of forming a UNP-led coalition. The President objected to a UNP government or a UNP-led coalition, and began negotiations with the radical, left-wing JVP. Eventually, the JVP agreed to support the government, and in early September, a memorandum of understanding (MoU) was signed binding the two parties for one year. It resulted in a PA-led minority government, sustained by JVP votes. The left-wing party had set twenty-eight conditions in the memorandum, one of which was a reduction of the Cabinet to twenty members. A twenty-two-member Cabinet was subsequently sworn in. But three senior Cabinet members refused to join, an indication of the continuing state of instability of the government. Adhering to the JVP's demands, the President also cancelled the referendum on constitutional reforms and ordered the Parliament to reconvene a day earlier. In addition, the JVP insisted that there should be no negotiations with the LTTE during the one-year period.

In October 2001, there was further evidence of instability within the SLFP when it removed its general secretary, S.B. Dissanayake, when the government faced a vote of no-confidence which was to be held on 11 October. It had become clear that the government will be defeated in this parliamentary vote after thirteen members of the coalition, including several ministers, defected to the Opposition. President Kumaratunga, therefore, dissolved the Parliament a day before the scheduled vote and announced that a general election would be held in early December. The dissolution was condemned by the Opposition, as it was prevented from proving its majority. However, the decision was constitutional, as the President had waited until one year after the previous election before dissolving the legislature. Meanwhile, violence between the LTTE and the government continued and showed no signs of abating.

The general elections of 5 December 2001, like that of October 2000, were marred by malpractices, the blatant exploitation of state resources—taking plentiful advantages of incumbency—and vote-rigging (often crude and sometimes adroit) on the part of the outgoing PA. In addition, during both these elections, the state's print and electronic media were fully and almost exclusively reserved for the campaign of the government candidates. Furthermore, both elections were blighted by systematic violence directed against Opposition members under the alleged instruction of senior government personalities. The December 2001 parliamentary elections were assessed to be the more violent of the two. However, on this occasion, the electorate turned against the outgoing government and the rigging of votes failed decisively.

The UNP-led coalition won a comprehensive victory, securing most of the polling divisions and all but one of the polling districts outside of the northern province. The UNP won 109 of the 225 seats (45.6 per cent of the votes) and the PA obtained seventy-seven seats (37.2 per cent). The JVP secured sixteen (9.1 per cent), while the Tamil National Alliance (TNA) won 3.9 per cent of the seats. Political analysts believed that the margin of victory for the UNP and its allies would have been much wider had the election been free and fair. In order to ensure a majority in the Parliament and in recognition of the support received from and through the coalition partners, the UNP leader, Ranil Wickremasinghe, formed a United National Front (UNF) government with the SLMC, TNA and several members of the former PA administration who had defected to the UNP after the election.

The political cohabitation between the President and the UNF government proved to be uncomfortable. The Sri Lankan polity was not especially accustomed to an arrangement wherein the prime minister and the President represented opposing parties (the last time this had occurred was in 1984). So the conventions and practices that would reduce friction between the two parties had not yet developed. One essential factor was the right of the President to dissolve the Parliament after one year from the date of the last election. Confronted with the prospect of an election called at the President's convenience after 5 December 2002, the UNF government proposed that future elections be called on the basis of a parliamentary resolution and that the President's right to dissolve the Parliament be nullified if the government had a majority in the legislature. However, the relevant constitutional amendment to sanction such a proposal was not introduced for debate in the Parliament, with the result that the President was able to dissolve the Parliament in February 2004, although the UNF had a majority in the legislature.

The Cease Fire Agreement and Peace Talks

One of the principal political developments that followed the UNF's accession to power was a strengthening of the peace process. An informal ceasefire took effect in December 2001. On 22 February 2002, Prime Minister Ranil Wickremasinghe and the LTTE leader, Velupillai Prabhakaran, signed a Cease Fire Agreement (CFA[1]) for an internationally monitored indefinite ceasefire period, with the Norwegian government serving as facilitator. The CFA committed the two sides to specified courses of action and stipulated the conditions required for the commencement of peace talks.[2] A Sri Lanka Monitoring Mission (SLMM), operated by several Scandinavian countries and led by Norwegians, conducted the supervision of the implementation of the CFA.

The assumption was that the two parties would abide by the ceasefire agreement and commence peace talks on or before 2 August 2002. This deadline was missed, but the cessation of hostilities was maintained. On 4 September, the UNF government removed the official ban on the LTTE, a condition that the LTTE had insisted upon as a prelude to negotiations. The three-day peace talks began nearly two weeks later in Thailand. During the negotiations, the LTTE unexpectedly gave signs of abandoning their long-standing demand for a separate state[3] and appeared to be prepared to accept regional autonomy and regional government. These apparently successful talks ended with both sides agreeing to establish a committee to deal with the return of more than 8,00,000 internally displaced people to what was declared as High Security Zones (HSZs) operated by the Sri Lankan military. An agreement was also reached to form a joint task force for humanitarian and reconstruction activities. As for these latter purposes, it was decided to make an appeal to international donors for support. These talks in Thailand were continued in October–November 2002 and again in January 2003.[4]

Talks were also held in Norway in December 2002, in Germany in February 2003 and in Japan in March 2003. However, the LTTE abruptly withdrew from the talks in April 2003 and did not participate in any further peace negotiations. While the governing coalition elected in February 2004 seemed anxious to continue with the talks, the LTTE did not reciprocate.[5]

Fresh Elections and a Quarrelsome Coalition

In February 2004, the SLFP reached an agreement with the JVP concerning an electoral pact for future elections and the formation of a coalition government with an agreed programme. This new alliance, the United People's Freedom Alliance (UPFA), defeated the UNF at the parliamentary elections held on 2 April 2004. The coalition secured 45.6 per cent of the vote, while the UNP share declined to 37.83 per cent. The coalition won 105 seats in the Parliament, falling short of a majority by eight seats. All subsequent efforts to secure a majority with the support of some Opposition parties failed. A key element in the Parliament then was the Jathika Hela Urumaya (JHU), which held nine seats. This party, dominated by bhikkhus, won nearly 6 per cent of the total vote. Mahinda Rajapaksa, a senior member of the UPFA and former fisheries minister, became the prime minister[6] of this rather unstable minority government.

The government established on the basis of the parliamentary elections of April 2004 was expected to bring about a decisive shift in the politics of Sri Lanka, as a coalition with leftist leaning was seen to be in place, with the JVP assuming a position of great influence in the making of policy and in policy implementation. The JVP also took over the left-wing leadership of the trade unions (with the exception of those in the plantations). In its early stages, the government seemed intent on radicalizing administrative affairs, if necessary with a new Constitution or alternatively with an amended Constitution. All it lacked was a majority in the legislature or rather the two-third majority needed for constitutional reforms. As a result, the government initiated a policy of persuading the UNP's allies to 'cross the floor' in the legislature. It succeeded in this objective to some extent, but it still failed to secure a majority, not to speak of the coveted two-third mandate. The UNP was greatly weakened by these defections, especially because the courts ruled in favour of those who defected when the UNP had challenged the defections as illegal.

Despite the initial success of the government, it soon proved to be no more than a quarrelsome, unstable coalition, which lasted for just over a year after its establishment. The crux of the problem was that the JVP proved to be an unreliable coalition partner, anxious to radicalize government policies but averse to sharing the blame that inevitably resulted from exaggerated expectations of change. Two problems persisted—high and rising prices, and high levels of unemployment. While the economy had shown signs of improvement under the previous UNF-led coalition,[7] by mid 2004, very early in the term of the new government, it became clear that the government had no viable policies to cope with a deteriorating economy.

The Tsunami and a Government in Crisis

The electoral pendulum, which had swung so decisively in favour of the UPFA coalition during the 2004 election, thus began its inevitable swing away from it. The government's problems multiplied when the devastating Asian tsunami struck Sri Lanka in the last week of December 2004. Historically, Sri Lanka had been an island free of tsunamis, volcanoes and earthquakes, and was affected only by the occasional floods. However, on this occasion, one-third of the coastline was severely affected by the huge waves. More than 30,000 lives were lost, and over one-fifth of the population either lost their homes or livelihoods or suffered substantial losses of income. After some early success in helping people to cope with the devastation, government rehabilitation policies were seen to be inadequate and lacking in focus. The tsunami left an unpopular government even more out of favour with the electorate, and it had to deal with a severe crisis of confidence.

The December 2004 tsunami was the worst natural disaster to hit Sri Lanka for centuries. The Sinhalese areas in the densely populated south, and in the not-so densely populated south-east, suffered severely. But the north-east under the control of the LTTE was even more badly affected—whether it was the east coast, with its large Muslim population or the south-east, with Muslim, Tamils and some Sinhalese population, all suffered loss of lives, livelihoods and income. In a grim parallel with the island's ethnic tensions, the government faced severe criticism from people in the south and south-east who had voted for the coalition in large numbers, while people of the north-east who had largely not voted for the government, were no less vociferous in their criticisms. Rehabilitation funds were sufficient, but the mechanisms for transfer of funds and supervision of rehabilitation work were either non-existent or utterly inadequate. The government's perceived ineptitude in the face of the tsunami added greatly to its unpopularity.

Fortunately for Sri Lanka, the tsunami did not affect the most productive parts of the country—the south-west coast was not severely damaged, nor were the plantations in the hills of the centre of the country. However, the tourism industry was badly affected, as were the coastal fisheries.

All the while, the coalition-building exercise with the JVP proved to be exceedingly difficult. Apart from its left-of-centre radicalism, the JVP was inflexibly opposed to the LTTE and, throughout the entire period of its association with the administration, it undermined every government effort to devise a policy of accommodation with the LTTE as part of the existing peace process. Faced with the severity of the task of reconstruction in the wake of the tsunami, the government introduced a proposal for an administrative device that could bring the government and the LTTE together in the reconstruction of areas damaged by the tsunami—and, indeed, in all the affected areas. The device was restricted in its scope to the north and the east of the island and to a narrow two-kilometre strip along the coast. From the outset this mechanism, better known as the Post-Tsunami Operations Management Structure (P-TOMS), became a controversial issue within both the government and the country as a whole. Nationalists objected to the principle of including the LTTE in the reconstruction process and expressed fears that the P-TOMS could become the basis of a separate state.

The LTTE agreed to work within the new structure. The UNP, for its part, supported the government's new device but insisted on its amendment. However, the JVP condemned the P-TOMS and threatened to resign from the coalition if the government signed the draft agreement. By the end of June 2005 the draft had been signed, and the JVP consequently left the coalition. The government was thus left with a minority in the legislature and was forced to depend on the various groups within the legislature for support of its political agenda.

Under normal circumstances, the UNP would have insisted on the formation of a new government. However, the problem was that the President's term of office was coming to an end, either at the end of 2005 (as the UNP insisted, on the basis of the requirements of the Constitution) or by November 2006 (as President Kumaratunga insisted, based on the fact that although she had come to power in 1999, she had been sworn in later, in 2000). Either way, this 'lame duck' presidency complicated the calculations with regard to the government and the legislature. After several attempts to accommodate the President's wishes had failed, the SLFP decided to put forward a proposal to nominate a successor to the President. After much internal wrangling, the party nominated the prime minister, Mahinda Rajapaksa, as its presidential candidate, while Anura Bandaranaike was its prime ministerial candidate. While Rajapaksa went on to serve as the executive President, Bandaranaike never became the prime minister.

Under the terms of the Constitution, the date for the presidential election had to be determined by the election commissioner. In late August 2005 the Supreme Court ruled that, constitutionally, a presidential election should be held by November 2005, rather than 2006. It was subsequently announced that the poll would take place on 17 November 2005.

In early August 2005, the ongoing peace process with the LTTE suffered a significant setback after its cadres were suspected of involvement in the assassination of the minister of foreign affairs, Lakshman Kadirgamar, at his home in Colombo. Kadirgamar was an influential Tamil. His assassination prompted the declaration of a state of emergency in the country. Anura Bandaranaike succeeded Kadirgamar as the minister of foreign affairs, after relinquishing his industry and investment promotion portfolios to the minister of finance and planning, Sarath Amunugama. Later in that month, the LTTE agreed to hold their first high-level talks with the government since 2003. The talks were to be on the issue of the ongoing ceasefire. However, disputes arose over a satisfactory venue for the talks, with the government insisting that they take place in Sri Lanka, while the LTTE demanded that they be held either in the Tamil-dominated north of the country or at a neutral venue abroad,

In September 2005, Prime Minister Rajapaksa concluded an agreement with the JVP whereby, in return for its support in the forthcoming presidential election, he would abandon both the P-TOMS and the government's commitment to work towards a power-sharing arrangement with the Tamils, and would also review the existing CFA. Thus, it was feared that, in the event of his election as President, Rajapaksa could return Sri Lanka to a state of war. Meanwhile, the presidential candidate for the UNP, Ranil Wickremasinghe, stressed his commitment to reviving the stalled peace process.

On 17 November 2005, fourteen candidates contested the presidential election. Mahinda Rajapaksa secured a narrow victory over his closest rival, Ranil Wickremasinghe, winning 50.3 per cent of the vote, compared to 48.4 per cent for Wickremasinghe. The election was notable for the low turn-out amongst the country's Tamil population, particularly in the LTTE-controlled northern and eastern areas. This was thought to have played a significant part in Wickremasinghe's defeat, as he had stressed his commitment to the ongoing ceasefire agreement during the electoral campaign. While the LTTE had stated that it would not prevent people from voting, there was widespread evidence to the contrary. Rajapaksa subsequently nominated the minister of agriculture, public security, law and order and of Buddha Sasana, Ratnasiri Wickremanayake, as prime minister. Neither the JVP nor the JHU were awarded any Cabinet portfolios. In June 2006, Rajapaksa was appointed chairman of the SLFP.

10

The LTTE'S Last Phase: 'No War No Peace'

By the end of 2005, Sri Lanka had entered a new phase in the 'cold war' between the government and the LTTE. The governing coalition did not have a majority in the legislature, thus making it vulnerable to pressure from the JVP, which used its links with the government to urge an end to the Cease Fire Agreement (CFA) and called upon the government to embark on what it called an 'all-out war' with the LTTE. However, the government adhered to its policy of maintaining the peace, despite the deaths of servicemen and policemen in attacks by the LTTE in various parts of the north-east of the island. The UNP, on its part, backed the government in its policy of peace. Thus, there was no danger of the government weakening on the matter of peace under pressure from the Opposition. The result was that the stalemate between the government and the LTTE continued into 2006, as did the pressure on the government by the JVP, which advocated war as the alternative to the phase of peace at all costs.

By early 2006, the government and the LTTE expressed readiness to resume the peace talks. These took place in Geneva in February 2006. It soon became clear, however, that the talks were not a succession to those held between the UNF government and the LTTE. The LTTE repeatedly highlighted the need for a clear look at the CFA and put forward two demands.

First, it urged that the army withdraw from certain areas in Jaffna and other parts of the northern province—declared as High Security Zones—so that the legitimate owners of these lands and buildings could return and resettle there. Second, the government was asked to disarm the so-called paramilitaries, by which the LTTE meant the Karuna dissidents of the LTTE within the eastern province.

Tamils of the eastern province had been a significant force among the fighters of the LTTE—they had once formed the virtual backbone of the LTTE's army. Karuna had been a senior figure in this army, and a trusted aide of the LTTE leader Prabhakaran. But once the Tamils of the eastern province broke away from the LTTE in 2005–06, the LTTE suffered a severe setback from which it never really recovered.

The LTTE had originally described the issue of the Karuna dissidents as an internal matter. But by the time the peace talks were held in early 2006, the LTTE insisted that it was the government's responsibility to disarm the Karuna faction. This suggested the LTTE's discomfort with its own inability to do so. The government agreed to disarm the paramilitaries. But its subsequent failure to do so, particularly in the case of the Karuna faction, was to cause difficulties in its negotiations with the LTTE. When the preliminary talks between the government and the LTTE ended in another stalemate, the LTTE went back on its offer of holding a further set of peace negotiations.

The LTTE then suffered a diplomatic reverse when in May 2006 the European Union (EU) included it on a list of proscribed organizations deemed to be involved in, or linked to, acts of terrorism. This entailed, inter alia, a 'freeze' on the LTTE's financial assets in all the then twenty-five states of the EU, and a ban on fundraising by the group within the EU, as well as the prevention of LTTE representatives from visiting countries of the EU. Subsequently, in July 2006, following LTTE demands in response to this ban, Finland, Denmark and Sweden chose to withdraw their ceasefire monitors from Sri Lanka.

In the meantime, the LTTE continued with its policy of official commitment to the CFA and to peace but engaged nevertheless in acts of violence. On 15 June 2006, an explosion killed more than sixty persons—men, women and children— travelling on a bus at Kebithigollewa, a small township near Anuradhapura. This could only be described as the worst massacre of civilians since the signing of the CFA in 2002. Questions were asked whether this incident marked the beginning of yet another spell of direct confrontation between the government and the LTTE or whether it heralded the beginning of another war for Eelam. After the victims of the explosion were buried in a mass grave, however, the stalemate continued—a stalemate of 'no war and no peace'. The LTTE's denial of any involvement in the incident was received with much scepticism. There was widespread international condemnation of the 'massacre' from India, the USA, Switzerland and France, among numerous other countries. The Indian government dispatched its foreign secretary, Shyam Saran, to Colombo on 3 August to urge the government and the LTTE to resume the peace talks.

In mid July 2006, an even more serious breach of peace occurred when the LTTE blocked the passage of water at Maavil-Aru, a minor irrigation project in the eastern province. Eventually, owing to pressure from the local Sinhalese population who threatened to use force to get the Maavil-Aru system working, and also because the army was anxious to intervene since the livelihoods of 1500 or more families—Sinhalese, Tamils and Muslims—were at stake, the Rajapaksa government agreed to use force through the army to open the channel.[1] Some viewed the LTTE action as an attempt to compel the Sinhalese and Muslims to leave the area served by the waters of the Maavil-Aru channel (i.e., an attempt at 'ethnic cleansing').

The army's campaign which began at Maavil-Aru continued into 2008 and 2009. Soon after the campaign began, the LTTE launched an attack on Muttur, a Muslim port-town in the eastern province. Although the attack was repulsed, there was widespread destruction of property. There was also an attack at Maavil-Aru in which large numbers of Muslims were killed. The events at Muttur and Maavil-Aru represented serious setbacks for the LTTE, although the 'no-war' pledge appeared to be in force. The government justified its resorting to armed force as purely a defensive action against aggression and as part of a humanitarian attempt to provide water to the paddy lands in the region.

The LTTE had barely recovered from the setbacks at Maavil-Aru and Muttur when it began another attempt to capture Jaffna town and bring it under its control. Hundreds of people were reported to have been killed in the ensuing violence and tens of thousands fled the area. As the battle for Jaffna continued in October 2006, it was difficult to assess what impact the renewed conflict would have on the CFA and the peace process. Although the parties involved in the fighting declared themselves to be committed to peace, there was no consensus on how peace was to be managed or on the constitutional framework required for Sri Lanka to move towards peace on a long-term basis.

In October 2006 the Supreme Court, in a landmark decision, declared that the amalgamation of the northern and the eastern provinces, which had taken place in 1988 under President J.R. Jayewardene and under pressure from the Indian government[2], had been unconstitutional. Tamil parties protested this decision. But the government accepted the ruling and proceeded to appoint a separate Governor for the eastern province (following the merger, there had been one Governor for the north-eastern province[3] as a whole). Local government polls were also declared for this province.

In 2007, the government strengthened its position in relation to the Opposition parties in the Parliament. As part of its drive to obtain an overall majority, the government was able to secure the support of a faction within the UNP, resulting in the defection of nineteen MPs, and a major Cabinet reshuffle in January. The reshuffle saw Cabinet berths being given to Karu Jayasuriya, former deputy leader of the UNP, who now became minister of public administration and home affairs, and to Rohitha Bogollagama, who was now the minister of foreign affairs. In October 2006, the UNP had signed an MoU with the government, in which both parties agreed to pursue a peace policy and adopt other measures to stabilize the country. Following the UNP defections, however, this MoU reportedly became non-functional. The net effect of the crossing over of MPs was a diminution in the UNP's position in the Parliament rather than an actual strengthening of the government to any significant extent. In addition, the JVP failed to become the principal Opposition party despite the decrease in the number of UNP parliamentary seats.

Meanwhile, the LTTE finally decided to join the peace talks. These were to be held in Geneva, in October 2006. In doing so, the LTTE insisted that the discussions be confined to the 2002 CFA. The government accepted this stipulation and sent its negotiators to Geneva with the hope that the CFA could be amended. However, little was achieved through these talks, although both sides agreed to uphold the terms of the CFA.

An Undeclared War

Under pressure from the international community, the LTTE agreed to a second round of peace talks. But by the end of August 2007, no such negotiations had been held. The LTTE's readiness for further peace talks was apparently designed to keep the government guessing as to whether regular and successive breaches of the peace process would lead to the resumption of an all-out war policy. As it was, the government and the LTTE both claimed to be upholding the official 'no-war' policy while, in reality, a policy of 'undeclared war' was being conducted by both sides.

For the LTTE, undeclared war amounted to a concerted attempt to cause unrest in the eastern province. Its principal target was the Muslim community, the largest ethnic group in that province. Thereafter the Sinhalese settlements in the region were targeted.[4] The government responded to this undeclared war by the LTTE with its own version of an undeclared war, in which the LTTE's strongholds came under military attack, with one after another of LTTE positions succumbing to the Sri Lankan army. One early target was the strategic centre of Sampur, which the LTTE had used as a base for attacking Trincomalee. After Sampur, the government forces besieged a number of smaller strongholds, and in early May 2007, the military targeted the forests of Toppigala. By mid July, the LTTE had lost control of its jungle bases in Toppigala. With that the army had captured virtually the whole of the eastern province from the LTTE.

In March and April 2007, the LTTE carried out its first air raids, against military targets around Colombo and elsewhere. During a span of eight to ten years, the LTTE had reportedly created a rudimentary 'air force' of five trainer aircraft, manufactured in the Czech Republic, along with the attendant infrastructure for these aircraft. This air force was said to be capable of bombing selected targets but no more than that. Some observers viewed its creation as an act of desperation rather than as an actual escalation of the war, while for others it represented a worrying new dimension in the conflict.

The bravado of the LTTE bombing targets close to Colombo, however, could not undermine the Sri Lankan army's successful campaign in the eastern province. One result of the undeclared war was the creation of a refugee situation estimated at between 2,00,000 and 4,00,000 people—the majority being Muslims, in addition to Tamils and some Sinhalese. Resettlement and reconstruction efforts commenced, but their immediate impact on the refugee problem in the eastern province was limited.

Proposals for a devolution package submitted by the SLFP in May 2007 envisaged the district as the core unit of the devolution exercise, and not the province, as had been the practice since 1987. According to the SLFP's proposals, the district would be the widest extent of power-sharing. When the SLFP recommendations were severely criticized, the party's response was that the proposals represented a basis for future discussions and not a final package. The SLFP stated that a final version of the devolution package would be drawn up, incorporating any necessary amendments in response to the criticisms and objections expressed. However, the proposals were rejected by the majority of the other parties, including the UNP. Nor was the SLFP's insistence on the retention of a unitary state acceptable to the majority, most of whom preferred the drawing up of some form of a federal Constitution. The SLFP proposals made provision for the amalgamation of the contiguous regions (this clause had been incorporated into the package prior to the Supreme Court's rejection of the amalgamation of the northern and the eastern provinces). Even so, the re-amalgamation of the two provinces—the northern and the eastern—was difficult to envisage given the need for a favourable majority in each province. There was no probability of such a majority in the eastern province, in view of the strong opposition of the Muslims and Sinhalese to such a merger. The Tamils were a minority of between 30 per cent and 35 per cent of the population of the eastern province. The Muslims were at least 40 per cent of the population there with the Sinhalese forming at least 10 per cent if not 15 per cent. Nevertheless the clause for possible amalgamation was expected to prove useful for the purposes of compromises regarding the constitutional proposals.

The early months of 2008 witnessed two major developments: the first of which was the government's abrogation of the CFA and the second, the election of members to the eastern provincial council.

A Cornered LTTE

By early 2008, the LTTE had lost control of the eastern region, and was reduced to controlling only parts of the northern province, particularly parts of the district of Mullaitivu. In January, the government had revoked the CFA and embarked on a policy of war against the LTTE. The army then won several encounters with the LTTE and the army Commander, Lt. Gen. Sarath Fonseka, claimed that the LTTE had lost its capability to fight as a conventional army. The LTTE forces went on to conduct sharp defensive campaigns against the army and continued with its tactic of guerrilla warfare, resorting to terrorist strikes in many parts of the country. However, the army maintained its superiority over the LTTE.

More significantly, the LTTE lost much of its foreign support. In addition to the EU's ban on its fundraising operations, the LTTE was included on the list of terrorist organizations compiled by the US Federal Bureau of Investigation (FBI). In the case of Canada, home to a large Tamil diaspora, it banned the World Tamil Movement, allegedly an LTTE front organization.

Thus, the LTTE became increasingly dependent on its home base for financial resources, but that support would prove to be inadequate to ensure its survival.

During mid 2008, the peace process was at a virtual standstill, with the government insisting that the LTTE disarm before the peace talks could be resumed and the LTTE showing no signs of accepting that position. The LTTE demonstrated its staying power by occasional bursts of fierce resistance to the army advances in the northern province, as also by indulging in terrorist attacks in various parts of the country wherein the victims were more often the civil population travelling in buses and trains than the police or other security forces. The LTTE made effective use of its supporters amongst the Tamils residing in the suburbs of Colombo and elsewhere for this purpose. In early April, the minister of highways and road development, Jeyaraj Fernandopulle (together with at least fourteen other people) was killed in a suspected LTTE suicide-bomb attack carried out near Colombo. The police and other security forces were unable to trace the LTTE operatives engaging in these terrorist strikes. Thus, a weakened LTTE remained a potent force. Moreover, it was unwilling to disarm. It was neither ready to resume the peace talks nor to surrender.

The creation of a provincial council for the eastern province was crucially important for the separation of the northern and the eastern provinces. The election itself, held in May 2008, was won by an SLFP-led coalition, which included the Karuna faction—Tamileela Makkal Viduthalai Pulikal or TMVP—led by Sivanesathurai Chandrakanthan, better known by his adopted name, Pillayan. The TMVP had contested as an armed militia, and most of the electoral abuses that had figured so largely in the election had stemmed from its activities[5]. After some discussions, Pillayan was appointed the chief minister of the eastern provincial council. Pillayan's elevation was evidence of the relative decline of the LTTE, which always claimed to be the sole representative of the Tamil minority.

Politically, a weakened UNP remained the government's main

opponent in the country and in the Parliament. In December 2007, the SLMC withdrew its support for the governing coalition. But this was offset by divisions in the ranks of the UNP and, more so, the division of the JVP into two factions. One was inclined to support the government, while the main group continued on a dual policy of opposing the government, especially by organizing trade union action, and yet remaining supportive of the government within the legislature. The result was that the government could survive within the legislature by manipulating the legislators to help it win a majority vote on crucial issues. This appeared to be a viable political policy over the remainder of Rajapaksa's tenure as President. The next presidential election was due in 2010 and the President was disinclined to test the possibility of a legislative election at a time when there was widespread labour unrest as well as discontent within the general population about the increases in the price of food. Unemployment remained another problem. It was better, therefore, for the government to persist with a wafer-thin majority than to risk everything at a legislative election. As a substitute for a national election, the government announced elections for some of the provincial councils—in particular for the councils of Sabaragamuwa and the north-central provinces (NCP), in both of which the government had earlier failed to win a majority. In late August 2008, the government regained control of the two provinces, winning twenty-five of the forty-four seats in the Sabaragamuwa provincial council, and twenty of the thirty-three seats in the north-central provincial council (NCPC). President Rajapaksa considered his party's victory in these elections to be an endorsement by the voters of the government's military policy against the LTTE.

In the meantime, the government hosted the fifteenth South Asian Association for Regional Co-operation (SAARC) conference. In its efforts to provide security for the visiting delegates, the government did not hesitate to demolish houses and shops in Colombo and its suburbs, wherever these were regarded as security risks. President Rajapaksa regarded the chairmanship of SAARC as a political bonus, even if the costs of the meeting and heading SAARC placed additional demands on an economically challenged government.

Externally, there was pressure from India for a revival of the peace process with the LTTE, while the EU in particular expressed concern about the government's perceived infringements of human rights, about which it was also being criticized by non-governmental organizations operating in the country. The Opposition parties were less vocal on the issue of human rights than with regard to attacks on journalists, especially on those critical of the government's conduct of war against the LTTE. In particular, these criticisms were directed against exaggerated claims made by the government on victories in battles against the LTTE. In these circumstances, the judiciary, particularly the higher judiciary, played a key role in defending the tenets of human rights and free speech, subjecting government decisions that appeared to contravene them to severe criticism, and often reversing them despite the embarrassment such judgements caused to the government.

Within eighteen months of the government's success at defying the LTTE over the waters of the Maavil-Aru in the eastern province, General Fonseka's forces were on the verge of annihilating the LTTE in the northern province. By this time, the LTTE had lost the manpower of the eastern province—the backbone of its army—and was in no position to challenge the purposeful march of Fonseka's forces, as they pressed forward to the early elimination of the LTTE as a fighting force. Facing a depletion of its manpower, the LTTE continued to resort to the practice of incorporating child soldiers into its ranks. This process had begun much earlier but now it saw a greater need than ever before. As the need for child soldiers increased, the LTTE went deeper into Mullaitivu.

General Fonseka was not only the most dynamic General in the Sri Lankan army of that time, he was also the one most determined to defeat the LTTE as General Ranatunga had done in 1986–87. Ranatunga's forces had routed the LTTE in 1987[6] and had been on the verge of capturing Jaffna and its neighbourhood when the Indians intervened with pressure on the Sri Lankan government to stop the advance of its forces into Jaffna.

Now, twenty-two years later, the Sri Lankan forces under General Fonseka were on the verge of doing what Ranatunga had done in 1987. Fonseka was also intent on going further than what Ranatunga had done on that occasion. The further Prabhakaran's forces went into the forested coasts of Mullaitivu, the more Fonseka kept adjusting the lines of his own forces, making it more difficult for Prabhakaran to escape. Moreover, the Sri Lankan navy, now a more energetic and enterprising fighting force than it was in the past, had cut off the LTTE's escape route across the seas and had also cut off its access to supplies of weapons from the LTTE's suppliers in South East Asia and elsewhere. By now, the navy was more than a match for the LTTE's dreaded Sea Tigers.

As 2008 drew to a close, the Sri Lankan armed forces had cornered the LTTE and were on the verge of defeating it. To put it differently, in 2009 Fonseka was on the verge of achieving what Ranatunga had been prevented from by the Indian government in 1987.

11

The Collapse of the LTTE

The dramatic collapse of the LTTE in the first half of 2009 took most political observers by surprise, none more so than western students—including senior politicians, administrators and diplomats—of the affairs of Sri Lanka. The rout of the LTTE at the hands of General Ranatunga in 1987[1] had long been forgotten as were the lesser defeats the LTTE had suffered at the hands of Ranatunga's successors in the 1990s[2]. Also forgotten was how the LTTE had been saved by the intervention of the Indian government in 1987. The Indians had saved the LTTE from Ranatunga's efforts to capitalize on his victory of 1987 and to move into Jaffna town and its suburbs. True, the Indian Peace Keeping Force (IPKF) that entered the north and the east of Sri Lanka in 1987 had fought the LTTE on Sri Lankan soil. After a prolonged effort[3], the IPKF had driven the LTTE away from the north of the island where its strongholds were believed to be, to the areas of Vanni just south of the southern borders of the Jaffna and Kilinochchi districts and into the jungles of the eastern province and Mullaitivu. There the LTTE had survived attacks by the IPKF for nearly two years. People tended to forget the defeats the LTTE had suffered at the hands of the IPKF. Nonetheless, they remembered how the LTTE had fought valiantly to prevent the Sri Lankan army from taking complete control of the A9 road that linked Jaffna with Kandy and the south of the country. The A9 remained under the control of the LTTE till 2008.

People remembered also the LTTE's victories over the Sri Lankan army, especially the capture of the Elephant Pass fort in 2000, the demolition of the army base in Mullaitivu and the seizure of army weaponry, including its prized heavy artillery.

The military campaign against the LTTE continued into the first quarter of 2009. Despite a spirited but increasingly futile resistance on the part of the LTTE, most areas of the northern province came under the control of the army by the first quarter of 2009. When the township of Kilinochchi, the administrative headquarters of the LTTE, fell to the army in the early months of 2009, it marked the end of the LTTE's hold on any substantial part of the northern province. One by one, other 'strongholds' of the LTTE virtually dissolved when confronted with the advancing army. There was a collapse of the LTTE as a military force, and by April 2009, the LTTE greatly diminished as a fighting force. So far as its territorial control was concerned, it was confined to small slivers of land on the coasts of Mullaitivu.

The Sri Lankan government set about capitalizing politically on the defeats suffered by the LTTE. The government held public meetings in several parts of the island to celebrate these victories. A feature of these celebrations was that the army was not given due credit for its role in the defeat of the LTTE. The government took all the credit. In addition, it revived its policy of holding elections to the provincial councils, so as to demonstrate the strength of the popular support it had gained from its victories on the war front. In those election campaigns, the government concentrated on appealing for support solely on the basis of the success of its war policy. In fact, it had little else to show as achievements. The election to the provincial council of the western province at which it won a decisive victory solely on the strength of its propaganda about victories over the LTTE was the last and perhaps the most significant of electoral triumphs till the presidential election of 2010 in which the celebration of the defeats of the LTTE received overwhelming prominence. These celebrations continued into the parliamentary elections of 2010 but on a more subdued scale.

The government's policy of war against the LTTE had two significant features. On the one hand, there was the increased manpower of the army (see chapters 4, 12 and 13) as a result of which the army now had the men to occupy territories abandoned by the LTTE. The army's domination was such that the LTTE made no attempt to recover these territories as they had done in the past.

Secondly, a revitalized navy took firm control over the coasts and prevented the entry by sea of military equipment purchased by the LTTE through its agents in Europe and South East Asia. More importantly, the navy had defeated the feared 'Sea Tigers', the LTTE's naval wing, and set about preventing the escape of the LTTE cadres and the LTTE leadership by sea from the embattled fragment of the northern province under the LTTE—particularly from the Nanthikadal lagoon in Mullaitivu.

LTTE on the Defensive

By the first quarter of 2009, the LTTE was very much on the defensive trying desperately to hold on to the fragments of territory on the Mullaitivu coast—the Nanthikadal lagoon— where they were holed up for what proved to be their last battle. The resistance struggle of the LTTE did continue but on a very subdued level. The army continued to capture LTTE strongholds in the northern province. As we have mentioned,

Kilinochchi, the administrative headquarters of the LTTE, fell to the army and did so without much resistance. Thereafter, other LTTE strongholds collapsed in the face of the relentless advance of the army, while the strip of territory held by the LTTE in Mullaitivu became narrower and narrower as the army drew near.[4]

The LTTE, in the meantime, faithful to its terrorist tradition, placed the people of Mullaitivu as a sort of human shield—ignoring their wishes—against the advancing Sri Lankan forces[5]. It hoped that the prospective collateral damage in the form of heavy civilian casualties might delay, if not prevent, the rapid advance of the army towards the LTTE positions in Mullaitivu. Meanwhile, in response to Indian pressure and also to protect non-combatant Tamil civilians, the army slowed down its advance. There was at the same time a decline in the number of terrorist attacks by the LTTE in the north and other parts of the country.

As in 1987, in the period 2008–09, the LTTE failed not only as a military force but also as a terrorist outfit. Now they resorted to diplomacy. The first and the most important part of this diplomatic initiative was to appeal to India either directly or through LTTE sympathizers in Tamil Nadu to intervene in Sri Lanka and insist on a truce or to mediate with the Sri Lankan government to stop its offensive, something which the Indians had done in 1987.

The fate of non-combatant Tamils in Mullaitivu now became a major source of concern in India and elsewhere. The hard truth was that most of these non-combatants were held in Mullaitivu by the LTTE who prevented them from moving out to safety, despite all efforts by the army to move them on to secure areas.

In response to pressure from India, the Sri Lankan army announced that it would not use heavy artillery in its Mullaitivu campaign, and made several pronouncements to this effect. But that was the only concession India could extract from the Sri Lankan government. The LTTE was still banking on its supporters in Tamil Nadu, especially the Karunanidhi government there, which gained greater influence in the power portals of Delhi during the general election campaign in full swing in April and May 2009. But the Indian government was firm in its refusal to intervene for a truce in the north of Sri Lanka. All that the Indian government would do was to express concern over the fate of non-combatant Tamils in particular and over the cause of the north-Sri Lanka Tamils in general. Once the general election in India culminated in a relatively strong Congress-led Central government, not very dependent on the Tamil Nadu constituency for its support in the Parliament, the LTTE was doomed.

The Capture of Mullaitivu, and the Humanitarian Problem

By May 2009, the army had moved into Mullaitivu in a three-pronged pincer movement that culminated in the demolition of the LTTE in its last stronghold.[6] The victory of the army was a comprehensive one, much like General Ranatunga's victory in 1987. The victory on this occasion was even more decisive than that of 1987. The LTTE high command had managed to escape and had then mustered the strength to fight again. In mid May 2009, Prabhakaran and the rest of the leadership of the LTTE were trapped in the Nandikadal area and were killed.[7] All this while, even as the army was fighting the LTTE, the navy prevented the LTTE leadership and cadres from escaping by sea.

Thus when Mullaitivu was captured, the LTTE was demolished as a military force and as a political entity. The situation was such that the LTTE had no regional units left in the north of the island through which it could continue any worthwhile resistance.

The army's victory created a humanitarian problem. This involved an enormous increase in the number of non-combatant Tamils in Mullaitivu and other locations in the north of the country. They or most of them had been held there by the LTTE. Now they were herded into refugee camps in close proximity to Mullaitivu, and to other locations in the northern province by the advancing Sri Lankan forces. They found themselves unable to make their way to their homes in Jaffna and the rest of the northern province, as the LTTE had earlier planted landmines in the area as a defensive measure. For one thing, the Sri Lankan army was reluctant to let these Tamils move to their homes until the mines had been cleared.

The fate of the non-combatant Tamils became the focus of a second diplomatic venture, this time by the Tamil diaspora groups in Canada and Europe. European countries with Great Britain and France in the lead, followed by Germany, first called upon the Sri Lankan government to halt its operations against the LTTE. But they met with a firm refusal from the government's side. When these European powers—Great Britain and France, in particular—met with little success in this initiative, they pioneered a demand for an international investigation into the alleged 'war crimes' committed by the Sri Lankan forces and the LTTE in the war's last phase. The emphasis was on the acts of the Sri Lankan forces and the reference to the LTTE came almost as an afterthought. The European powers had very little or no evidence about these war crimes, but they persisted with these charges well after it was shown that no war crimes had been committed.[8] As in any battle where civilians had been caught in the crossfire, some civilians had lost their lives at the hands of the advancing army. But more significantly, some had been killed by the LTTE.

On 25 May 2009, the United Nations Human Rights Commission convened in Geneva a special session on Sri Lanka following a request made by seventeen countries, mostly European. The proposed resolution sought to condemn the Sri Lankan government for its alleged disregard for civilian life during the last phase of the war against the LTTE. This resolution was voted down. Instead, a resolution tabled by the Sri Lankan government itself, commending its handling of the war and, in particular, its commitment to human rights, was passed by a vote of twenty-nine to sixteen. In an unmistakable rebuff to these western nations, the two Asian regional powers, China and India, voted for Sri Lanka, in addition to Russia, Pakistan, Egypt and Cuba. Sri Lanka also received support from nations that were once part of the non-aligned movement.

This resolution marked another defeat for the Tamil diaspora which had agitated in Canada—where it was a very powerful force—and in Great Britain, France and Switzerland, as well as other parts of Europe, in order to gain sympathy for the LTTE and the Tamil cause.

However, even after the collapse of the LTTE, the Tamil diaspora in western Europe and Canada—especially Canada—continued to be the principal advocates of the Tamil separatist cause. It was a cause for which they had provided some if not much of the funds over the last two decades. Some of those funds remained with the diaspora groups for their present diplomatic campaigns.

The victorious Sri Lankan government was now confronted with two important tasks. First of all, and on a short-term basis, it had to deal with the non-combatant Tamils in the refugee camps. Despite both the Sri Lankan government and other governments and humanitarian agencies spending substantially on these refugees, life in these camps was hard if not harsh. Improvements there were painfully slow. However, within six months to a year, most of the non-combatant Tamils did go back to their homes. The second problem was that of reconciliation with the Tamils and encouraging them to re-enter Sri Lankan public life, free of all the LTTE controls over life in Jaffna. (This latter theme is dealt with in greater detail in Part IV of this volume.)

The LTTE had existed for forty years in Sri Lanka, out of which for thirty years, it had been the principal force fighting on behalf of the Tamils and agitating for the establishment of a separate Tamil state in the north and the east of the island, an objective for which they had wide support also in the south Indian state of Tamil Nadu. Although the LTTE had primarily been a Sri Lankan entity, it had always been anxious to win the support of the Tamils living overseas. As we have seen, they had diaspora groups in Canada and western Europe (however, significantly, no such groups had existed in India, at least not on a similar scale). The LTTE had built a fleet of commercial boats, the only South or South East Asian separatist group to be so equipped. This fleet had served several purposes. First of all, these boats had been used to smuggle narcotics from the Golden Triangle in Asia to various parts of Europe. As long as this smuggling activity had thrived, the LTTE had a sizable income with which to support its political activities and its armed forces. Once the income from the narcotics trade dwindled, the LTTE had turned to another illegal activity to maintain its income—this involved 'people smuggling' of Tamils to Australia and western Europe and Canada. Thirdly, there had been the more legitimate but much less important activity of transport of commercial items in South and South East Asia. The diaspora groups had been a significant source of income for the LTTE, an income that supported their military and administrative needs. It had also been directed to the running of small businesses in Great Britain and western Europe, not to mention Canada. The north and the east of Sri Lanka had been other sources of income, especially from the rigorous taxes imposed on salaries and the fees that had been charged for transfer of property by Tamils and others who lived in the areas controlled by the LTTE.[9] All this had been taking place at a time when official salaries in Sri Lanka were tax-free, beginning from 1978.

However, the LTTE never had adequate resources to run its affairs in the north and the east of the island. For that they had been dependent on the Sri Lankan state which funded the schools, hospitals, clinics and other institutions in the LTTE-controlled areas. In short, the costs of administration in the north and the east of Sri Lanka had been met by the Sri Lankan government. A significant part of these costs had gone into the salaries paid to officials, including teachers and doctors serving in these areas.

The LTTE had been spared the need for funds required for the administration of the north and the east of the island controlled by them. The salaries paid by the Sri Lankan government in these areas had been on a par with those in other parts of the country. The LTTE did not have to bear any of these costs. Perhaps the only salaries and wages that were paid by the LTTE had to do with those of their cadres in the armed wing. Whether the LTTE had paid for the drugs and other materials needed in the hospitals and clinics is a matter on which no firm information is available. It had been the practice of the LTTE to transfer their sick and wounded cadres for treatment to Tamil Nadu if the local doctors and others felt they could not handle them adequately. Even when the IPKF had been present in the north and the east of the island, the wounded cadres of the LTTE would be smuggled across the Palk Straits to Tamil Nadu.

Despite the claims of the LTTE that a substantial part of

the weapons used by it had been captured from the Sri Lankan forces, those had actually been smuggled from India and from South East Asia. Admittedly, some of the weapons had been seized in LTTE raids on the Sri Lankan army bases during the presidency of Chandrika Kumaratunga. This included the heavy artillery at Mullaitivu. Also, some of the weapons used by the LTTE had been fabricated in the north and the east of the island by its cadres, who included engineers.

By 2007, the weaponry held by the LTTE had proved to be inadequate for its defence against General Sarath Fonseka's 'new model' army whose morale had been high and who had been intent on trouncing the LTTE forces. The weaponry of the Sri Lankan forces had come firstly from Pakistan, and more importantly, from China. Some of the boats for the Sri Lankan navy had come from Israel, but most of the small boats used for the defeat of the 'Sea Tigers' had been fabricated in Sri Lanka itself. Eventually, these boats had been more than a match for the very efficient small boats on which the LTTE had relied to transport their cadres and for carrying material from ships to smaller boats and through them to the coasts.[10] The navy's boats had proved to be more than adequate to prevent the escape of LTTE cadres and their leaders from the northern province and elsewhere in Sri Lanka.

As for dominance of the skies, the Sri Lankan air force, although small, had established early control in the areas dominated by the LTTE. In the early stages, till about 2000, the LTTE did make attempts to shoot down these planes. But after that, the Sri Lankan air force had dominated the skies, wreaking havoc on the LTTE especially by tying down its leadership to their hideouts and preventing them—including Prabhakaran—from moving about freely and leading the troops. Occasionally, some of the LTTE leaders would be located and killed by the air force[11] or by the army.

General Fonseka's Hour of Glory

The LTTE's principal difficulty had to do with the demographic imbalance that existed between itself and the Sri Lankan forces and people. At Independence in 1948, the Tamils constituted about 10 per cent of the Sri Lankan population. That figure shrunk to 7 per cent by 2009 and 2010. During the LTTE's fight for a separate state, a steady stream of Tamils had made their way to western Europe, Australia and Canada. Many had moved to western countries legally; then there were those who had fled to these parts of the world as economic refugees either through the LTTE or on their own. In fact, it had come to a point where Toronto in Canada had more Tamils than Jaffna or Colombo.

The Sri Lankan armed forces had been strengthened substantially in terms of numbers during the administration of Chandrika Kumaratunga (chapters 4, 12 and 13). These numbers increased once again under Rajapaksa, and to a greater degree than under Kumaratunga. As a result, General Fonseka had been able to use the army to occupy and hold territories abandoned by the LTTE or capture them from the LTTE. Significantly, the LTTE in its last phase had made no attempt to recapture these territories. Instead, the LTTE had moved further into the borders of the northern province towards the sea, especially in the Mullaitivu district. The demographic imbalance had become more pronounced after the defection of the eastern province Tamils. This had damaged the morale of the LTTE forces and they had been compelled to rely on child soldiers to fill the resultant gaps. This reliance on child soldiers had worked to the advantage of the Sri Lankan forces in their encounters with the LTTE.

The LTTE leader Prabhakaran had earned an enviable reputation in the 1980s for his daring and unorthodox tactics at war and for his meticulous planning as a guerrilla leader. However, after the Maavil-Aru encounter with General Fonseka, we see very little of this prowess. Although the LTTE persisted with their terrorist strikes, these became less frequent and effective after 2005. One of these terrorist strikes was at General Fonseka himself in his headquarters in Colombo. The attempt was, as usual, meticulously planned, but this time it failed in the sense that the victim survived the strike. There was also an attempt on the life of the President's brother, Gotabhaya Rajapaksa, but he escaped without any injuries. Grievously injured, General Fonseka recovered at the national hospital in Colombo and then he was moved for further treatment to Singapore. No sooner had he recovered fully, which happened rather quickly, than he turned his attention to planning the final attack on the LTTE and its leader. In this campaign which he directed in 2007–09, he demonstrated a daring and determination that few of his predecessors had shown as leaders of the Sri Lanka army. Thereby, the Sri Lankan government, under Rajapaksa, were able to reap the benefits of the army's efforts. General Fonseka used the army and its resources with remarkable skill, devising attacks by eight-man squads[12] of both the army and the special forces to move deep into the bases of the LTTE and to take its forces by surprise. This proved to be very effective, and the LTTE had no answer to these unorthodox tactics.

Faced with an unusually resourceful General, the LTTE failed both in terms of strategy and tactics. From Maavil-Aru onwards, the LTTE's efforts proved to be more defensive rather than offensive. This was the exact opposite of the nature of the tactics employed by General Fonseka's forces. The LTTE cadres found themselves abandoning one camp and one station after another to the forces of General Fonseka. Eventually, the LTTE had no strongholds left as its forces fled to the coasts of Mullaitivu where they were cornered by General Fonseka's forces and were unable to break through the lines that kept Prabhakaran and the LTTE high command covered.[13] After the defeat of the LTTE at Mullaitivu, the bodies of Prabhakaran and those of the leaders of the LTTE high command were discovered on 18 May 2009 in Mullaitivu.[14] Television images of Prabhakaran's body was proof to the world of the death of a master terrorist, a man who had held control over a third of Sri Lanka's territory and much of its sea coast for over thirty years.

The defeat of Prabhakaran and the LTTE was truly a historic development. No Tamil had posed so severe a threat to the Sri Lankan state as did Prabhakaran. He regarded himself as an iconic Tamil national figure—the Sun God itself—and thanks to the many victories he had won over sections of the Sri Lankan army over a thirty-year period, he tended to overestimate his skills just as he underestimated his opponents, including General Fonseka. He had survived the defeat the LTTE had received at the hands of General Ranatunga in 1987, and in many of his calculations of 2009, he hoped that the Indians would save the LTTE as they had done in 1987. He hoped they would forget that he had organized the assassination of Rajiv Gandhi. In the final stages, his forces were no match for General Fonseka's revitalized army. In Fonseka, he found a man as single-minded and as determined as he was when at his best. Fonseka's defeat of Prabhakaran was as carefully planned as anything the latter had done in his heyday, and the former's command over his own resources was indeed more impressive than Prabhakaran's.

12

After the Defeat of the LTTE

The annihilation of the LTTE in May 2009—with its leader and other senior leaders killed—constituted a decisive defeat. It was more than could have been expected even in the context of the defection of LTTE's eastern province cadres after 2004 and the resolute campaign conducted against the LTTE by General Fonseka and his officers at Maavil-Aru in 2006 and thereafter. Earlier, in 1987, faced with defeat from General Ranatunga's army, Prabhakaran and some of his associates had escaped to Tamil Nadu in a state of disarray but had returned to continue their struggles against the Sri Lankan state. Later, the LTTE had also taken on the IPKF. Three years after 2006, i.e., in 2009, Prabhakaran was killed. It's very likely he lost his life while attempting to break through the trap set for him and his associates by the Sri Lankan army and navy. The photographs we have seen of Prabhakaran's body would suggest he had suffered a head wound from a sniper's bullet. His son, Charles Anthony—his potential successor—had been killed a day or two (around 17 May) before him, along with virtually the whole senior leadership of the LTTE.

Prabhakaran's body was shown on national television after it had been identified by two of his former associates. These two men were either working with the Rajapaksa government or might have surrendered. They could even have been captured. To leave no possible opportunity for a 'Prabhakaran cult' to thrive based on his grave, the LTTE leader's body was cremated, not buried, and the ashes thrown into the sea. No clues were given as to the site or the sites at which the ashes had been dispersed. The attempt, clearly, was to leave no evidence of any remains of the LTTE's founding leader.

However, this careful elimination of evidence of his remains could not entirely remove from the collective memory of certain sections of the Tamils of Sri Lanka—especially those of Jaffna and the Jaffna peninsula and, of course, those belonging to the Tamil diaspora—his image and deeds. That said, today there is no political party of the Tamils in Sri Lanka that can really be linked to the LTTE. The closest we have are the remnants of the TNA, a group which had been linked to the LTTE and had carried out its behest within the national legislature. A few of them still remain in the Parliament. Their supporters won a significant, overwhelming majority in the elections of 2011 held for the village councils in the northern province. Even so, after the defeat of the LTTE and the death of Prabhakaran, the TNA has virtually lost its moorings. Although there are those who still call themselves members of this party, as far as possible they keep their pro-LTTE past and career carefully concealed.

The Tamil Diaspora[1]

The main source of pro-LTTE loyalties during the last days of the LTTE, and after its rout and the death of its leaders, is the Tamil diaspora. The Sri Lankan government confronted the pressures from this diaspora in the final stages of the battle with the LTTE in 2008 and 2009. This pressure was firstly exerted through LTTE sympathizers in Tamil Nadu and then through the diaspora's links with British and French politicians.

The current use of the term 'diaspora' by Sri Lankan journalists and politicians shows little evidence of an awareness of both its present and historical complexity. Instead, what we have is a one-dimensional reference to the political assertiveness of Tamils from Sri Lanka who had taken residence overseas in the post-Independence period and who have a record of opposition to Sri Lanka and the Sri Lankan governments, especially to the Rajapaksa government.

The size of this Tamil diaspora is estimated to be between 8,50,000 and one million, a sizable number in comparison with the total Tamil population in Sri Lanka. Currently, the Tamil diaspora is distributed in three continents. It is mainly concentrated in the following areas (the figures are based on the numbers mentioned in both Sri Lankan and overseas newspapers).

The largest segment of the Tamil diaspora is in Canada and the number is estimated to be around 2,00,000. The city of Toronto has about 1,00,000 to 1,40,000 of them. From these figures, one could conclude there are more Jaffna or Jaffna-peninsula-origin Tamils in Toronto than in another city in the world, including Colombo and the town and suburbs of Jaffna. The United Kingdom has about 1,20,000 Tamils in the diaspora, whose origins go back to the 1950s or the 1960s. Other European centres of residence of the Tamil diaspora are: Germany (around 60,000); France (around 50,000); Switzerland (around 35,000); the Netherlands (around 20,000); Norway (around 10,000); Denmark (around 9000) and Sweden (around 10,000). Most of these Tamils came into these countries after the 1960s. In Asia, the largest settlement of Sri Lankan Tamils is in India, with around 10,000 of them, most of whom are treated as refugees in that country, while Malaysia has around 25,000 of them. As for Australia, it hosts around 40,000 Sri Lankan Tamils.

The Sri Lankan government faces challenges of great complexity from sections of the Tamil diaspora. Some groups among this diaspora will indeed support attempts to further the now-demolished aims and objectives of Prabhakaran's LTTE. Some of these groups had been associated with the LTTE for a number of years and in a number of ways. Most of them had provided the LTTE with funds they had collected on its behalf. While some of these funds had been handed over to them voluntarily for transfer to the LTTE, some others had been extracted under various forms of duress, such as by putting pressure on the overseas Tamils through their relatives living in Jaffna and Colombo. A few in the diaspora had been involved in the LTTE's efforts at narcotics-smuggling and distribution. Some members of the diaspora had also been part of small business enterprises funded by the LTTE. In the present context, some may even be associated with the efforts to establish a transnational 'government' of the LTTE, especially in the United Kingdom, Canada and elsewhere. Such a transnational 'government' could be active, but its operations are unlikely to see fruition. It would carry heavy risks. There is little hope of success for this enterprise in the real world, especially after the comprehensive defeat of the LTTE and the physical elimination of its leadership. However, Sri Lankan diplomacy will have to keep this transnational 'government' very much in mind as it keeps up its struggle against the political aims and objectives of potential successors of the LTTE. Such a transnational 'government' would have access to what is left of the monetary resources accumulated by the LTTE, but these depleted resources may be inadequate for the purposes such a 'government' would have in mind. The prospects of replenishing these resources are more limited than in the past when Prabhakaran and the LTTE were active. The Sri Lankan foreign affairs ministry would do well to have a research unit which studies the record of the Tamil and other diasporas of the world.

It would be tempting to see the diaspora as a post-1980s phenomenon. It is not, except with regard to Canada. In the United Kingdom and Australia, the diaspora has origins that go well back into the 1950s and 1960s. So it is with regard to the Tamil diaspora in some parts of Europe. However, the origins of the Tamil diaspora in Malaysia go back to the early twentieth century. In the case of India, the Tamil diaspora's situation is unique. It is a large community, supported by remnants of the Sri Lankan Tamil political parties, and also has links with elements in the Tamil Nadu political system. Besides, it is very much under the influence of sections of the Indian administrative system, especially the RAW.

In almost every part of western Europe, the Tamil diaspora operates within the democratic political system of those countries. For instance, in the United Kingdom and France—as well as in Canada—it seeks to influence the host country's politics by providing a vote bank at the national elections. This vote bank works not only at the national level but also in constituencies which have a large Sri Lanka Tamil population. The community also seeks to influence non-governmental organizations ranging from Amnesty International and the International Crisis Group, to smaller groups more interested in charity and economic development, by carrying on with stories of the harsh policies and the unfair treatment meted out to them in Sri Lanka which had compelled them or their parents to leave the country and seek a better life elsewhere. There is, and will be, little mention of the reality of difficulties of living in Jaffna under the LTTE, and even in a Colombo that had to bear the pressures of the LTTE.

The Sri Lanka governments will have to treat the Tamil diaspora as a multifaceted phenomenon. This transcontinental grouping had first come together in response to the LTTE's appeals for assistance, especially financial assistance, but after the comprehensive defeat of the LTTE, the replication of such a situation would be difficult. The money extracted from the Tamil diaspora in North America and western Europe had been very substantial. Also, such fundraising had been a time-consuming affair because the diaspora is distributed over several continents. We do not know how the LTTE's administrative machinery achieved this feat, although there is some knowledge of the identity of the individual or individuals who had led these efforts. While some of the principal figures of this fundraising campaign have been captured, it will take some time—some years—before their funding methods and success can be properly assessed.

The Militarization of Sri Lanka

In part four of this monograph (chapters 14 and 15), we have dealt with the policies of reconstruction and reconciliation that need to be in place if the defeat of the LTTE is to pave the way for a return to the pre-1950s' pattern of national existence. One of the main themes we have dealt with is the issue of reintegration of the northern and the eastern provinces into the Sri Lankan state after these areas have been influenced and controlled for so many years by the LTTE. The LTTE was such a powerful influence in the affairs of Sri Lanka, especially of its north and east, and that its influence will linger. We need to recognize that it would take a generation, or at least one or two decades, before a functioning institutional structure, supporting a democratic system, would emerge and be sustained—especially in Jaffna and the northern province.

One of the key issues for post-LTTE Sri Lanka is a diminution of the role of the armed services. Earlier in this volume, I have dealt with the expansion of Sri Lanka's security services since the 1960s (chapter 4). Even after it was evident that by 2004 the LTTE had lost its eastern province leaders and cadres, and could be defeated militarily, there was a purposeful effort to expand the number of personnel in the armed forces (chapter 13).

A study of the growth of the army from around 1965 to 1995 shows that even in 1995 Sri Lanka had more security personnel per million of the population than other states in South Asia, including India and Pakistan. Thus, to increase the number of Sri Lanka's security forces even further, as happened between 2005 and 2009, was to make the militarization of Sri Lanka even more pronounced. This militarization process has become one of the principal issues in post-LTTE Sri Lanka. The reluctance on the part of the government to reduce the size of the army, in particular, after the defeat of the LTTE is explained in part by a determination to prevent any prospect of a revival of the LTTE in the northern province and in the Jaffna peninsula principally. An article entitled 'Sri Lanka Army: In Bigger Barracks', *The Economist*, in its 4 June 2011 issue, provided some information on how the armed forces have been kept occupied in this new post-LTTE environment.[2] The use of the armed services, to back the police and the administration, has become a fact of life in post-LTTE Jaffna and the northern province. This, as well as the frequent use of the army in other areas, including Colombo and its suburbs, has led to criticisms in the Parliament. These criticisms are likely to become more frequent the longer the government takes to reduce the presence, if not the size, of the security services and lower their profile. One could argue that in the context of high unemployment in the country, even a principled reduction of the security services against the background of the defeat of the LTTE would need to be planned carefully.

The post-Prabhakaran situation calls for the preparation of a White Paper by the government on Sri Lanka's security services. Nothing of the sort has been forthcoming in post-Independence Sri Lanka, especially since the 1960s when the country began moving from being a virtually demilitarized entity to one that was being militarized at a level unmatched in the whole of South Asia.

A reduction in the size of the security forces needs to be attempted urgently now that the LTTE has been defeated. This reduction in the size of the security services has to be attempted along with efforts to reduce the overwhelming Sinhala-Buddhist identity of the security forces (see chapter 4). While the fact of such a distortion taking place was found to be accurate as early as 1995, its continuation has been outlined in recent research articles.[3] A purposeful attempt to reduce this distortion, if not to eliminate it, reconstruction is an essential part of the post-LTTE Sri Lanka. Once the government decides on the scale of this reduction of the overwhelming Sinhala-Buddhist domination of the Sri Lankan security services, the actual steps to be taken could be organized by the leadership of the security forces. We have seen in other chapters (chapter 4, for instance) of this monograph how the officer corps of the security services had been dominated by ethnic and religious minorities prior to Independence and in the early years of Independence. But it is unlikely that a return to this pattern of the minorities as a significant force in the security forces could occur now. What is necessary is that the composition of the security forces ought to reflect something of the current ethnic and religious diversity of Sri Lanka.

The structure of this identity will become clearer after the national census of 2011. The previous national census of 2001 was seriously disrupted by the actions of the LTTE which had prevented enumeration for the census in the northern and the eastern provinces. With the defeat of the LTTE, the country can now get back to the traditional pattern of a comprehensive national census every ten years.

The army and the security services will remain a powerful presence in Sri Lanka. They were a popular force in Sri Lanka during the struggle against the LTTE. By restructuring these security forces so that they would have representation from all the ethnic and religious minorities, the forces are likely to acquire a truly national character and thus no longer be a predominantly Sinhala-Buddhist one.

A similar restructuring will need to be attempted in the police force, and in the bureaucracy, especially the national government's bureaucracy.

The bureaucracies of the provincial councils ought to generally reflect the ethnic and religious structure of the population in the provinces. As we have seen, the LTTE had prevented the enumeration of the population in the northern and the eastern provinces at the time of the census of 2001. The 2011 census is likely to show a drop in the population of the northern province, particularly of Jaffna and the Jaffna peninsula. This is because large numbers of Tamils from Jaffna and the northern province have left for Canada and western Europe, and in smaller numbers to Australia.

They have also left for towns and townships close to Colombo. This shift of the Tamil population to Colombo and its suburbs is currently estimated at 12 per cent of the Tamil population of Jaffna and the Jaffna district. It is a change that will affect the composition of the population of the city of Colombo, and the Roman Catholic areas close to the national airport at Katunayake—especially during election time.

Once the results of the census of 2011 are made available, it would be possible to adopt a policy of making the country's bureaucracy reflect, more accurately than it does now, the ethnic and religious diversity of Sri Lanka's population. It is very unlikely that the Tamil minority, especially those from Jaffna and the Jaffna peninsula, will ever see a return to the prominent position it held in the bureaucracy in the two or three decades before the transfer of power in the 1940s. But the new structures in the bureaucracy will have more Tamils in them than there were in the years of the ethnic conflict, especially once the LTTE took over the leadership of the Tamils and proclaimed themselves as their sole spokesmen.

Next, there is the issue of the position of the hill-country Tamils, those from the plantation areas. With the death of their powerful and long-time leader, S. Thondaman, a few years ago, the Indian Tamil community seems to be adrift politically. Moreover, as an ethnic group, it seems to be less interested in working in the plantations than its previous generation. Large numbers of them are moving away from the plantations and are seeking employment in and around Colombo and Kandy and in towns in the plantation areas. Meanwhile, the state has improved the education opportunities for the children of 'plantation Tamils', and with education available virtually on the same scale as in other parts of the island, they will be competing for jobs with the Jaffna and Colombo Tamils. They are also moving into trade in all parts of the island.

In the years that lie ahead in terms of reconstruction and reconciliation, the Indian Tamils pose as many difficulties to the Sri Lanka Tamils as they do to the Sri Lankan state. For the state, there is the delicate problem of managing the shift of the 'plantation Tamils' from being almost entirely a working-class group to one which has a class structure similar to that of other ethnic groups. This means, in effect, expectations of positions in the Sri Lankan bureaucracy and in the education system. This would be difficult enough at the best of times but would be more difficult in the post-LTTE era because the 'plantation Tamils' would be competing with the Jaffna Tamils not only for employment but also for the opportunities that present themselves in capitalist enterprises. The 'plantation Tamils' have generally been more ready to compromise, if necessary, with regard to political objectives, an attitude they have shown over language and the changes in the language policy. Living as they do among the Sinhalese, they have demonstrated a sensible preparedness to adjust to changing circumstances. Surprisingly, they have shown themselves to be less attracted than the Sri Lankan Tamils to the pull of Tamil Nadu politicians, if not to Tamil Nadu politics. Sri Lanka will need to watch the plantation Tamils' gradual transition towards equality with Sri Lanka Tamils in all areas of activity, with interest.

In Retrospect

One of the issues emerging from a study of Sri Lanka's prolonged ethnic conflict is that separatist/terrorist groups are vulnerable to military defeat at the hands of a determined government and army. This was seen as early as in 1986–87 when General Cyril Ranatunga routed the LTTE in his Vadamarachchi campaign. Ranatunga had reorganized the army, and the then government had expanded its numbers from 15,000 to 30,000 for this purpose. The army was reconstructed for the battle with the LTTE. When the LTTE was routed in the Vadamarachchi campaign, its cadres fled in disarray, with Prabhakaran and some of his close associates fleeing in haste through the port of Velvetithurai—well-known for its links with the smuggling trade—to hideouts available to them in Tamil Nadu. As we have seen, Ranatunga had planned to move to

Jaffna and townships close to Jaffna in order to destroy the administrative structures of the LTTE, but he was prevented from doing so by the intervention of the Indian government which pressurized President J.R. Jayewardene to get Ranatunga to desist from the next stage of his attack on the LTTE. As it turned out, the LTTE survived to fight for a much longer time—for another twenty-two years before General Sarath Fonseka crushed it in 2009, killing Prabhakaran and most of the other LTTE leaders.

If General Ranatunga's success in the Vadamarachchi campaign provides one lesson, it is that a military campaign is one way to deal with the threat from a separatist and terrorist movement. The Indian effort to prevent him from moving into Jaffna and townships close to Jaffna proves another point—namely, that the LTTE's long-term survival depended as much on its own stubborn resistance as on the folly of politicians, both Indian and Sri Lankan. The Indians—politicians, administrators and diplomats—saved the LTTE in 1986–87 and on other occasions. President R. Premadasa helped the LTTE survive the onslaught of the IPKF in the final phase of the Indian force's tenure in Sri Lanka, during 1989–90. The Indian government in 1990 expected the Sri Lankan forces to move in and occupy the camps and buildings vacated by the IPKF. Instead, Premadasa permitted the LTTE to move into these vacated places. When the IPKF was in the north and the east of Sri Lanka, Premadasa had provided the LTTE with money and weapons. During that time, although General Ranatunga was the defence secretary, he was not consulted on these matters. However, even if he had been consulted, his objections would have been overruled. Premadasa's hostility to the Indians and the IPKF was such that he had articulated the theory that the Sri Lankan government under his leadership had one thing in common with the LTTE, and that was their shared animosity towards the IPKF.

When Chandrika Kumaratunga took over as executive President in 1994–95, her attitude to the LTTE was more favourable than that of the SLFP in general. Treating the LTTE as a worthy foe, she agreed to participate in negotiations with them in Jaffna. During the conference that followed, LTTE flags and photographs of Prabhakaran were prominently displayed, apart from other LTTE insignia, in a careful assertion of its equal status with the Sri Lankan state, a pattern that Premadasa had adopted. However, both sets of negotiations failed (the one with Premadasa lasting much longer than that with Chandrika Kumaratunga). Premadasa was assassinated by the LTTE in 1993, while its attempt on Chandrika Kumaratunga's life failed, leaving her with a damaged eye. The executive President's attitude towards the LTTE changed with Mahinda Rajapaksa's victory in 2005, and especially after the Maavil-Aru incident.

In the meantime, the army had taken over the reins of leadership in the struggle against the LTTE. In 2002, Sarath Fonseka led the army against the LTTE's efforts to expel the Sri Lankan forces from Jaffna. Thereafter, there was a stalemate till 2004 when the eastern province cadres of the LTTE broke up with Prabhakaran, leaving him considerably weakened in the continuing struggle against the revamped Sri Lankan army. This new balance of forces, with the LTTE very much on the retreat, became evident even to the LTTE once the Sri Lankan army had succeeded in pushing the LTTE back at Maavil-Aru in 2006. The LTTE would continue to fight the Sri Lankan security forces, but the odds were against it.

As we have seen, General Sarath Fonseka's victory at Maavil-Aru marked the beginning of a three-year campaign which ended with the destruction of the LTTE and with the deaths of Prabhakaran and its other senior leaders. With the LTTE forces pinned down on the waters of Nanthikadal in Mullaitivu and facing certain defeat, there had been efforts to get external agencies to intervene so as to end the war and call once more for peace talks. The LTTE itself sought Indian intervention, as in 1987, but the Indian government declined to intervene. Sections of the Tamil diaspora sought the assistance of British and French politicians, if not the British and French governments themselves, to get the Sri Lankan government to halt the campaign against the LTTE and then engage in negotiations for a ceasefire. These efforts failed. Mahinda Rajapaksa did listen to these calls but rejected them. The Tamil diaspora then continued with their campaign, this time with sections of the UN bureaucracy. That too did not save the LTTE and its leadership, although the Sri Lankan government had been presented with an uncomfortable, short period of diplomatic struggle with the UN bureaucracy.

The last stage of the campaign against the LTTE provides invaluable data for those who study the issue of how a war, as part of a prolonged ethnic conflict, ends. This present volume provides a brief introduction to such a study. Much more work needs to be done as more evidence appears for scholars, with the passage of time. Such evidence will also be available as a by-product of the ongoing conflict between General Sarath Fonseka and the Mahinda Rajapaksa government. That conflict will continue beyond the end of the tenure of the Rajapaksa government, as one more controversial issue in the divisive politics of Sri Lanka and in the revival of its once rigorous democracy. It would, of course, be part of any study of how wars end.

The Challenges of Militarization: 1986–2011

With the establishment of the executive presidency in 1978, the President of the republic of Sri Lanka became the commander-in-chief of the armed services. The post of secretary of the ministry of defence went to a political associate of President Jayewardene, a colonel in the army reserve service, while for the first time since Independence, the head of government ceased to be the foreign minister, with that position being occupied by another MP. The appointment of the defence secretary breached a well-established tradition under which this position had been held by a senior member of the higher bureaucracy. In 1981, however, the retiring head of the army was brought in as the secretary of defence, evidence of the government's perception that military expertise was essential in this key post under the changed circumstances. From 1981 to the end of 1994, a succession of retired army chiefs held this post. With the victory of the PA at the elections of 1994, Chandananda de Silva, the former commissioner of elections, a senior member of the higher bureaucracy, was brought in as the defence secretary, a reversion to the practice that had prevailed before 1977. However, between the years 1981 to 1994, despite the elevation of senior army officers to the post of secretary of defence, there was no relaxation of civilian control over security affairs, and all major decisions were taken by the Cabinet and the President of the republic.

There was, in addition, a deputy minister of defence, whose task was the oversight of the security services. This was Anuruddha Ratwatte, a cousin of Mrs Bandaranaike (her father's brother's son). Despite the controversial nature of his appointment to the army and of the various stages of his promotions therein, he retained the post of defence secretary till the election of Mahinda Rajapaksa as President in 2000.

From the last quarter of 1983, there was a qualitative change in the nature of the separatist threat to the Sri Lankan government. There was a purposeful challenge from the Tamil separatist forces, with their attacks becoming more daring in scope and powerful in impact. The government responded as it did in the case of the JVP insurgency by a resort to force through the security services, and by an institutional structure for these services and new policies established in 1986. For the first time since Independence, an urgent need was felt for a rapid increase in the number of personnel in the armed services and the police as well as for modernization of their equipment to match those in the possession of the Tamil separatists, all of which resulted in a substantial increase in the budgetary allocation for defence. In the early stages of the rapid expansion of the army, discipline was often poor and there was also a lowering of morale in the face of setbacks. There were frequent charges of attacks on civilians, and certainly there was evidence to support some of these charges.[1]

The Army and Tamil Separatism

By the early part of 1984, the army was the only law enforcement agency left in Jaffna in the north of the island, and the main separatist stronghold. The guerrilla forces were now much larger, much better trained, and much better equipped than they were before. This training—much of it in India under the auspices of the Research and Analysis Wing (RAW) and other agencies of the Indian government—and equipping of the guerrilla forces had begun well before the riots of July 1983. But there is no mistaking the intensification of these processes as a result of the violence inflicted on the Tamils in July 1983. Tamil Nadu had always been a ready haven for these guerrilla forces, but now the support they received was strengthened immeasurably, as was the extent of the protection they enjoyed.

The perception, particularly in Jaffna, that the army consisted of a group or groups of ill-disciplined young men with a predilection for violence directed against civilians, was something new. It was a change that emerged as a result of a confluence of two others: a change in the composition of the forces—they became largely Sinhalese and Buddhist—and a fundamental change in the nature of the problem they confronted in their traditional role as peacekeepers employed as a last resort. In the earlier phases of Sri Lanka's post-Independence cycles of ethnic violence, that is to say in the mid and late 1950s, the army had earned the plaudits of the Tamils as a tough and impartial peacekeeping force that cracked down hard on troublemakers and refused to be intimidated by politicians, however highly placed they may have been, when such persons sought to protect those who disturbed the peace.[2]

The regular use of the armed forces to quell disturbances did not lead to any relaxation of civilian control over them. From 1977 to early 1983 the government, quite deliberately, abstained from imposing a state of Emergency during outbreaks of violence since it was felt that the use of the Public Security Act may give the armed services too much independent authority despite the control over them by the civilian executive.

There was a distinct improvement in the state of discipline and morale of the army by the beginning of 1985. That was before the post of the general officer commanding the Joint Operations Command was created to take overall charge of the security forces, and to coordinate security operations. The new post was also necessitated by the rapid increase in the size of the armed services between 1982 and 1986 when the number of the personnel increased from around 15,000 to 30,000[3]. The most significant increase in the strength of the security services came between 1986 and 1996, as the following table would show.

Table I: Security Forces in Sri Lanka (selected years)

	1986	1987	1988	1993	1994	1995	1996*
Army	30,000	40,000	40, 000	90,000	1,05,000	1,05,000	1,18,890
Navy	3960	4000	5500	10,100	10,300	10,300	11,831
Air Force	3700	3700	3700	10,700	10,700	10,000	12,292
Total	37,660	47,700	49,200	1,10,800	1,26,000	1,25,300	1,43,013
Police Force	21,000	21,000	21,000	40,000	40,000	80,000	
Paramilitary Force	5000[1]	5000[1] 1500[2]	5000[1] 2000[2]	3000[2]	3000[2]	3000[2]	

Source: ICES data
1. *National Auxiliary Volunteer Force* 2. *Special Task Force (Police)*
* Provisional estimates from official Sri Lankan sources

Figure I below shows a substantial escalation in defence expenditure between 1981 and 1998, reflecting a massive increase in the number of personnel enrolled in the security services and an increase also in expenditure on materiel, purchased mainly from Pakistan and China, and to a lesser extent from other sources as well. Even as late as 1978, the annual expenditure on defence was only $40 million, or 1.5 per cent of the Gross National Product (GNP). In 1985, Professor J.W. Bjorkman, an American observer of Sri Lanka's welfare policies, made the point that Sri Lanka 'unlike its South Asian neighbours or even most other countries of the third world is virtually demilitarized'.[4] Saadet Deger, in a study of the economic effects of military expenditure on the Third World, made the same point a year later, even more emphatically.[5] Ironically, just at the time when these comments were published, i.e., in 1985–86, large sums of money were being diverted to the expansion and modernization of the armed services in response to the threat posed by the Tamil separatist activists as well as the guerrilla and terrorist groups associated with them.

Figure I: Defence Expenditure 1981–98

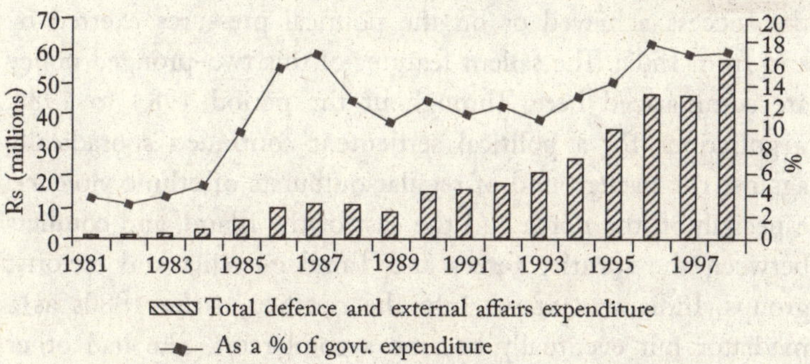

☒☒☒ Total defence and external affairs expenditure

◆ As a % of govt. expenditure

By 1985, expenditure on the armed services[6] had risen to $ 215 million or 3.5 per cent of the GNP. This steep increase was maintained since then, thus diverting to defence purposes money that would normally have gone to the maintenance and expansion of Sri Lanka's welfare state or on roads and telecommunications. Defence expenditure as a proportion of the annual national budget reached 16.8 per cent in 1987, by which time the total number of security personnel had reached around 75,000, consisting of the army, navy, air force, police and paramilitary forces.[7] By this time, the police had developed its own paramilitary wing, the Special Task Force (STF), which combined police duties with security operations in the eastern region. The other paramilitary group was the home guard, armed peasants given the task of defending their villages in the periphery of the Tamil districts or within them, from attacks by Tamil guerrilla bands. In these attacks, unarmed civilians were the deliberate targets, and it was felt that it was only by employing the home guards that these incursions could be checked.

As we have seen in the earlier chapters, successive Sri Lankan governments resorted to a two-pronged policy in dealing with the threat posed by the Tamil separatist activists. A military response was often accompanied by political negotiations, while the priority given to one or the other of these depended on the success achieved or on the political pressures exerted by and from India. The salient features of this two-pronged policy are summarized here. Throughout the period 1984 to 1986, negotiations for a political settlement continued sporadically against the background of regular outbursts of ethnic violence, especially in the north and the east of the island, and conflicts between the security forces and Tamil guerrilla and terrorist groups. India was drawn into the conflict in the 1980s as a mediator but eventually became a combatant. She had other roles as well, especially in internationalizing the conflict through the use of her diplomatic missions in the more important capital cities of the western world, and in initiating or lending support to moves at the UN and in UN sub-committees to espouse the cause of Sri Lanka's Tamils. This was apart from providing assistance, moral, financial and military—including training facilities and the supply and shipment of arms—to the Tamil separatist groups. India's involvement in Sri Lankan affairs reached its apogee with the Indo-Sri Lanka peace accord of 1987.[8]

Indian Intervention and the Security Services

With the signing of the Indo-Sri Lanka accord on 29 July 1987, the Indian Peace Keeping Force arrived in the island. As we have seen, the peacekeepers soon became combatants and grew from a small force of 5000-7000 men into an Indian army of around 1,00,000 men, almost as large as the Soviet army then in Afghanistan, and bigger than the British content of the Indian army of the Raj in its heyday.[9] The Indian forces operated independently of the Sri Lankan forces. Despite assertions by the then Sri Lankan President (J.R. Jayewardene) that the IPKF was subject to his direction and authority, the ground reality was that the IPKF forces took their orders from the Indian government.

The Indo-Sri Lanka accord of July 1987, like the other well-publicized accords negotiated by Rajiv Gandhi in India (in Punjab and Assam), failed in nearly all its objectives. Worse still were the consequences that flowed from it: apart from the failure to pacify Jaffna, it precipitated a serious political crisis in the Sinhalese areas of the country. The signing of the accord had led to violent protests, in and around Colombo and parts of the south-west coast. They were among the most serious anti-government riots since Independence. The government forces took three days to a week to quell the riots and they were able to do so only because of the rapid transport by air (by the Indian air force) of several thousand Sri Lankan troops from Jaffna.

Although the IPKF was never seen outside the north and the east of the island (save perhaps in the north-central province on their way to the east coast), its shadow lay across the country's political landscape. Its presence in the country was exploited, politically, to the detriment of the government by a combination of the SLFP and the revived JVP—most of all by the JVP. The opposition to the IPKF thus became the catalyst for political confusion and sporadic but calculated acts of violence in the Sinhalese areas of the country.

The IPKF's presence in the north and the east of the island was not without its advantages to the Sri Lankan government. Sri Lanka's expenditure on defence dropped noticeably after mid 1987. The Indian government bore the heavy expenditure involved in the pacification of the north and the east. However, this decline in defence spending on the part of Sri Lanka might have been more substantial if the threat posed by the JVP had not proved to be so serious. As it was, no reduction in the number of defence personnel was possible. On the contrary, because of the JVP threat, the army was expanded—by 1990, it had three divisions instead of the two that had existed up to that time—as was the police.

With R. Premadasa's election as President in December 1988, the IPKF's presence in the island became a point of contention between the Sri Lankan and Indian governments. The negotiations on the removal of the IPKF from the island were both long-drawn-out and acrimonious. Eventually, the IPKF was withdrawn on a timetable determined by the Indian government. The process was completed in March 1990. By that time, there had been a surprising rapprochement between the government of Sri Lanka and the LTTE, drawn together by a common opposition to the IPKF, and in the hope that the hostilities of a decade could be overcome by negotiations. These latter were cordial enough at the beginning, and this period of peace (after May 1989) enabled the army to devote its attention to meeting the challenge posed by the JVP. It is grimly ironic but nevertheless true that the continued presence of the IPKF in the island, and peace talks between the government and the LTTE, helped the Sri Lankan security forces, and in particular the army, to meet and overcome the threat posed by the JVP.

In June 1990 just when the LTTE seemed to be on the verge of winning at the bargaining table what it had not been able to win on the battlefield, the hostilities between it and the Sri Lankan government were renewed. The LTTE broke the ceasefire pact, and its battle with the Sri Lankan armed services raged since then with the inevitable consequence that Sri Lanka's defence expenditure increased to meet the costs of the war in the form of purchase of military hardware from abroad (especially between 1996 and 1998) and the expansion of the manpower resources of the security services. On 1 May 1993, President Premadasa was assassinated by the LTTE. Subsequently, the presidential post was held for fifteen months by D.B. Wijetunga. When he called a presidential election in 1994, the UNP went on to lose a parliamentary election for the first time since 1977.

A Change of Regime

The PA coalition, elected in 1994, inherited these problems of war and security. The PA government's immediate response was to place greater emphasis on the restoration of peace in the country. Its leader projected herself as the peace candidate in the parliamentary and presidential campaigns of August and November 1994. After a narrow victory at the parliamentary elections in August 1994, she went on to secure an overwhelming majority in November that year at the presidential election. One of the principal features of this victory was the massive vote she received from the Tamil minority—including the

Indian Tamils—wherever it was possible for the Tamils to vote (i.e., outside the Jaffna peninsula). With this solid mandate, the government almost immediately went about resuming negotiations with the LTTE. These negotiations, which had begun in the wake of the victory at the parliamentary elections, had been interrupted briefly after the assassination by the LTTE of Gamini Dissanayake, Kumaratunga's UNP opponent at the presidential election. The government was now intent on exploiting its electoral triumph to devise a political settlement. Thus began the second set of direct negotiations with the LTTE by a Sri Lankan government. The first one had taken place in 1989 and 1990 under R. Premadasa, which lasted for a year before breaking down. On this occasion, however, the talks collapsed within a few weeks, by 19 April 1995. The failure once again had to do with the intransigence of the LTTE and its attacks on the Sri Lankan security forces notwithstanding the formal ceasefire agreement. Later, this violence was directed against the Sinhalese living in the eastern province.

Eventually, the PA government decided on a more vigorous course of action, a military campaign in the Jaffna peninsula, the LTTE's stronghold. The campaign began in early July 1995, and despite some early setbacks, its first stage culminated later in the year with the capture of Jaffna town and parts of the Jaffna peninsula, with a surprisingly small number of civilian casualties. The next stage began in May 1996 when the army drove the LTTE out of the whole of the Jaffna peninsula. This was the second time in the space of ten years that the Sri Lankan army was engaged in a military campaign in the Jaffna peninsula. In mid 1986 when the first attack was made, it was stopped in its tracks, after some early success, by the threat of Indian intervention. On this latter occasion—1996—India maintained a studied silence, evidence that it had no intention of intervening. The third phase began in May 1997, involving an attempt on the part of the Sri Lankan government to establish control over the A9 road, in particular the section of it from Vavuniya to Jaffna, the main supply route as it was known. After some initial success, this campaign, Operation Jayasikuru, faced stiff resistance from the LTTE, and it was terminated later in 1998.

As it had done in 1987–90 when the Indian army brought the Jaffna peninsula under their control, the LTTE moved its operations headquarters to the areas just south of the peninsula, to Kilinochchi and Mullaitivu, and retained control of these till the withdrawal of the IPKF. In September 1996, the Sri Lankan army captured the Kilinochchi township after a long battle with the LTTE (but lost control of it again by mid 1998). The Mullaitivu district served as the last LTTE stronghold and its soi-disant administrative capital till 2009. The low-intensity conflict in the country's north-east continued into the last quarter of 1999. Then in a brief and brisk campaign in November 1999, the LTTE recaptured the townships and villages that it had lost to the army eighteen months ago. Over ten years earlier, the LTTE forces had survived in the forests of the Kilinochchi and Mullaitivu districts for over two years overcoming the efforts of the IPKF to dislodge them.

The PA government's military campaign was based on the assumption that the LTTE could be defeated militarily or at least weakened to a point wherein it would settle for something much less than the separate state for which it had been fighting for so long. Certainly, the fall of Jaffna town in 1995 and the loss of control over the Jaffna peninsula had been significant reversals for the LTTE, reversals that could have resulted in a decisive defeat had it been unable to prevent the Sri Lankan armed forces from consolidating their hold on that densely populated region. However, the Sri Lankan forces had been unable to achieve such a consolidation.

Militarization and Its Problems

The increase in defence expenditure over the period 1985–99, was cause for concern on many fronts. The social and economic costs of this arms build-up were becoming severe as scarce resources were being diverted into the defence budget. The prospects of returning to the defence expenditure levels of the early 1980s seemed remote.

However, despite the rapid strengthening of the defence services since the mid 1980s and constant use of the army and other services against the Tamil separatist guerrillas and against the JVP in the period 1988–90, Sri Lanka was spared any significant militarization of its politics. On the other hand there was, regrettably, the emergence of what the American scholar Stephen P. Cohen, an expert on the military of India and Pakistan calls, 'civilian militarism', which is to say, 'the adoption of military-like values and public style by civilians'.[10] Moreover, it was a refined version of 'civilian militarism' that had emerged in Sri Lanka, posing a serious threat to the country's democratic system. On account of genuine or perceived threats to government ministers—especially those with defence responsibilities—by way of assassination attempts by the LTTE, there was a proliferation of security men, including commandos, accompanying them wherever they went. A conspicuous example of this was the country's deputy minister of defence, Anuruddha Ratwatte, who generally travelled with a huge entourage of security men armed with automatic weapons. When he took this security entourage with him for the humdrum business of canvassing support at election time, or even more humdrum—and private—matter of casting his vote, it had an intimidating effect on the electorate and the average voter, especially his political rivals and opponents. Many other ministers also had a security entourage, generally smaller than his, and not a few of them travelled around their constituency at election time accompanied by a very visible security staff. Thus the line between genuine security needs, and the deliberate use of such security forces for party political purposes became blurred.

While the policy of civilian control of the military was maintained, the constitutional, political and administration mechanisms were often changed. The legislature scrutinized the defence budget at the annual budget review, and whenever supplementary estimates were presented for approval. While it was the rule that the Parliament must approve of military expenditures, most governments found ways of using budgetary allocations of other ministries, especially those related to defence, for security purposes. The civilian executive (but not the legislature) always exercised the power to override military decisions, including both strategic and tactical decisions. More to the point, the civilian executive occasionally imposed its own views and priorities with regard to both strategy and tactics on the security services.

The politicization of the military one saw under the Bandaranaikes, both husband and wife—Mrs Bandaranaike in particular—was kept under careful check in the far more turbulent 1980s and early 1990s. Under the PA government, there was little evidence of politicization of the military. The civilian executive continued to have the final say on promotions to the top positions in the services, especially the army, and, of course, on matters such as recruitment and enlistment of officers and other cadres. These recruitment and enlistment procedures also had institutional checks and balances which effectively prevented any blatant attempts to favour political party supporters or children of party supporters.

Ethnicity and the Security Services

One feature of the expansion of the armed services—the dominance of the Sinhalese—is often referred to but seldom actually quantified. The situation as of 1995 with regard to the ethnic composition of the armed services is set out in Figure II. What it shows is how minuscule the representation of the minorities in the armed services had become. The transformation of the armed services into ethnic soldiers, sailors and airmen (with a sprinkling of women) began in the late 1950s. It was accelerated in the 1960s, and reached its present position of total Sinhalese dominance largely as a result of the conflict between the Sri Lankan armed forces and the Tamil separatist activists which assumed its recent form from the mid 1980s.

Figure II: Ethnic Composition of Armed Services as of 1996*

	Ethnicity	Number	Total	Percentage
AIR FORCE				
Officers	Sinhalese	690		95.6
	Tamils	10		1.4
	Muslims	20		2.8
	Burghers	2		0.3
			722	
Other Ranks	Sinhalese	11,300		97.7
	Tamils	90		0.8
	Muslims	150		1.3
	Burghers	30		0.3
			11,570	

ARMY				
Officers	Sinhalese	4700		97.3
	Tamils	40		0.8
	Muslims & Malays	70		1.4
	Burghers	20		0.4
			4830	
Others Ranks	Sinhalese	1,13,050		99.1
	Tamils	150		0.1
	Muslims & Malays	820		0.7
	Burghers	40		0.04
			1,14,060	
NAVY				
Officers	Sinhalese	700		97.1
	Tamils	10		1.4
	Muslims & Malays	10		1.4
	Burghers	01		0.1
			721	
Other Ranks	Sinhalese	11,020		99.2
	Tamils	20		0.2
	Muslims	40		0.4

Malays	10		0.1
Burghers	20		0.2
			11,110	

* Computations based on Sri Lankan official sources.

So long as the ethnic conflict continued in the form of an armed struggle, Tamils would not join the armed services or the police because their families were vulnerable to threats, if not direct attacks, from the LTTE and its allies. The LTTE quite deliberately targeted Tamil officers and those in other ranks in the services and the police force. The few Tamils who served in the army, navy and air force had their homes in the Sinhalese areas of the country. They and their families were relatively safe from reprisals by the LTTE. But these were not the only reasons. In the reality of Sri Lanka's prolonged ethnic conflict involving the armed services engaged in battle against Tamil separatists, Tamils were treated with suspicion by the recruiting officers at the point of entry, and by their peers once they joined.

In contrast, the Indian army has demonstrated how effective ethnically mixed forces are in dealing with situations of violent ethnic conflict, such as in Assam, the north-eastern states, Punjab and Kashmir. Although the situations in India and Sri Lanka would not be strictly comparable in view of the greater ethnic diversity in India, the Sri Lankan armed services too would benefit from an infusion of minority representatives in much larger numbers than in the 1990s and 2000s. The pendulum that had swung so far against the Sinhalese and Buddhists in the early days of Independence has swung so dramatically in the opposite direction that even a moderate reversal of the swing would benefit the country and the armed forces.

With Mahinda Rajapaksa's victory at the presidential election in 2000, the controversial Anuruddha Ratwatte ceased to be the deputy minister of defence.[11] Instead, Rajapaksa's younger brother, Gotabhaya Rajapaksa, a former Lt. Col. in the army and an American citizen, became secretary to the ministry of defence, and for the first time since 1984 or so, there was no deputy defence minister or a Cabinet minister with oversight over defence and security affairs in addition to his own portfolio. Thus since 2000, the portfolio of defence and security affairs has been under the purview of the defence secretary who is responsible to the President in the latter's role as defence minister. While this arrangement has strengthened civilian control over the security services, the exercise of this control falls under the President's jurisdiction. The other side of the story is that, in effect, the Cabinet has lost any independent authority or influence it may previously have had in matters of defence and security policy. This has also created the very real factor of an overly powerful official who wields more influence than the Cabinet ministers, merely because he is the President's brother.

In a presentation at an official seminar[13] conducted by the Sri Lankan government in order to provide an official version of how the LTTE had been defeated, Gotabhaya Rajapaksa, speaking as the defence secretary, first revealed that there had been a substantial increase in the size of the army between the end of 2005 and the end of 2009—and he then proceeded to provide some significant details and statistics. The army's nine divisions had been increased to twenty. Its forty-four brigades expanded to seventy-one and its 149 battalions were raised to 284. The number of personnel in the army increased from 1,20,000 in 2005, at the end of Gotabhaya Rajapaksa's first term as defence secretary, to over 2,00,000 by the time the LTTE was defeated in 2009; with a 1,20,000-strong force, the army was more than a match for the resources of the LTTE. After all, the army had increased its number of personnel from a mere 15,000 to 30,000 at the time of the Vadamarachchi campaign in 1987. That had been a doubling of the army's size—and it had proved to be more than adequate then to inflict a severe defeat on the LTTE. So the increase that came in 2005 could be described as superfluous considering that the LTTE had been severely weakened by the defection of its eastern province cadres and by several defeats at the hands of the army.

AFTER THE ROUT OF THE LTTE: RECONCILIATION AND RECONSTRUCTION

While it was the military that had defeated the LTTE, Mahinda Rajapaksa made it seem as if it was all his own doing. The electorate responded by giving him a resounding mandate at the presidential election of 2010—he won with 57 per cent of the vote. He used the same triumphalist campaign at the parliamentary election a few months later, at which his party, the United People's Freedom Alliance (UPFA), won a decisive victory, falling just short of a two-third majority.

His rival at the presidential election was none other than General Sarath Fonseka who had been chosen by the Opposition parties as their common candidate. After his victory, Rajapaksa turned on Fonseka and instituted a variety of charges against him in the courts and at a court martial.[1] The legal battle that followed lasted over a year. This very unusual development in Sri Lanka's parliamentary life introduced a new element of acute discord in national politics, one which among other matters, could hamper the policies of reconciliation in the northern and the eastern provinces which are essential in any programme of peace-building in Sri Lanka.

---

1. A court martial found him guilty of some of these charges, and he was sentenced to a term of three years' imprisonment, subsequently reduced to two and a half years. Fonseka was released from jail in 2012, but the terms of his release have become controversial. The fact is that Fonseka's civic rights were not restored in full.

The Passage to Reconciliation

Aclue to understanding the essence of the Sri Lankan ethnic conflict is to view it as a contest between a majority (the Sinhalese) with a minority complex, and a minority (the Tamils) with a majority complex. In addition, there is the fact that the Tamils became a privileged minority under British rule and were intent on resisting any or all measures taken after Independence that seemed likely to reduce their advantageous position. Many of the issues in contention have been referred to in earlier chapters of this present monograph and in my earlier monograph, *Reaping the Whirlwind: Ethnic Conflict, Ethnic Politics in Sri Lanka*. We have seen how Sinhalese-dominated governments introduced changes in the language policy and on admission of students to universities that were seen to be harmful to the interests of the Tamils or were seen to show no concern for the Tamils. This was best seen in regard to the language policies introduced in 1956–58 where the policymakers of the government elected in 1956 completely ignored the language policy settlement negotiated in the 1940s. We have also noticed how the language policy changes of the 1950s were later modified till over time they travelled a full circle from being 'Sinhala Only' in 1956–58 to 'Sinhala and Tamil'. A similar lack of concern for minority interests was seen in the changes in the university admissions policy introduced in the 1970s. We have seen how the controversial policies of the 1970s in university admissions were systematically modified thereafter and how the rivalries between the minorities—the Tamils and the Muslims—affected these modifications. These rivalries affected attempts to modify the university admissions policy. In addition, there were the regional compulsions at play in these changes, which reflected not merely the rivalries between the minorities but also pressures from sections of the Sinhalese majority.

At the heart of those changes in the language policy and the university admissions policy, as originally effected, were the powerful influence of Sinhalese-Buddhist rural values and traditions. These influences triumphed with regard to the changes in the language policy in 1956–58 and were not without significance thereafter in the changes made in the university admissions policy. The Sri Lanka Freedom Party reflected these Sinhalese-Buddhist rural values and traditions in the 1950s as it does under President Mahinda Rajapaksa today. Rajapaksa's election victory over General Fonseka for the presidency in 2010 and over the UNP in the subsequent parliamentary elections illustrated the continuing influence of these forces on the electoral process. While these Sinhalese-Buddhist rural values and traditions prevailed in the mid 1950s, and in 2009–10[1], they are an obstacle in introducing policies of reconciliation and effecting policies of reconstruction as regards the Tamil minority now and in the future.

The Formidable Task of Reconciliation

As the current government of Mahinda Rajapaksa surveys the problems of the island after the security forces' successful campaign against the LTTE, it has learned very early that it is much more difficult to plan and implement a policy of reconciliation with the Tamil minority than it had been to plan the defeat of the LTTE.

For thirty years or more, about a third of the land area of Sri Lanka, and fully two-thirds of the coasts had been dominated by the LTTE or lay beyond the control of the Sri Lankan state. To bring these areas under the control of the state again is a formidable task, something amounting to a fundamental reconstruction of the territorial structure of the island, and the effective reintegration of the northern and the eastern provinces with the rest of the country. These were matters which were difficult, if not impossible, so long as the LTTE was in control of these areas. These are two of the nine provinces of the island, a structure built by the British in the period 1833 to 1889. After Independence in 1948, the Sri Lankan governments attempted to treat the districts—of which there are now twenty-five—rather than the nine provinces, as the largest units of administration. The provincial structure was revived in and after 1987 partly in response to pressure from India in association with the Sri Lankan Tamil leadership.

Quite apart from envisaging resistance to the renewal of a possible military challenge posed by any Tamil group, local or overseas, which the government is engaged in doing at present, it would be imperative to deal with the grievances, real or imaginary, of the Tamils, which had given the LTTE so firm a grip on the Tamil people, especially those living in the north and the east of the island. The northern province is overwhelmingly Tamil, while the Muslims are a substantial minority—at least 40 per cent of the population—in the eastern province (where they are larger in number, by far, than the Tamils).

For better or for worse, the LTTE proclaimed itself to be the sole representative of the Tamil people of Sri Lanka, a position it adhered to for thirty years or more, at much cost to the Tamil people and to the Sri Lankan state. Earlier, the FP and TULF had adopted a similar attitude. Thus, the larger community of Tamils in Sri Lanka had to pay a huge price—both in terms of losing democratic alternatives in political contests, as well as in terms of having to cope with the authoritarianism of the LTTE under which they were compelled to live for a few decades. There was a systematic destruction of the democratic traditions of the Tamil community, and with no compensation for them in the form of an improvement in living standards. On the contrary, there was a decline in living standards. Ever since the introduction of universal suffrage in Sri Lanka in 1931—or even earlier than that—Tamil political leaders had contributed substantially, first to the construction and then to the sustenance of Sri Lankan democracy. The LTTE put an end to this and reduced the relationship between the Tamil minority and the Sinhalese majority to a confrontational and military one—a defiant Tamil minority (around 10 per cent or less of the people) posing a separatist challenge to the Sri Lankan state, with the separatist challenge becoming a military one and the military challenge becoming a terrorist one. This is quite apart from leaving the Tamil people without a political party or parties to help in their re-entry to democratic politics.

Ever since the LTTE established itself as the predominant force among the Tamils, the relationship between the Tamil minority and the Sinhalese majority (over 70 per cent of the people) was converted into a conflict-ridden association wherein the economic resources of the island were drawn into destructive purposes with little or no attention being paid to economic growth or safeguarding of the integrity of the institutional framework and the infrastructure of the island. The destructive aspects of this decline were more prominent in the areas controlled by the LTTE than in the rest of the island. Nevertheless, the destructive impact of this conflict was not without its influence in the Sinhalese areas of the country[2]. One consequence was that instead of any substantial economic growth in the island, one saw a slowing down as economic resources were consumed by the conflict.[3]

For one thing, Sri Lanka which, at one time, was virtually a demilitarized nation, was forced to build up an army, indeed a larger army, per million of the population, than other parts of South Asia, including India and Pakistan. This massive militarization proved to be a heavy burden on the country but one that was inevitable given the formidable nature of the LTTE challenge to the Sri Lankan state. This was the price the country had to pay in standing up to and defeating the LTTE. It will take many years before the army can be reduced in size. However, the present Rajapaksa government shows no signs of initiating such a reduction. In part, this can be attributed to fears about the revival of an armed challenge to the Sri Lankan state. However, the prospects of a renewed armed challenge to the state emerging from the Tamil areas of the country are exaggerated. These have been based on a tendency to give credence to the fanciful threats being made by sections of the Tamil disapora in Australia, western Europe and North America. In any event, these threats from the Tamil diaspora could be met more effectively by systematic diplomatic activity rather than continued militarization. That said, the Sri Lankan state does not need to let down its guard, but it should make a careful and realistic assessment of the potential damage from the aims of the fringe groups in the Tamil diaspora. As we have seen, this diaspora amounts to about 8,50,000 people or about a third or more of the Sri Lankan Tamil population.

Despite the destructive effects of LTTE rule in the Tamil areas of the country, which involved the diversion of regional and other resources to the maintenance aspects of the LTTE cadres, and to their military and naval campaigns—even by putting pressure on Tamil families to let their children, both male and female, join the LTTE forces as soldiers or as child soldiers—there was also the neglect of the local infrastructure and the decline of any prospects of economic growth. Nevertheless, the Tamil people were not without pride in the LTTE and in the challenge it posed to the Sri Lankan state. Its violent and destructive ways were viewed as some sort of compensation for the apparent injustices suffered by the Tamils at the hands of the Sri Lankan state and its officials. The large-scale presence of the Sri Lankan state machinery—the administration, the police and the defence forces—in Jaffna and the Tamil areas of the country was a source of resentment. The LTTE's defiant response to this presence was admired, and regarded as a defensive measure against what were seen as the illegitimate demands and pressures of the state and its officials. The result was that the defeat of the LTTE and the death of Prabhakaran as well as other top LTTE leaders, were treated as an unbearable loss to the Tamil community. Memories of the more positive features of the LTTE are likely to remain fresh in the minds of the Tamil people for a long time and, more to the point, would affect the government's attempts at reconciliation—whether this be through policies or gestures. How long these positive memories about the LTTE and its role in the Sri Lankan polity would stay in the minds of the Tamils would depend on their receptivity to the Sri Lankan government's reconciliation measures.

The Lessons Learned and Reconciliation Commission

The Rajapaksa government made a start by appointment of something like a truth and reconciliation commission—the 'Lessons Learned and Reconciliation Commission'. How long this commission took in its deliberations and how it conducted these deliberations were vitally important factors in any programme of reconciliation and reconstruction. If the South African model of the Desmond Tutu-led truth and reconciliation commission would serve as a point of reference, much could have been achieved. But the ground realities in Sri Lanka would not support any idea of a comparison with the South African situation. Moreover, in Sri Lanka's case, there was no personality of the stature of Desmond Tutu to guide the affairs of such a commission nor was there any credible number of Sinhalese or Tamil personalities to give evidence before such a commission. For one thing, the death of Prabhakaran and other top LTTE leaders, as well as the absence of a Tamil leadership that would be acceptable to the Tamil people, posed a serious obstacle to the work of the commission. While a few leaders of Opposition parties and independent Sinhalese have given evidence before the commission, its processes were time-consuming, although great deliberation went into the matters at hand. Just as time-consuming was the preparation of a report or reports of its deliberations. Moreover, Sri Lanka's recent record in commissions of inquiry does not provide any grounds for optimism about the formulation of proposals and the assessment of charges about policies and measures taken.

A more practical alternative would have been for a group of advisers of the government to have examined the literature on the Sri Lankan conflict that has emerged over the last thirty years or more, and having examined this literature, the government could have proceeded to prepare and implement policies of reconciliation and reconstruction. This process would have been quicker and more realistic than the methods adopted by the Lessons Learnt and Reconciliation Commission. Another practical alternative would have been to regularly invite the Tamil political leadership that has emerged after the destruction of the LTTE, and other Tamils as well as representatives of other minorities, such as the Muslims and the Christians, for discussions on measures of reconciliation and reconstruction. These two processes would have been subjected to the ebb and flow of the ongoing arguments and discussions as well as the evolving political demands, which would have been an advantage. In addition, these processes could have been carried out alongside the Lessons Learnt and Reconciliation Commission, and if properly handled, could have reduced the time necessary for the formulation and implementation of an effective policy of reconciliation and reconstruction by such a commission.

The situation the Rajapaksa government has to deal with is more complex than merely a conflict between the Sinhalese and the Tamils. One practical problem that needs to be kept in mind in preparing policies for reconciliation and reconstruction is that the Tamil areas in the north of the country and the Tamil and Muslim areas of the east are among the most underdeveloped parts of the island. This is not a recent or a contemporary problem but a historical fact. These areas lack the wealth of resources that the Sinhalese areas of the country have and have had. For example, these areas did not have the benefits of plantation agriculture that the Sinhalese areas of the country enjoyed.[4] There was no coffee industry, no tea and no rubber industries in these areas, only coconut production on a limited extent of land. This situation is not likely to change in the near future, indeed, for years to come. The only possibility is to bring more land in the north under coconut cultivation, if possible.

Under British rule, the rapidly increasing population in the Tamil areas of the north and the east—in particular, in the north—had been accommodated in the lower rungs of the administrative structure that evolved in the country, especially in the Sinhalese areas in the south-west of the country. As a result, the Tamils had come to dominate the administrative structure of the country for much of the nineteenth and the early part of the twentieth century. Under the British rule, the Tamils had also gained employment in the clerical grades in the developing commercial houses in Colombo. As we have seen in part two of this monograph, the Sinhalese opposition to the Tamil domination of the public services had become a major political factor of discord in the period of negotiations with the British on the matter of transfer of power in the 1930s and the 1940s. In the 1920s and earlier, and till the 1930s and 1940s, the Tamils had constituted at least 40 per cent of the workforce of the lower rungs of the public services. Today, this figure is around 4 per cent or less. This latter figure needs to be increased. In any policy of reconciliation and reconstruction, measures would need to be taken to accommodate such an increase through the equivalent of an affirmative action policy on a long-term basis. The reduction of openings for Tamils in state-sector employment since the mid 1950s has been cause for grievance among the Tamils.

The Rajapaksa government has accepted the fact that a comprehensive analysis of the processes of recovery and reconstruction of the areas of the north and the east of Sri Lanka, especially areas formerly controlled by the LTTE, needs to take into consideration that only one act of 'ethnic cleansing' took place during the whole period of conflict between the LTTE and the forces of the Sri Lankan government. That was the expulsion of the Muslims of the northern province (about 80,000 people) by the LTTE in 1990 and seizure of their property, including houses, other buildings, and jewellery and cash.[5] These Muslims have been living since then as refugees in the south of the country, especially in the Muslim areas of the north-western province, as also in the north-central province. They also moved to other parts of the Sinhalese areas, especially to the central province to live among the Muslims there.

Whatever excuses or reasons the LTTE gave for this exercise in 'ethnic cleansing', the question of compensation for losses never arose. We do not know whether the Muslims did formally ask the LTTE for such compensation, but we do know that the LTTE never paid any compensation. Some Muslims expelled by the LTTE from the northern province have expressed a wish to go back there and reclaim their houses, shops and other buildings. Now that the LTTE has been defeated, the prospects of the Muslims going back are more realistic. However, in any event, there is little prospect of the Muslims receiving compensation from the resources of the LTTE or from its successors. The compensation would have to be provided by the Sri Lankan government as part of a wider or an overall settlement of the problems of the north and the east by way of recognizing the give-and-take nature of electoral politics.

There is also the question of the expulsion of Sinhalese from various parts of the northern and the eastern provinces. But as the numbers affected are far smaller than those among the Muslims, and as the victims among the Sinhalese are largely peasants, this problem would be easier for the Sri Lankan government to handle than the problem posed by the expulsion of Muslims.

Another set of persons who may want to go back to Jaffna are the Sinhalese bakers who had dominated that trade in Jaffna for decades. A small group, they were not expelled—they just moved away in the 1980s. They have now expressed a wish to go back to their businesses in Jaffna. But in any event, their return is a matter of economic or social forces at work, and not one that just concerns those in political power in Jaffna.

Infrastructure and its Revival

The thirty years or more of LTTE domination of the northern and the eastern provinces were a period that saw neglect of

SRI LANKA AND THE DEFEAT OF THE LTTE   251

infrastructure. For instance, the LTTE removed the railway lines in the northern province and used the steel for its own purposes, especially for fortification in the form of bunkers. These railway lines are now being replaced by the Indian government and this replacement will not involve too much time as the track is still in place. Indian assistance is envisaged also for the repair of the port of Kankesanthurai—perhaps the most important port of the northern province—and the Palali airport in Jaffna.

That would leave only the matter of reconstruction of roads to be undertaken by the Sri Lankan government. The roads of the northern and the eastern provinces have been neglected and are badly in need of repair—whether it be the strategically important A9 linking Jaffna with Kandy and the Sinhalese areas of the country or the roads in the northern and the eastern provinces linking the interior with the coast. This is one of the principal areas of reconstruction and would require grants from the Sri Lankan government. Grants would also be necessary for any expansion of the highway system in the northern and the eastern provinces. This is an expensive and time-consuming matter. However, it is required not only as a gesture of reconciliation but also for welding the road system of these provinces with that of the rest of the country for the wider purposes of national and economic regeneration.

The repair of the roads and railways will involve several years of activity. Grants from the Indian government and soft loans from the Asian Development Bank (ADB) will ease the burdens on the Sri Lankan government. But even with money coming in from India, the ADB and elsewhere, the processes will be long-drawn-out and will take many years of purposeful effort.

Fortunately, the weather pattern in the north and the east of the country is favourable to long periods of work in road reconstruction. Only the period of the north-east monsoon will affect this work, but this is only for three or four months of the year—January and February, and from October to December.

All that said, we need to emphasize the point that the economic reconstruction of the northern province requires more than the rehabilitation and expansion of the existing network of roads. The process of reconstruction would benefit from the construction of other roads linking Jaffna and the coastal areas of the northern province, with the interior of both the northern province and the eastern province and these with the Sinhalese areas of the country. Nothing of the sort had been attempted over the last thirty years or more. This could involve the legal business of acquiring land—and perhaps some houses and other buildings—and therefore it confronts the complex emotional issues involved in gaining the consent of the owners of these properties. The costs of purchase of properties would need to be negotiated as an essential preliminary. If the compensation is adequate, the process would not require much time. But negotiation would be a time-consuming business especially because the owners of these properties would need to be convinced of the benefits of these roads for themselves and for the wider purposes of reconciliation and of economic growth of the north and the east of the island. The model for these acquisitions should be the procedures adopted in road-building in other parts of the country.

Linked to this process of acquiring land in the north and the east of the island for the regeneration of the road system is the complex issue of moving the security forces, especially the army, out of lands and property controlled by the security forces in what are called the High Security Zones.[6] The issue of HSZs is a highly sensitive matter in any policy of reconciliation with the Tamils, in particular with the Tamils of the Jaffna peninsula. The properties taken over had been among the most valuable in the Jaffna peninsula. While the security forces regarded these properties as essential for defence against the LTTE, the property owners could only think of the losses they incurred. The HSZs have been a matter of acute concern to both the security forces and the people whose houses and land had been taken over by the security forces. As long as the LTTE had remained a threat to the army and other security forces, there had been reluctance on the part of the security forces to return the houses, land and other buildings acquired for the HSZs to the owners of these properties. Now that the LTTE has been defeated and no longer pose a threat to the security forces and the state, the return of these properties is a matter of urgency and an essential part of the processes of reconciliation and reconstruction. The return of property within the HSZs to their legitimate owners could be negotiated without much difficulty. However, the question of compensation for use of these properties by the security forces would need to be negotiated. The principles involved in assessing the compensation have to be defined and negotiated, and along with that, the more difficult issue of compensation for damages to these properties at the hands of security forces. It would be necessary to determine how much of this damage could be attributed to the LTTE and how much to the security forces.

15

Reconstruction

The defeat of the LTTE at the hands of the Sri Lankan army came more rapidly after 2006–07 than even the government had expected. As we have seen, the LTTE's 'army' collapsed, as did its 'navy'. After the rout of the LTTE in 2009, there has been no LTTE-controlled political structure left in Sri Lanka, and certainly not an LTTE-controlled political party even if the lingering influence of the LTTE can be seen in the Tamil National Alliance (TNA). Thus the absorption of the LTTE-controlled territory in the north and the east has proved to be easier than one could have expected given the long period of LTTE 'rule' in these parts of the island. Nevertheless, in order for the Sri Lankan state to re-establish control over the 'LTTE territories' for the long term, it will have to face lots of challenges. This despite the fact that the present Rajapaksa government controls more of Sri Lanka than any Sri Lankan regime had done from 1948 to 1980. The Rajapaksa government has not yet paid much attention to any clearly defined policy of reconciliation and reconstruction for the north and the east of the island. It has instead resorted to ad hoc policies. Except for the grants and loans from India, it keeps a tight control over grants and allocations from other countries.

The LTTE left behind no political structure in Sri Lanka nor a large number of committed supporters other than the loosely knit diaspora groups in Canada, Australia and western Europe. Moreover, the LTTE had systematically destroyed every Tamil political party or group in Sri Lanka, either compelling them to join its wing or seek a subordinate alliance. The LTTE claimed for itself the position of the sole spokesmen of the Tamil people and jealously guarded this position by ruthlessly eliminating any Tamil who sought—or was believed to seek—an independent political role in any part of Sri Lanka. It ruthlessly destroyed any semblance of a democratic tradition in the north and the east of Sri Lanka.

The defeat of Prabhakaran and his LTTE forces was a truly historic achievement. In the annals of Sri Lankan history, no Tamil had posed so severe a threat to the Sri Lankan state as Prabhakaran had done. He regarded himself as an iconic Tamil national figure—the Sun God—and thanks to his terrorist incursions and to the several victories he had won over sections of the Sri Lankan army over a thirty-year period, he had overestimated his skills just as he had underestimated his opponents, including General Fonseka. He had survived the defeat the LTTE had received at the hands of General Ranatunga in 1987. In many of his calculations while facing defeat in 2009, he had hoped that the Indians would save him as they had done in 1987 forgetting that he had organized the assassination of Rajiv Gandhi. But in Fonseka, he had found his match. In fact, the general's command over his own resources was more impressive than Prabhakaran's.

In the post-LTTE phase, the Rajapaksa government has treated the reconstruction process as an essential feature of renewing the national and regional political systems. However, the central problem in any policy of economic reconstruction is that the parts of the northern and the eastern provinces formerly controlled by the LTTE are some of the most backward areas of the island in terms of economic resources. The British who presided over the transformation of Sri Lanka into a dynamic plantation colony had virtually ignored the northern and the eastern provinces. The coffee plantations that had transformed Sri Lanka's economy in the nineteenth century were all located in the central hills and in Uva. With the collapse of the coffee industry in the 1870s, the renewal process of the economy that followed from 1880s onwards till the 1920s came by way of the tea and rubber industries, all of them located in the central hills and the western, southern and north-western provinces. Then there was the coconut industry, with the main areas of production being in the western and north-western provinces, and to some extent in the Jaffna peninsula and other parts of the northern and the eastern provinces. All this while, the administrative centre of the plantation industry as a whole continued to be in Colombo. As in the 1830s to the 1880s, the northern and the eastern provinces remained a backwater so far as the plantation economy was concerned.

There was no change in this situation even after Independence except for some significant developments in industry—cement and chemicals—in the early years of Independence. These industries were developed by the state in the northern province. However, by and large, there was little else in terms of industry in the northern province after 1953. Even after the northern and the eastern provinces came under the control of the LTTE, no industrial development took place there. The LTTE's record as managers of economic resources of the areas they controlled was dismal. The records show it did nothing in the sphere of economic development, nothing that could be considered as a useful contribution to economic growth. The rich rice-producing areas of Mannar in the northern province and the more significant and productive rice-producing areas of the eastern province were neglected while being exploited. The profits that came from rice production there went largely to the LTTE and to those favoured by the LTTE.

Thus, at this point, when the LTTE has collapsed, the northern and the eastern provinces are in need of rejuvenation as part of a wider objective to integrate these areas into the national economy. In evolving a set of principles for economic growth in the areas formerly controlled by the LTTE, the Sri Lankan state would need to provide substantial economic resources through the annual budget for a decade or more in a spirit of reconciliation. It is only then that the plan for stabilization and economic reconstruction of these areas would achieve success. This would mean that the Sri Lankan state would have done much more for these areas than the British, and especially the LTTE.

The post-Independence political elite in the north and the east had generally done little for the economic development of their provinces. The one exception was the Tamil Congress leader, G.G. Ponnambalam. In the early years of Independence, Ponnambalam was the most important Tamil political leader of the time (from the 1940s to 1955 or so) and a member of the Sri Lankan Cabinet. He deftly used his influence as the leader of the Tamils and his power as a Cabinet[1] minister to embark on a policy of developing industries in the northern province. The cement factory in Jaffna, the establishment of which he oversaw, is still the largest in the island. Although somewhat run-down, it is still viable as a source of commercial production and as a source of employment. This employment is largely, if not solely, for Tamils and it would remain so for years to come as the largest employer of Tamils, in industry in Jaffna and its neighbourhood. Ponnambalam's role as the creator of industrial employment in the northern province should serve as a model for those engaged in the economic regeneration of this province. It is an encouraging record and something worth examining in the arena of economic reconstruction in these post-LTTE days.

A Development Agenda for the Northern and Eastern Provinces

There are two areas in which there is substantial room for development in the northern and the eastern provinces—tourism and fisheries.

The beaches of the eastern province have always attracted large numbers of domestic and foreign tourists. But the struggle between the Sri Lankan security forces and the LTTE saw the destruction of many of the hotels in this province and Trincomalee. The responsibility of the LTTE for this destruction surpassed that of the security forces. These hotels are now being repaired, and there is room for a larger investment in hotels in the area. On a larger note, investment in the hotel industry should come both from Sri Lankan sources—especially in the case of hotels in Colombo and the western province—and possibly from the Tamil diaspora with surplus funds at their disposal, funds which once went to the LTTE. However, so far the Tamil diaspora has not made any significant investment in this industry.

The northern and the eastern provinces have rich fishing resources. These resources even attracted small numbers of Sinhalese people who lived on the coasts of the western province. They would use the period of the south-west monsoon (May to September) to move to localities in the coasts of the northern and eastern provinces where the seas are much calmer than on the south-western coasts. Some of them have settled permanently there. The island's fishing industry was badly affected by the conflict between the security forces (both the army and the navy) and the LTTE. The fisheries of Jaffna were especially disturbed by both the LTTE and the Sri Lankan forces. There was, in addition, a special problem of Indian fishermen encroaching on Sri Lankan waters, a problem more pronounced in Jaffna than in other parts of the coast. This is likely to continue.

Potentially, the fisheries of the northern and the eastern provinces would be a rich source of wealth and employment for the people of that region. These fisheries, like the fisheries in the rest of the island, are in need of modernization. Together, these fisheries would prove more than adequate to meet the needs of the local population. At the moment, the island imports tinned fish from western Europe and elsewhere to supplement local supplies. The conflict with the LTTE is partly responsible for the poor state of the fisheries today. But now that the LTTE has been defeated, a modernization and expansion process of the fisheries should be attempted, both as part of a policy of reconciliation with the Tamils and as a segment of a policy of economic reconstruction in Sri Lanka as a whole.

As for the agriculture sector, the Mannar district in Jaffna and the eastern province as a whole are rich rice-producing areas. Both are surplus producers that supply the densely populated Jaffna peninsula with its rice. However, as both these areas have suffered from neglect and worse at the hands of the LTTE, they need a regeneration programme. For this, the expertise could come from the research centres in the Sinhalese areas of the country which have a proud record of success in making the island virtually self-sufficient in the area of rice production, a process that took many decades. If proper regeneration measures are undertaken, Mannar and the eastern province can add substantially to the rice-production sector of the island. The harvests in these areas could then move beyond supplying merely to the needs of Jaffna and the heavily populated areas of the northern province. The profits would go to the cultivators of Mannar and the eastern province.

The Jaffna peninsula and the northern province, in general, are some of the driest parts of Sri Lanka. Nevertheless, the Tamils of the Jaffna peninsula have developed an efficient system of agriculture dependent on underground sources of water. This system is efficient largely because of the hard and scientific work that goes into these small plots of land. Here, cultivation is a much harder proposition than in the wetter Sinhalese areas. In the early twentieth century, engineers in Jaffna were debating the merits of exploiting the water resources of the Jaffna lagoon and the Elephant Pass areas for meeting the needs of Jaffna and the Jaffna peninsula. These schemes were forgotten partly because of the expenses involved and partly because the development of irrigation in other parts of Sri Lanka, culminating in the complex Mahaveli project of the 1970s and 1980s, took priority. These early twentieth century schemes for the supply of water to Jaffna and the Jaffna peninsula could be revived and funded as part of an imaginative policy of reconciliation and reconstruction. This is likely to capture the imagination of the people of Jaffna, something akin to the impact of the Mahaveli scheme on the Sinhalese population. In recent times, there have been proposals for a diversionary canal to take some of the water from the Mahaveli scheme to parts of the Tamil areas—in particular, the Vanni region of the northern province. However, this project is not only very expensive but also carries the disadvantage of excessive evaporation. In any event, this scheme would take much longer to bear fruit than an attempt to transfer water from the Jaffna lagoon and the Elephant Pass areas to Jaffna and the Jaffna peninsula.

This discussion of irrigation and diversion of water illustrates some of the difficulties that confront the government of Sri Lanka in any systematic attempt at economic development and reconstruction in the Tamil areas of the country. This process of development and reconstruction is something that would go beyond anything attempted by the British during their rule in the island. The tasks at hand are difficult, expensive and time-consuming, but they need to be undertaken in any genuine attempt at reconciliation and reconstruction. These schemes could be discussed with the World Bank and the Asian Development Bank so funds are made available either through grants or soft loans. The model would be the more ambitious nature of the funding of the various features of the Mahaveli scheme in the 1970s and 1980s. However, such grants and soft loans were easier to obtain in the 1970s and 1980s than in the present times. The political objectives of such grants and soft loans—underlining a policy of reconciliation of the Tamils and also the reconstruction of the northern province if not of the northern and the eastern provinces—would make it more likely that such grants would be made than they would be if this reconstruction of the territories of an aggrieved minority was not emphasized.

There is also the issue of rebuilding small- and medium-scale industry in the northern and the eastern provinces. The capital for this could come from several sources beginning with local investors, then from foreign sources and from allocations in the annual national budget, from banks now moving into these areas, and possibly also from the Tamil diaspora. Local Tamil businessmen could invest in the small- and medium-scale industries in these areas, either by themselves or in association with outsiders.

The rehabilitation of industry and agriculture in the northern and the eastern provinces would need to be accompanied by the repair and expansion of the school system in these areas and also by the expansion of the University of Jaffna into a major university of the country. In addition, there's the task of expanding the facilities of universities in the eastern provinces—especially in the Muslim majority areas—established and developed in the 1980s and 1990s. These need to become full-fledged institutions rather than be largely Muslim or Islamic ones as they are today. The funding for these universities has come mainly from the government through the University Grants Commission. Grants have also come from the Islamic world.

The northern province has one of the most significant private universities in the island, the Jaffna College, the oldest in the country, established by missionaries in the nineteenth century. As a part of the policy of reconciliation, its faculties could be improved and expanded wherein it becomes a major university of the country or takes on an independent status. The grants for this ought to come from the state.

India and the Rehabilitation Programme

Meanwhile, the Indian government has shown an interest in the rehabilitation of Sri Lankan Tamils, especially the Tamils of the northern province affected by the conflict. This has partly to do with a concern for the rehabilitation of Tamils held as refugees by the Sri Lankan state in the last stages of the conflict with the LTTE. The return of these Tamils, housed in camps in the northern province, has proved to be a slow process. The Sri Lankan government has expressed commitment to permitting these refugees to return to their homes even in the face of minefields constructed by the LTTE. In a policy statement made in June 2010 in New Delhi, President Rajapaksa had assured the Indian government these refugees would all return to their homes by the end of 2010. And many, if not most of them, have done so.

Then there's the issue of helping the Tamils in the northern and the eastern provinces to repair their homes and other buildings damaged in the course of the Sri Lankan government's campaign against the LTTE. This damage is quite extensive, and their repair is part of the policy of reconciliation and reconstruction. The governments of Sri Lanka and India have announced their commitment to building 50,000 houses as part of this programme of rehabilitation.[2] This is a comprehensive programme for which most, if not all, funds would come from India, either as a loan or as a grant.

However, this Indian commitment to a policy of encouraging and funding programmes for the rehabilitation of the Tamils of the northern province could prove to be a controversial one if it does not include the Muslim minority in the area. Of course, there is the wider issue of the Muslims of the eastern province. The Indian policy of concern for the welfare of the Tamils of the northern province is the continuation of a policy that evolved in the 1960s and 1970s as part of India's response to the Sri Lankan ethnic conflict and efforts made for the protection of the Tamil minority. This Indian concern for the Tamil minority is currently part of a wider issue: New Delhi's fears of the burgeoning influence of China over Sri Lanka, an influence that arose principally with Beijing providing arms and ammunition for the Sri Lankan forces in the latter's fight with the LTTE. The Indian role in the contest with China will be dealt with later in this chapter. All we need to say here is that the Indian response to this Chinese influence would be grossly inadequate if it consists largely of a concern for the affairs of the Sri Lankan Tamil minority.

The Restoration of Democracy in the Tamil Areas

Reconciliation and reconstruction would lose much of their appeal if they were not accompanied by the rehabilitation of democracy in the Tamil areas of the country. The LTTE is primarily responsible for the systematic destruction of democracy among the Tamils. At the same time, the so-called Tamil moderates cannot be absolved of all blame in so far as the support they gave the LTTE is considered, as well as the fact that demands and claims by the Tamil moderates were the source of some of the programmes of the LTTE and of their political objectives. The separatist claims of the LTTE such as the concept of a Tamil homeland, go back to the Federal

Party of the 1950s and 1960s. However, even in recent times when Tamil moderates voted at parliamentary or presidential elections, they tamely permitted the LTTE to dictate matters. For instance, they would not vote if the LTTE declared they should not vote. Tamil candidates for the Parliament would either be chosen by the LTTE or in consultation with it—and always with its approval. Such parliamentarians would be guided by the instructions or wishes of the LTTE in their votes in the Parliament. This subordination of the moderates to the demands of the LTTE is a factor in the decline and collapse of democracy among the Tamils of the northern province. The Tamils in other parts of the island did not succumb to the pressures of the LTTE to the same extent. The Tamil plantation workers were generally free of LTTE pressures although they were not inconsiderate of LTTE interests.

The virtual collapse of the system of local government in the northern and the eastern provinces, in particular the collapse of the village councils, for which the Tamil moderates[3] and the LTTE—as well as the Sri Lankan government—must share the blame, contributed very much to the general decline of democracy in the northern and the eastern provinces. The LTTE were not enthusiastic about local government institutions, while both the Tamil moderates and the Sri Lankan government accepted this situation as an inevitable consequence, first of all of the political settlement advocated by the Indians in 1987 and then of the domination of the LTTE in the areas it controlled. The culpability of the government was seen most prominently in its failure to establish a provincial council for the northern province. The fear was that such a council would be controlled by the LTTE. A provincial council for the eastern province was established after the Tamils of this province broke away from the LTTE. These local government bodies have now been restored, and elections held, elections which have been won by the Tamil National Alliance. When elections were held for the provincial council of the eastern province, former LTTE cadres captured power at the expense of the Tamil moderates and the Muslims. The Tamil groups that contested these elections were part of an armed militia. Their inevitable victory was not an example of the operation of democracy so much as an attempt to secure the eastern province as an area free of the LTTE but not free of an armed militia. This Tamil militia operated with the consent of the government. Democracy was no part of this whole sequence of events. It was largely a matter of a group of Tamils breaking away from the LTTE and working with the Rajapaksa government. While this may have yielded practical advantages in terms of the government's larger struggle with the LTTE, there was no question of any democratic practices entering the picture.

The disarming of Tamil groups now in control of the provincial council of the eastern province or those operating elsewhere within the eastern province is an essential prelude to the democratization of the province. These armed groups are primarily used as shock troops for the manipulation of elections in the northern and the eastern provinces. This manipulation is carried out either for their own purposes—not confined to electoral politics—or on behalf of the Rajapaksa government.

If the LTTE was an important factor in the decline and destruction of democracy in the northern and the eastern provinces, the government's culpability lies in its tolerance of the armed Tamil groups in the eastern province and elsewhere. The justification has been that these erstwhile LTTE cadres need to be protected from retaliation by the LTTE. But now that the LTTE has been demolished, these Tamil groups should be compelled to hand back their arms to the police or the army. Should these groups be disarmed by the state, it would also be necessary to hold fresh elections to the provincial council there.

In fact, the Tamils are a minority of about 20 per cent of the population in the eastern province. The fact that the Tamil groups control the provincial council serves to exclude the Muslims who are a dominant minority in the eastern province (as much as 40 per cent of population) from either their legitimate share in power or any share at all.

The democratization process will also require the establishment of a provincial council for the northern province. Elections to that provincial council will enable political parties and individuals to vie for positions in the council. Such a council will give the Tamils opportunities in influencing, if not fashioning, the development policy of the northern province. The Tamils could play a big role in the democratization process of the province.

Along with a provincial council for the northern province, there had been the need for establishing or re-establishing village councils in both the northern and the eastern provinces. As we have seen, these councils went on to be established in 2011. This should provide all segments of the population of these provinces—Tamil, Muslim and Sinhalese—with opportunities to manage the affairs of their localities on their own. It would not only contribute to the democratization process of the country as a whole but would also give the local population a voice in the development of their regions. These councils could serve as a check on the bureaucracy, both state and provincial, and would also be a source of information on the needs of the people. They would be a platform for the maturation of alternative sources of leadership and could diminish the power and influence of parliamentarians.

The processes of democratization are necessarily slow-moving. However, the formation of these councils could provide another layer of leadership to Sri Lankan democracy. That said, they could also become centres of parochial interests and obstacles in the path of the wider democratic process. But that is a price that democratization has always got to pay.

Fortunately, what is required is not the establishment of democracy de novo but the re-establishment of democracy, a return to democratic systems and practices that had been in vogue before the advent of the LTTE. The right to vote had been in existence in Sri Lanka since 1931 and along with it parties, individuals and associations that appealed to the electorate on the basis of a political platform, as also organizations that sought places in these councils on the basis of programmes and promises. For instance, the Tamil Congress was established in 1944 to win the support of Tamils in all parts of the island. It had worked to fashion a programme of action during the national debates on the transfer of power. The Tamil Congress dominated Tamil politics till around 1955. Its rival, the Federal Party, was established in 1951 and survived till the 1970s as the main political group of the Tamils. In the mid 1950s, the Federal Party had electorally defeated the Tamil Congress. Like the latter, the former spoke on behalf of Sri Lanka's Tamils. Both were also separatist in their outlook—the Federal Party much more so than the Tamil Congress. The LTTE's separatism sprang from that of the Federal Party and the Tamil Congress—more so from the former. Subsequently, the Tamil Congress and the Federal Party were driven into the political wilderness by the LTTE, with some of their leaders (especially leaders of the Federal Party) even being assassinated by the LTTE. Currently, with the destruction of the LTTE by the Sri Lankan army—as also because of the decline of the Federal Party and the death of the Tamil Congress leader, G.G. Ponnambalam (in 1976)—the political landscape in the Tamil areas of the north and the east lacks any significant political party, other than the TNA. The national political parties based in Colombo and elsewhere have been unable to establish themselves in the Tamil areas of the island. The present lack of any major political parties in the north and the east is likely to benefit these national parties. However, much more likely is either the emergence of new political parties seeking to build on resources left behind by the Tamil Congress and the Federal Party or a revival of either of these parties. Whether these political groupings will continue to be purely regional or ethnic in their aspirations, or search for a national role either on their own or in association with the more prominent national parties, will play a part in the revival of the democratic process in the Tamil areas of the country. Of course, such a revival will depend on the health of democracy in Sri Lanka as a whole.

The Tamil areas of the country were not the only parts affected by the collapse of democracy that followed in the wake of LTTE's rise to influence. Sri Lankan democracy as a whole lost much of its integrity and spirit in the long struggle with the LTTE. While the country which had its first election under universal suffrage as early as 1931 continued to have elections even when the LTTE was a prominent political factor, over the passage of time the national elections started getting plagued by malpractices.[4] The exit of the LTTE from the national scene will now help in the revival of democracy both in the Tamil areas which the LTTE had dominated and in the broader Sinhalese areas where they had not. The major political parties now have the responsibility of helping in the revival of past standards of electoral politics in the Sinhalese areas of the island, and in the renewal of the democratic process in the northern and the eastern provinces. This latter agenda will depend heavily on the democratic traditions of the island.

One institutional change that will help in the renewal of the democratic traditions of Sri Lanka is the establishment of an election commission based on the Indian model. This commission ought to enjoy the kind of powers that its Indian counterpart has. Sri Lanka has had a commissioner of elections and a department of elections but both lack the standing of the Indian counterpart. An election commission based on the Indian model is likely to reduce, if not eliminate, corrupt practices in Sri Lankan elections, and will help to keep in check governmental interference in the conduct of elections.

Regional Rivalries

Currently, Sri Lanka is caught up in the web of rivalry between India and China. When India was perturbed at the seemingly increased Chinese influence in Sri Lanka, the relative importance of the assistance that China gave to Sri Lanka in its conflict with the LTTE was the principal cause. When Sri Lanka needed a regular supply of materiel for its army, India's attitude was ambivalent at best, while Pakistan, first of all, and China, to a much greater degree, provided the arms. The army's victory against the LTTE would have been much more difficult without Pakistani and Chinese, in particular, arms supplies.

Moreover, Chinese supplies and assistance were made available without applying any pressure on Sri Lanka with regard to measures required for the management of the island's ethnic conflict—principally in terms of legislation and institutions, which had been the case with India. In 1987 when the LTTE had been routed by the Sri Lankan army under General Ranatunga and an attack on Jaffna—to seal the victory—seemed the next step, the Indian government intervened on behalf of the LTTE and warned the Sri Lankan government against any attack on Jaffna. The LTTE survived and moved across the Palk Straits to Tamil Nadu and elsewhere in India, and it took Sri Lankan governments another twenty-two years before they could decisively defeat the LTTE again. (General Fonseka, who fashioned the defeat of the LTTE between 2006 and 2009, was a Lt. Col. with the army in 1986.)

Had the Indian government not intervened on behalf of the LTTE in 1986, Sri Lanka would have been spared twenty or more years of bitter conflict. But it is also true that a political settlement of the conflict had been negotiated by the Sri Lankan and Indian governments—in 1986 and 1987. Some two decades later—in 2009—the LTTE was again anxious to get the Indian government to mediate in Sri Lanka. It not only wanted New Delhi to insist on a halt to the army's campaign against it but also sought a renewal of the peace talks. However, on this occasion, the Indian government did not intervene—it only declared an interest in the welfare of the Tamils in Sri Lanka, especially in the welfare of those rendered homeless by the conflict, by which it meant the Tamils of the Jaffna peninsula and the northern province. This was an appropriate response because a political settlement had been negotiated under the Indian auspices in 1986 and 1987. Earlier, in 1979–80, a 'domestic' settlement to the conflict had been attempted—between the Sri Lankan government and the TULF.

After the defeat of the LTTE, the Indian government has declared its concern for the welfare of the Tamils displaced by the conflict. New Delhi had announced that it would provide grants or loans for the construction of 50,000 houses, with the construction being jointly managed by the two governments concerned. Negotiations on this agreement commenced in late 2010. While there's pressure from the state of Tamil Nadu to get New Delhi to insist on a system of devolution of power in Sri Lanka, one which would benefit the Tamils—presumably those of Jaffna and the northern province—so far the Indian government has refrained from endorsing this demand. The Indian government's reluctance is understandable because Sri Lanka's system of devolution based on provinces, introduced in 1987, was modelled on the Indian system of provincial governments. It was introduced at the insistence of India—more to the point, it was introduced on behalf of the Tamil minority. Before the days of the provincial system, Sri Lanka had a system of district councils, which came into place in 1979–80 after much discussion and with the support of the Tamil leadership. The Tamil leadership preferred provincial councils over district councils. Having secured the provincial councils system in 1987, the Tamils pushed for the larger objective of an amalgamation of the northern and the eastern provinces. As we have seen, this amalgamation was brought into place by President Jayewardene in 1988 using his special powers. Nearly twenty years later, the procedure in the amalgamation process was challenged before the Supreme Court as unconstitutional, by sections of the Opposition. The Supreme Court decided in favour of this application. The Rajapaksa government accepted the decision with much enthusiasm and moved to create a council for the eastern province. But what it has not been able to do is to create a council for the northern province. The lack of a provincial council for the northern province leaves a significant gap in the devolutionary process in Sri Lanka.

Meanwhile, in response to Chinese economic assistance to Sri Lanka, the Indian government has offered economic assistance of its own, thus engaging in a rivalry with the Chinese. In seeking to influence Sri Lanka in a situation of a rapid expansion of Chinese power and influence in Asia,[5] the Indian government has two obvious disadvantages. First, its continued concern for the Tamil community makes others in the island suspicious of Indian policies. Second, and perhaps even more disadvantageous, is the pressure from sources in the state government in Tamil Nadu, not just the government and the Opposition there but also from fringe groups more enthusiastic than the government and the Opposition and much less responsible in utterances and aspirations as regards what needs to be done on behalf of Sri Lankan Tamils. So, in this context of rapidly increasing Chinese interest in Sri Lanka, India would do well to be more expansive in its concerns, to move from being merely advocates of Tamil interests, to consider also other minorities, especially the Muslims and, of course, the interests of the Sinhalese majority as well as the island, as a whole.

In the meantime, Sri Lanka will have to insist on safeguarding its own national interests as it confronts the rivalry between India and China. It would need to sharpen its diplomatic skills in its efforts to protect its interests from being submerged in this rivalry between Asia's two powerhouses.

Conclusion

This monograph provides an analysis, in previous chapters, of the emergence, maturation and defeat of the LTTE, the well-known separatist, terrorist force in Sri Lanka. The emphasis in the monograph is on the defeat of the LTTE between 2006 and 2009. Given the current controversies over the events relating to the last phases of the annihilation of the LTTE, it will be a few more years before something like a definitive study—based on a wide range of interviews with Tamil civilians trapped in the war zone as well as with officers of the Sri Lankan army and navy who were involved in strategizing and effectively implementing plans to destroy the LTTE forces—can be written.

For this present monograph, I searched for and located as much material as possible on the last phase of the attack on the LTTE. But certain gaps still remain. For instance, it would have been extremely useful to have had an interview or interviews with General Sarath Fonseka who led the campaign which saw the annihilation of the LTTE and the deaths of almost all the LTTE leadership, including its leader V. Prabhakaran. Unfortunately, in its anxiety to gather all the credit for the defeat of the LTTE, the Rajapaksa government prosecuted Fonseka on a number of charges, and succeeded in securing his conviction on some of these. Fonseka was till recently in jail, virtually a political prisoner. He was released in May 2012, but the restoration of his civic rights remains. In the context of the Rajapaksa government's blitzkrieg against Fonseka, many senior officers—especially army officers—involved in the destruction of the LTTE are reluctant to talk freely about these events. Most are disinclined to talk. We hope the time will come when they will be able to speak freely. Given the volatility of Sri Lanka's political world, that time will come sooner than the Rajapaksa loyalists think it would. It would then be possible to piece together a more comprehensive study of the way in which the LTTE was finally destroyed.

The Rout of the LTTE, 2006 to 2009

The overwhelming defeat of the LTTE by General Cyril Ranatunga's revamped Sri Lankan army came as much of a surprise to the LTTE, just as it did to commentators on Sri Lanka's political scene. These events have been dealt with in earlier chapters of this book. The LTTE's defeat in 1986 could well have marked its effective destruction as a political and military force as early as 1986–87. However, with the intervention of Rajiv Gandhi and the Indian government—a colossal blunder for which, in 1991, Rajiv Gandhi paid with his life—the group had been spared to survive and fight another day. Indeed, for two decades more.

The process of LTTE resuscitation that came after 1989 was also facilitated by two Sri Lankan executive Presidents, in succession: first, R. Premadasa who was elected to office in 1989[1], and later, President Chandrika Kumaratunga whose electoral victory in 1994 marked the beginning of the Sri Lanka Freedom Party's long reign in its many manifestations. The SLFP continues to rule Sri Lanka to the present day. Both Premadasa and Kumaratunga, but more particularly the former, sought to absorb the LTTE into the Sri Lankan party system. This policy, such as it was, benefited the LTTE much more than it did the two Sri Lankan Presidents who attempted it. One has only to consider the LTTE's responses to these overtures. They assassinated Premadasa (in 1993) after working with him for two years or more, and failed in their attempt to assassinate Kumaratunga in 1994.

Surprisingly, the stunning defeat inflicted on Prabhakaran and the LTTE as well as the former's hasty departure to Tamil Nadu in 1986—he escaped in a smuggler's boat—does not figure at all in the works of M.R. Narayan Swamy, an Indian journalist who established himself as an authority on the LTTE and on Prabhakaran.[2] The full effect of Ranatunga's victory over the LTTE was lost because the Vadamarachchi campaign was closely followed by the controversial Indian intervention in Sri Lanka from around July 1987.[3] The arrival of the even more controversial Indian Peace Keeping Force (IPKF) in the north and the east of Sri Lanka drew far more attention and more widespread criticism. Amidst this clamour, what happened with regard to stopping the second phase of the Vadamarachchi campaign was thus virtually ignored. This vociferous criticism of the Indian intervention and, in particular, the arrival of the IPKF became part of a more widespread opposition to the Jayewardene government on these policies and its association with India. Moreover, one of the most controversial conditions imposed on Sri Lanka as part of the Indo-Sri Lanka 'agreement' of 1987 was the dispatch of the Sri Lankan forces—in particular the Sri Lankan army—to its barracks, something which the officer corps of the army deeply resented.

Chandrika Kumaratunga's enthusiasm for working with the LTTE did not last very long after its botched assassination attempt on her. Premadasa's enthusiasm for the LTTE lasted for a few years after its initiation. The most surprising part of this was his successful initiative in ordering or persuading the Sri Lankan police forces in the eastern province to surrender[4] to the LTTE, thereby facilitating the latter's gaining complete control of the eastern province. The 600 policemen who surrendered to the LTTE—a consequence of his quixotic move—were butchered in cold blood by the eastern cadres of the LTTE. The blame for this does not rest with Prabhakaran but with the LTTE's eastern province cadres and their leaders who broke away from the LTTE. These leaders eventually moved on to an association with the Rajapaksa government. Some even went on to hold high office in the Rajapaksa government—positions they continue to hold to the present day.

Then the Indian government, with the help of President Jayewardene, successfully applied pressure on General Ranatunga to abandon his plans to move into Jaffna town, or anywhere in its vicinity, in order to destroy the administrative structure of the LTTE. Following this, the General eventually retired from the army. After taking on a number of civilian positions including that of secretary of defence, he retired to his farm at Mawanella close to Kandy.

The appearance of Ranatunga's memoirs in 2000[5] and the wide publicity they received, particularly in the officer corps of the Sri Lankan army and among retired officers, brought the Vadamarachchi campaign into sharp focus among critics of LTTE.[6] Apart from anything else, it helped to shatter the myth—propagated by the LTTE and its sympathizers and, more to the point, accepted by defeatist individuals in the Sri Lankan forces, politicians, journalists and academics—of the group's invincibility. One needs to remember too that General Sarath Fonseka who planned and executed the defeat of the LTTE in 2009 had been a Lt. Col. in Ranatunga's forces in the Vadamarachchi campaign, as was President Rajapaksa's younger brother, G. Rajapaksa, who became secretary of defence in 2005 and later secretary of defence and urban development. He too had been a Lt. Col. in General Ranatunga's army at the time of the successful Vadamarachchi campaign.

With General Ranatunga in 1986, the army expanded from a force of merely 15,000 men to one of just over 30,000. At the time of Prabhakaran's decisive defeat and death in 2009 the army had over 2,00,000 men. These numbers increased to over 3,00,000 even after the defection of the eastern province cadres of the LTTE.

Once the eastern cadres of the LTTE moved away from the main force, the LTTE was severely weakened, not merely by the loss of numbers but due to the growing disharmony amongst the cadres—the eastern cadres argued they had no option but to move out of the LTTE because the group's Jaffna-based leaders believed that the Jaffna Tamils were superior to the Batticoloa Tamils. Thus the LTTE, a force which claimed to be the genuine voice of the Sri Lankan Tamils as a whole, could not treat its Batticoloa forces—which, in effect, were the principal fighting force within the LTTE—as equals.

The leadership of the Sri Lankan army understood the significance of the split in the LTTE—and the virtual revolt of its Batticoloa cadres—before most other sections of opinion in the country. As discussed earlier in this book, the leadership of the army redoubled their campaign against the LTTE after the eastern cadres in the LTTE split with the main force under Prabhakaran. But it took longer for the Sri Lankan press to grasp the importance of the split in the LTTE and the virtual revolt of its Batticoloa cadres. The press preferred to be discreet on this development, unlike the army leadership which grasped very early that the LTTE forces were now more vulnerable to a determined attack than they had been since their defeat at the Vadamarachchi campaign of 1986. The more optimistic leaders of the army, including General Sarath Fonseka, calculated that the LTTE could be routed in the years after 2006 as they had been in 1986. Even the more cautious elements in the army and in the other services went along with General Sarath Fonseka and backed him in his campaign strategy and tactics. As for the academic world and the political commentators, we have Professor Gerald Peiris publishing a monograph titled *The Twilight of the Tigers*.[7] Written around 2006, the monograph was published only in 2009, by which time the twilight had turned to night. The monograph appeared for sale in Sri Lanka just when the LTTE had been virtually destroyed as a military and terrorist force.

Moderates and Extremists

Having examined, from the data available, the LTTE's emergence and rise to a position of dominance among the Tamil separatist forces in Sri Lanka, it would be seen that there was no real difference between the so-called moderates among Tamil political groups such as the Tamil United Liberation Front (TULF)—the principal political force among the Tamils of Sri Lanka since the mid 1950s—and the LTTE.[8] Large numbers of the cadres of the LTTE had originally served as foot soldiers in the political campaigns and agitation of the TULF. Gaining experience and respectability in the process, they moved on to overtake the TULF and other moderate forces and to establish an early dominance over them, a position established in the late 1970s and well before the traumatic anti-Tamil riots of 1983—generally regarded as the point at which the LTTE's separatist and terrorist campaign emerged as the principal and virtually unchallenged force among the Tamil political organizations.

From the early and mid 1980s to around 2006, the LTTE was very much the sole spokespeople of the Tamils of Sri

Lanka. They adopted this position and refused to countenance the claims of rival Tamil groups to any prominent position in the Tamils' struggles in Sri Lanka. The LTTE—sometimes operating as a group but mostly on an individual basis—killed the leadership of the TULF from 1990 to 1999, just as they had earlier eliminated the leadership and even the members of other Tamil separatist groups smaller than the TULF. However, the LTTE's political objectives and claims were kept simple and, principally, could be located in those of the TULF. These include the issues of Tamil separatism and the creation of a Tamil state in Sri Lanka. Neither the Federal Party (FP), the TULF nor the LTTE published a comprehensive position paper on the implications of federalism for Sri Lanka.[9] At no stage since the FP's rise to prominence in the early 1950s, or the LTTE's in the 1970s, has there been a study on the implications of establishing a separate state in Sri Lanka. There was no monograph either by persons in these groups or by independent scholars. The TULF spoke eloquently about what it called the 'Traditional Homeland' or '"Homelands" of the Tamils in Sri Lanka'.[10] The LTTE took over this political concept and enthusiastically advocated it. The TULF's advocacy of the amalgamation of the northern and the eastern provinces was eventually adopted in Sri Lanka in 1988 under great pressure from India. The LTTE also campaigned for this amalgamation often with even greater fervour than the TULF.

In the time of its control and administration of some of these areas in the north and the east of Sri Lanka, the LTTE did not make any contribution by way of new institutions and administrative structures. They simply continued the Sri Lankan system that existed. As discussed earlier in this book, they did not provide much by way of funds—or any funds at all—for the administration of the areas under their control. The finances required came mainly from the Sri Lankan government. In the areas they controlled, their administrative personnel—few in number—held more or less the same titles as those in the Sri Lankan state.[11] Even at the height of their control over these territories, the town of Kilinochchi, their administrative capital, was a pale imitation of a small Sri Lankan town under the control of the government. In the wider area of LTTE administration one sees the whole of it simply as an imitation of the Sri Lankan system or systems.

The one major contribution they made was the successful conversion of a powerful terrorist organization to a virtual quasi-state, one with external dimensions which included a 'navy' of about twenty commercial vessels (used for a number of purposes including the collection and distribution of narcotics) and which sent its personnel on a worldwide quest for arms, in support of its aim of establishing a separate state. (The principal LTTE official in the search for arms was captured after the defeat of the LTTE.[12]) At their best, these LTTE 'officials', including those who gathered arms, operated with a zest and with an efficiency that a small sovereign state would have relished.

Another area of LTTE expertise that needs examination is the search and collection of money in many parts of the world, in particular western Europe and North America. Some or much of this money was used for arms purchases. Some of the money still remains in the hands of LTTE sympathizers, especially in western Europe, and some of these financial resources were invested either on behalf of the LTTE or for LTTE sympathizers. Clearly some of these resources are available to sections of the Tamil diaspora for their present and future activities.

A review of the LTTE's activities is a case study in the transformation of a group which specialized in terrorist activities into something like a conventional military force. They were more effective as a terrorist force than as a conventional army. Not every terrorist force could claim to have assassinated the former—and potentially the future—prime minister of a regional power,[13] the executive President of the state against which the LTTE was in conflict,[14] as well as several important politicians of that state.[15] This is apart from several prominent Tamil politicians in Sri Lanka, including the leadership of the TULF.

In 1986 General Ranatunga took up the LTTE's challenge. He fought them as he would a conventional military force. He believed that the LTTE's feared terrorist activity would wither once it was defeated as a conventional military force. He succeeded in this in 1986 and although he was prevented from completing the job of destroying the LTTE's 'administrative' base or bases, he had inflicted a comprehensive defeat on them in his Vadamarachchi campaign. Twenty years later we see General Sarath Fonseka adopting the same line of strategy and tactics against the LTTE.

1620 and 2009: Years of Destruction

With the destruction of the LTTE, the issue of reconciliation between the majority Sinhalese section of the Sri Lankan population and the Tamil minority has come up for discussion and implementation. Historically, this is not the first time the Tamil minority had suffered as severe a setback as it suffered in 2006–09. It had suffered a more severe setback in 1620 when the Portuguese destroyed the Tamil kingdom of Jaffna which had existed from the thirteenth century onwards till 1620, and which had controlled the Jaffna peninsula and strips of territory in the present northern and eastern provinces. In 1620 the Portuguese destroyed the Jaffna kingdom. Its monarchy, institutions, and administrative units and cadres were totally eliminated. The Jaffna kingdom never reappeared in any form. In the wake of Jaffna's destruction in 1620, the principal issue for the Tamil people was not reconciliation as it is today but simply one of recovery.

It took 200 years from 1620 before the Tamils were able to see any recovery. It came as the emergence of some sort of political status. The phrase 'some sort of political status' is deliberately chosen, after much reflection, to indicate the provision of a political identity within the new administrative structure which the British set up in the island and the incorporation of territories that formed part of the erstwhile kingdom of Jaffna within the British administrative structure. Thus the recovery of the Tamils as an ethnic group was part of the sociopolitical engineering which the British initiated in the 1820s in the process of consolidating their rule in the island, then known as Ceylon. The principal aim was to destroy all that was left of the Kandyan kingdom which had successfully resisted the Portuguese, the Dutch and in the early stages, the British themselves. The Colebrooke–Cameron reforms of 1832 which accomplished this are remembered primarily for their unification of Sri Lanka and in initiating the modernization of Sri Lanka. They should also be remembered for facilitating the re-emergence of Tamils as a Sri Lankan ethnic group.

One little-remembered part of this process of unification was that of bringing the Tamils into the political structure that Colebrooke and Cameron sought to establish. In the Legislative Council the British established in 1832, there was a Tamil non-official representative just as there was one Sinhalese representative, although the Sinhalese were about six times the Tamil population at the time. Significantly, there was no representative for the Muslims or for the Kandyan Sinhalese. A Muslim and Kandyan Sinhalese representative came into the Legislative Council in the 1880s. The point is that the Tamils were among the principal beneficiaries of the British social engineering in the 1830s.

There were other features of this social engineering we need to mention. There were the schools that came up in Jaffna and the north of the island under British rule. These included the schools of the American mission instituted after the mission, with its headquarters in Boston, came to Sri Lanka. The American mission was issued strict limits by the British. They were limited to the Jaffna peninsula and some other parts of the northern province. Schools and hospitals of the American mission were not permitted in other parts of the island. As a result of these schools, the Tamils of Jaffna had a head start in modern education in Sri Lanka, much to their advantage in the nineteenth and twentieth centuries. Then, again, there was another piece of social engineering. When the British in Malaya (now Malaysia) were short of the support staff for their emerging administrative infrastructure in the 1860s, the British encouraged the movement of Tamils from Jaffna to Malaya for this purpose. Whether the British extended a similar invitation to others from Sri Lanka is not known. But it would be historically accurate to say that the principal—if not the sole—beneficiaries were the Tamils of Jaffna.

The recovery of the Tamils from the destruction of the Jaffna kingdom was not simply a matter of an up–down movement beginning with the social engineering of the British. The Tamils made better use of the opportunities they were provided by way of education than most others in Sri Lanka, including the Sinhalese and certainly the Muslims. Similarly, they made effective use of their presence in the Legislative Council to fashion a leadership role in public life and the emerging political life of the country. This Tamil dominance in public life and in political life continued well into the early part of the twentieth century. [16]

For our purposes in bringing the present book to a conclusion, the Portuguese destruction of the Jaffna kingdom serves several useful purposes. First, and most surprisingly, this episode in the history of the Tamils of Sri Lanka gets little attention in the debates on the future of the Sri Lankan Tamils—particularly the debate on reconciliation. This is especially significant in the context of the defeat—indeed, the destruction—of the LTTE who dominated the public life of the Tamils, if not of Sri Lanka itself, for the last twenty years. On other issues such as the rise and defeat of the LTTE, the focus remains on the events of early to mid 1986, the Vadamarachchi campaign and the LTTE's defeat at the hands of General Ranatunga's army, while the debate fails to examine the effect of the Portuguese campaign of 1620s. Just as the Portuguese elimination of the Jaffna kingdom was seldom or never mentioned and therefore hardly ever considered in all their propaganda about the 'Traditional Homelands of the Tamils of Sri Lanka', neither the LTTE nor the Tamil political class that has grown up in the shadow of the LTTE speak of the destruction of the Jaffna kingdom by the Portuguese. Not even the Tamil scholars who write on the history of the Tamils in Sri Lanka speak in detail of that event. This event has contemporary relevance in the light of the discussions of the consequence of the defeat suffered by the LTTE. For those who speak about the need for a policy or policies of reconciliation after the defeat of the LTTE, the destruction of the Tamil kingdom by the Portuguese ought to be used in reflections on the issue of reconciliation today. If the history of the Portuguese destruction of the Jaffna kingdom provides any lessons for the present day, it is that reconciliation is a long-term process in which the Tamil people will play as important a role—rather a more important role—than the Tamil political elite. The internal and external pressures to initiate policies of reconciliation today are ill-defined. We need to remember that, in the wake of Jaffna's destruction in 1620, it took the better part of 200 years to even begin fashioning such a process of recovery. In this context the reconciliation planned today will take much longer than the politicians imagine.

Secondly, just as the British government's social engineering in the 1820s had a role in stimulating the Tamil recovery, so too will the current Sri Lankan government's policies and efforts in stimulating economic growth in the north and the east of the country serve a very useful role in the process of reconciliation. But more important than the efforts of the political elite in the north of the island and the political class as a whole are the people's efforts at reconciliation. For one thing, the Sri Lankan government of Mahinda Rajapaksa does not have the time the British had in initiating a recovery from the 1820s. Again the Rajapaksa regime will be under continuing pressure from external forces to expedite reconciliation even when it is obvious that reconciliation is a slow process in which people's attitudes and aspirations are more important than the government's policies, whether initiated on its own or under pressure from external sources. These external forces have no understanding of the contradictory forces at work in fashioning the processes of reconciliation. Reconciliation is not a one-way process. The initiatives being taken by the government is one part of the process, however enthusiastic it may be in talking of reconciliation. One could argue that the Tamils themselves need to have a clear notion of what they can contribute to the reconciliation process. Moreover, such notions will keep evolving and changing as responses to emerging issues. These are matters best developed as responses to people's demands. For instance, the Tamils in the north and the east of Sri Lanka would have different conceptions of reconciliation than the Muslims and of course the Sinhalese.

Policies of reconciliation need to include the 80,000 or so Muslims brutally expelled from the Tamil areas of the north under pressure from the LTTE.[17] They have lived in conditions of extreme poverty among the Muslims of the north-western province and among the Sinhalese in other parts of the country. With the defeat of the LTTE, some of these Muslims are gradually making their way back to their former homes. Some of the difficulties and complexities of reconciliation were demonstrated in the attitude of the Indian government which is building 50,000 houses for the people of the northern and the eastern provinces. So far, they have not allocated any significant section of these houses to the Muslims, and the latter are protesting against this failure on the part of the Indian government.[18] Thus, reconciliation is not a matter solely of reconciliation between the government and the Tamils or the Sinhalese majority and the Tamils. It needs to include reconciliation between the Tamils and the Muslims, as recompense to the Muslims for the only act of ethnic cleansing during the long struggle between the LTTE and the Sri Lankan state. By concentrating all their attention on the Tamils of the north and the east, the Indian government is making a grievous mistake. In regard to Sri Lanka's ethnic conflict, the Indian government is still concentrating, as in the recent past, on the Tamils alone.

How a War Ends

In addition to everything else, I intend this monograph to provide a useful, if not rare, study of how a long separatist war ends. It supplies valuable data on the various phases of bringing such a long war to an end. Earlier chapters would show how the war was brought to an end in mid 1986 with the successful conduct of the Vadamarachchi campaign. The Indian intervention in its first form—which entailed pressure on the Sri Lankan government to get General Ranatunga to stop the second stage of the Vadamarachchi campaign to move to break up the LTTE's administrative/military structures in the town of Jaffna and its surrounding towns—is hardly spoken of today. Had this initial phase of the process of Indian intervention not occurred, the campaign against the LTTE would probably have resulted in another round of diplomatic negotiations. Such negotiations could well have gone on for a year of two or even more. The prospects are that the LTTE would have been persuaded by the combined pressures of military defeat and Indian diplomacy to accept a political settlement. One consequence of such a diplomatic settlement could well have been a longer lifespan for the LTTE leadership and its LTTE leader. These are the might-have-beens of history.

As it happened, the second and more prolonged phase of Indian intervention gave the LTTE a new lease of life, and one in which they hardly ever reflected on the defeat they had suffered in the Vadamarachchi campaign. The studies published so far of the Indian intervention in Sri Lanka in 1987–90 and the introduction of the IPKF to the north and the east of Sri Lanka fail to reflect on the defeat suffered by the LTTE at the hands of General Ranatunga in the Vadamarachchi campaign. Having survived the battles they had with the IPKF, the LTTE believed they were more than a match for the Sri Lankan army. This explains their overconfidence, if not arrogance, during their negotiations with representatives of the Sri Lankan government in the 1980s and 1990s. It accounts in part for their arrogance in planning and executing the assassination of Rajiv Gandhi in India itself. It was that arrogance in attempting to gather a photographic record of the assassination that led Indian investigators of the Rajiv Gandhi assassination to successfully focus on the LTTE's responsibility for this, and to locate almost all the persons involved in the Rajiv Gandhi assassination within India. Only Prabhakaran and the other principal planner-conspirator remained beyond the reach of the Indian government and in Sri Lanka. Eventually they were both killed in Sri Lanka in their struggle with the Sri Lankan army.

After the departure of the IPKF from Sri Lanka in 1999–2000, the LTTE reasserted itself and, for a period of six or seven years, inflicted several defeats on units of the Sri Lankan army. This included successful raids on some of the army's units in the north of the island. They had some significant successes and, in the early part of 2000, the LTTE seemed poised for a campaign to take control of Jaffna town and to expel the Sri Lankan army from Jaffna. The Sri Lankan army successfully resisted the LTTE. From 2000 onwards, the new leadership of the army not only kept the LTTE at bay but readied themselves to defeat the LTTE in a military campaign.

The army's final push against the LTTE began with the successful Maavil-Aru campaign in 2006, following which the army, under General Sarath Fonseka, set about the business of destroying the LTTE forces. I have already discussed how he succeeded in defeating the LTTE, inflicting on the latter a defeat on the scale of the victory General Ranatunga achieved in 1986. Considering the scale of the defeat inflicted on the LTTE, including the death of its leader Prabhakaran and the rest of the LTTE high command in 2009, it went beyond anything achieved in 1986, and was somewhat comparable in impact to that inflicted by the Portuguese in 1620.

In the campaign against the LTTE from 2001 to 2009 neither the Rajapaksa government nor the army under General Fonseka were responsive to LTTE proposals for a ceasefire and a fresh set of negotiations. The emphasis was on a comprehensive defeat of the LTTE, and not a negotiated settlement. Thus the war would end with the total defeat of the LTTE. While this total defeat of the LTTE led to charges of human rights violations during the final stages of the war against the LTTE, there is very little evidence from credible sources to support these charges. Most, if not all, of these charges are derived from the charges made by sections of the Tamil diaspora, which are not backed by any substantial evidence from unimpeachable sources. But these charges will persist because of the receptivity of some western governments to these. In fact, one of the principal factors in operation is the pull of support at electoral levels in some of these countries.

Notes

Introduction

1. Several interviews and discussions with President J.R. Jayewardene in 1987 and 1988. At that time, I was gathering material for a political biography of President J.R. Jayewardene.
2. Ibid.
3. He was for a while secretary of defence.
4. The publication of G.H. Peiris's *Twilight of the Tigers: Peace Efforts and Power Struggles in Sri Lanka*, Oxford University Press (OUP), New Delhi, 2009, alerted us to the impending collapse of the LTTE.
5. See particularly S. Tammita-Delgoda, 'Sri Lanka—The Last Phase in the Eelam War VI', Manekshaw Paper, no. 13, New Delhi, 2009.

Chapter 1

1. Walter Laquer, *A History of Terrorism*, Traction Books, Rutgers—The State University of New Jersey, Piscataway, NJ, and Covent Garden, London, 2001; and *The New Terrorism: Fanaticism and the Arms of Mass Destruction*, OUP, 1999, and Phoenix Press, 2001.
2. See the discussion in Austin T. Turk, 'Social Dynamics of

Terrorism'; and Philip E. Devine and Robert J. Rafalko, 'On Terrorism' in *The Annals of the American Academy of Political and Social Science*, special issue on International Terrorism, vol. 463, September 1982, pp. 119–129, and pp. 39–53 respectively. See also G. Wardlaw, *Political Terrorism*, Cambridge, 1982, and P. Wilkinson, *Terrorism and the Liberal State*, London, 1979.

3.   Laquer, *The New Terrorism*, pp. 5–6.

4.   Devine and Rafalko, 'On Terrorism', p. 44.

5.   Fred Halliday, 'Terrorism' in J. Kreiger (ed.), *Oxford Companion to the Politics of the World*, Oxford, 1993, pp. 403–04.

6.   Ibid.

7.   There is an easily accessible account of these assassinations in Shashi Tharoor, *India from Midnight to the Millennium*, Penguin Books India (PBI), New Delhi, pp. 16-49.

8.   Jyoti Sen Gupta, *Bangladesh: Blood and Tears*, Naya Prakash, Calcutta, 1981; Lawrence Lifschultz, *Bangladesh: The Unfinished Revolution*, Hodder and Stoughton, London, 1986; Anthony Mascarenhas, *Bangladesh: A Legacy of Blood*, London, 1986.

9.   Maurice Collis, *Last and First in Burma, 1941–1948*, London, Faber and Faber Frederick A. Prasger 1956; Frank N. Trager, *Burma: from Kingdom to Republic*, New York, 1966. For a very recent assessment of the implications of this incident, see Amitav Ghosh, *Dancing in Cambodia: At Large in Burma*, Ravi Dayal, Delhi, 1998, pp. 71–73. See also Kin Oung, *Who Killed Aung San?* 2nd expanded edition, White Lotus, Bangkok, 1996.

10.   In the adoption of Mrs Sirimavo Bandaranaike as leader of the Sri Lanka Freedom Party for the parliamentary election of July 1960, an election which her party won with ease.

11.   As the daughter of S.W.R.D. Bandaranaike, and the widow of Vijaya Kumaratunga; assassinated in 1959 and 1988 respectively.

12.   Sisir Gupta, *Kashmir: A Study in India–Pakistan Relations*, Asian Publishing House, Bombay, 1967; Prem Shankar Jha, *Kashmir 1947: Rival Versions of History*, OUP, New Delhi, 1996; Alastair Lamb, *Kashmir: A Disputed Legacy, 1846–1990*, Roxford Books,

Hertfordshire, 1991; and *Birth of a Tragedy*, Roxford Books, Hertfordshire,1994; Victoria Schofield, *Kashmir in the Crossfire*, I.B. Tauris, London,1996; Navnita Chadha Behera, *State, Identity and Violence: Jammu, Kashmir and Ladakh*, Manohar, New Delhi, 2000. See also R.G.C. Thomas (ed.), *Perspectives on Kashmir*, Westview, Boulder, Colorado, 1992, and Sumit Ganguly, *The Crisis in Kashmir: Portents of War, Hopes of Peace*, Woodrow Wilson Center and Cambridge University Press. Among the early accounts of the Kashmir dispute is Joseph Korbel, *Danger in Kashmir*, Princeton University Press, Princeton, NJ, 1966.

13. Richard Sisson and Leo E. Rose, *Pakistan, India and the Creation of Bangladesh*, University of California Press, Berkeley, California, 1990.

14. Tahir Amin, *Mass Resistance in Kashmir: Origins, Evolution, and Options*, Islamabad, Institute of Policy Studies, 1995; and Sumantra Bose, *The Challenge in Kashmir: Democracy, Self-Determination and a Just Peace*, Sage Publications, New Delhi, 1997.

15. The Hizbul Mujahideen (HUM) is often described as the largest Kashmiri militant group. For a convenient list of such groups, see Zaffar Abbas, 'A Who's Who of Kashmir Militancy', *The Herald*, August 2000, pp. 29–31.

16. George Fernandes, 'India's Policies on Kashmir: An Assessment and Discourse' in Raju Thomas (ed.), *Perspectives on Kashmir*, p. 286.

17. Fernandes, 'The Global Fight against Terrorism: Where to Begin and Where to End', in K.P.S. Gill and Ajay Sahni, *The Global Threat of Terror*, Bulwark Books, New Delhi, 2002, pp. 7–14.

18. R.G. Wirsing, 'The Siachen Glacier Dispute: Can Diplomacy Untangle it?' *The Indian Defence Review*, New Delhi, July 1991, pp. 95–107.

19. K.M. de Silva, *Reaping the Whirlwind*. PBI, New Delhi 1998.

20. 'Profile of a Tiger', *India Today*, 30 June 1986. Durayappah was unarmed at the time of being killed—he was returning from a *kovil* (a Hindu temple). He was unsuspecting as well.

21. On the LTTE, see M.R. Narayan Swamy, *Tigers of Lanka: From Boys to Guerrillas*. See also, G.H. Peiris, 'Secessionist War and Terrorism in Sri Lanka: Transnational Impulses', in K.P.S. Gill and Ajay Sahni, *The Global Threat of Terror*, op. cit., pp. 85–126; Rohan Gunaratna, 'Asia Pacific: Organised Crime and International Terrorist Network', in K.P.S. Gill and Ajay Sahni, *The Global Threat of Terror*, op. cit., pp. 241–68. Pages 257–62 deal with the LTTE; K.M. de Silva, 'Separatism and Political Violence in Sri Lanka', in K.M. de Silva (ed.), *Conflict and Violence in South Asia: Bangladesh, India, Pakistan and Sri Lanka*, Kandy, ICES, Sri Lanka, 2000, pp. 379–430.

22. K.M. de Silva, *Managing Ethnic Tensions in Multi-Ethnic Societies: 1880–1985*, University Press of America, Lanham, Maryland, 1986, pp. 313–14, 325, 347.

23. Dayan Jayatilleka, 'The LTTE and Tamil Separatism in Sri Lanka', and G.H. Peiris, 'Prospects for a Negotiated Settlement of Sri Lanka's Ethnic Conflict' in K.M. de Silva and G.H. Peiris (eds), *Pursuit of Peace in Sri Lanka: Past Failures and Future Prospects*, Kandy, ICES, in association with the United States Institute of Peace, 1999, pp. 231–62 and 263–88 respectively.

24. Helena Cobban, *The Making of Modern Lebanon*, Hutchinson, London, 1985, pp. 202–03.

25. Swamy, *Tigers of Lanka*, pp. 241–42.

26. K.M. de Silva, *Reaping the Whirlwind*, p. 268.

27. Ibid., p. 269. See also H.S. Hasbullah, 'Ethnic Conflict and Prospects for Rehabilitation and Reconstruction: The Eastern Province' in K.M. de Silva and G.H. Peiris (eds), *Pursuit of Peace in Sri Lanka*, op. cit., pp. 337–39.

28. Swamy, *Tigers of Lanka*, pp. 147–48.

29. Ibid., p. 329, fn. 10 for a reference to the RAW instigation behind the attack.

30. John F. Burns, 'A Sri Lankan Evoked Pol Pot: Asia's Latest Master of Terror'. *The New York Times*, 28 May 1995. On the LTTE as a terrorist organization. See also W. Laquer, *The New Terrorism*, OUP, New York, 1999, pp. 191–96.

31. A.G. Noorani, 'LTTE Menace—An Impossible Negotiator' in an op-ed piece in *The Statesman*, 5 June 2000.

32. Swamy, *Tigers of Lanka*, pp. 331–32.

Chapter 2

1. Swamy, *Tigers of Lanka*.

2. K.M. de Silva, *A History of Sri Lanka*, London (revised edition), Penguin Books India, Delhi, 2005.

3. Jane Russell, *Communal Politics under the Donoughmore Constitution 1931–1947*, Tisara Printers, Dehiwala, 1983.

4. K.M. de Silva, *Sri Lanka: Problems of Governance*, ICES, Kandy, 1993, pp. 24–32.

5. K.M. de Silva, *Separatist Ideology in Sri Lanka: A Historical Appraisal of the Claim for the 'Traditional Homelands' of the Tamils of Sri Lanka*, International Centre for Ethnic Studies, Kandy, 1987, revised 2nd edition, 1994.

6. For a short but rather uncritical biography of Chelvanayakam, see A.J. Wilson, *SJV Chelvanayakam and the Crisis of Sri Lankan Tamil Nationalism, 1947–77: A Political Biography*, C. Hurst, London, 1994. Wilson who died in 2000 was Chelvanayakam's son-in-law. This extract is from p. 21 of the book, citing a report from *The Times of Ceylon*, 16 January 1956.

7. K.M. de Silva, *Traditional Homelands*, for a comprehensive study of this problem, and for the background to the Cleghorn Minute.

8. Ibid., pp. 30–31.

9. *The Journal of the Royal Asiatic Society, (Ceylon Branch),* hereafter *JRAS (CB)*, n.s., vol. 3, 1954, p. 131.

10. C. Manogaran and B. Pfaffenberger (eds), *The Sri Lankan Tamils: Ethnicity and Identity*, Westview, Boulder, Colorado, 1994, p. 92; M. Gunasingam, *Sri Lankan Tamil Nationalism: A Study of Its Origins*, MV Publications, Sydney, 1999, p. 54; A.R. Arudpragasam, *The Traditional Homeland of the Tamils: The Missing Pages of Sri Lankan History I*, Kanal Publications, Kotte, 1996, merely assumes the existence of a Tamil homeland as defined by the TULF and

other Tamil political groups, and makes no attempt to respond to scholarly criticisms of the evidence advanced in support of the concept of traditional homelands.

11. K.M. de Silva, *The Traditional Homelands of the Tamils,* op. cit., pp. 9–10.

12. G.H. Peiris, 'Prospects for Negotiated Settlement of Sri Lanka's Ethnic Conflict', K.M. de Silva and G.H. Peiris (eds), *Pursuit of Peace in Sri Lanka: Past Failures and Future Prospects*, ICES, Kandy, 1991.

13. K.M. de Silva, 'Coming Full Circle: The Politics of Language in Sri Lanka, 1943–1996', *Ethnic Studies Report*, (hereafter *ESR)*, XIV (1), 1996, pp. 11–48.

14. These issues are reviewed in Partha S. Ghosh, 'Language Policy and National Integration: The Indian Experience', and Tariq Rahman, 'Language Policy in Pakistan' in *ESR* XIV(I), 1996, pp. 49–72 and 73–98 respectively.

15. These issues are discussed in K.M. de Silva, *Managing Ethnic Tensions in Multi-Ethnic Societies: Sri Lanka, 1880–1985,* University Press of America, Lanham, Maryland, 1986; W. Howard Wriggins, *Ceylon: Dilemmas of a New Nation*, Princeton University Press, Princeton, NJ, 1960.

16. On the politics of Tamil Nadu during this period, see Lloyd Rudolph, 'Urban Life and Populist Radicalism: The Dravidian Movement in Madras', *The Journal of Asian Studies*, XX, 1961, pp. 283–97; and Robert L. Hardgrave Jr., 'The DMK and the Politics of Tamil Nationalism', *Pacific Affairs*, XXXVII, 1965, pp. 396–411 and 'Riots in Tamilnadu: Problems and Prospects of India's Language Crisis', *Asian Survey*, V, 1965, pp. 399–407.

17. C.R. de Silva, 'The Politics of University Admissions: A Review of Some Aspects of the Admissions Policy in Sri Lanka, 1971–78', *Sri Lanka Journal of Social Sciences* 1(2), pp. 85–132; 'Weightage in University Admissions. Standardisation and District Quotas in Sri Lanka', *Modern Ceylon Studies*, V (2), pp. 152–78.

18. K. Loganathan, *Sri Lanka: Lost Opportunities*, CEPRA, University of Colombo, 1996.

19. K.M. de Silva, *Managing Ethnic Tensions in Multi-Ethnic Societies*, 1986, pp. 181–90.
20. K.M. de Silva and Howard Wriggins, *J.R. Jayewardene of Sri Lanka: A Political Biography*, vol. II, The University of Hawaii Press, Honolulu and Leo Cooper Publishers, London, 1994, pp. 143–49, 178–80.
21. On this see Sessional Paper V of 1980, Report of the Presidential Commission on Development Councils; see also K.M. de Silva, *Managing Ethnic Tensions in Multi-Ethnic Societies*, pp. 313–18.

Chapter 3

1. K.M. de Silva, *Managing Ethnic Tensions in Multi-Ethnic Societies*, pp. 256–341; A.J. Wilson, *The Break-up of Sri Lanka: The Sinhalese–Tamil Conflict*, C. Hurst, London, 1988.
2. Swamy, *Tigers of Lanka*, and K.M. de Silva, *Regional Powers and Small State Security: India and Sri Lanka*, Woodrow Wilson Center Press, Washington DC, 1995, pp. 283–337.
3. K.M. de Silva, *Regional Powers and Small State Security*.
4. Ibid.
5. Ibid. S.D. Muni, *Pangs of Proximity: India and Sri Lanka's Ethnic Crisis*, Sage Publications, New Delhi, 1993.
6. C.A. Chandraprema, *Sri Lanka: The Years of Terror, The JVP Insurrection 1987–1989*, Lake House, Colombo, 1991.
7. Richard Sisson and Leo E. Rose, *War and Secession: Pakistan, India and the Creation of Bangladesh*, University of California Press, Berkeley, California, 1990.
8. K.M. de Silva, *Regional Powers and Small State Security*.
9. A. Balasingham, *The Politics of Duplicity: Re-visiting the Jaffna Talks*, Fairmax Publishing Ltd, Mitcham, Surrey, 2000.
10. Laurent Crellsamer, 'Tamil Emigrants Could Be Europe's Major Source of Heroin', *The Guardian Weekly*, London, 11 August 1985. See also 'Drugs, Guns and Tamil Terrorism', *The Asian Wall Street Journal*, 9 September 1985.

11. I owe this point to the researches of my former colleague Professor G.H. Peiris into the sources of LTTE funding. See his chapter 'Prospects for a Negotiated Settlement', K.M. de Silva and G. H. Peiris (eds), *Pursuit of Peace in Sri Lanka: Past Failures and Future Prospects*, ICES, Kandy, in association with the United States Institute of Peace, 1991, pp. 274–78. For a more extensive study by him on the LTTE's sources of funding, see 'Secessionist War and Terrorism in Sri Lanka: Transnational Impulses', in K.P.S. Gill and Ajai Sahni (eds), *The Global Threat of Terror*, Bulwark Books, New Delhi, 2002.

12. Christopher McDowell, *A Tamil Asylum Diaspora: Sri Lanka Migration, Settlement and Politics in Switzerland*, Berghahn Books, Providence, 1996; Olivind Fuglerud, *Life on the Outside: The Tamil Diaspora and Long-Distance Nationalism*, Pluto Press, London, 1999.

13. *Patterns of Global Terrorism*, The US Department of State, Washington DC, 1995, pp. 48–49.

14. Ibid., p. 48.

15. *Perspectives–International Terrorism: The Threat to Canada*, Ottawa, May 2000. A pointed reference is made in this document to the LTTE, and its fundraising activities in Canada.

16. In its issue of 15 June 2000, the Sri Lanka daily, *The Island*, published a letter by Martin Collacott to the *National Post* of Canada, in which he complained that he was appalled by the way in which Tamil Tigers and their supporters have abused and exploited Canadian hospitality.

17. Collacott was Canadian high commissioner (ambassador) in Colombo at the time of the riots of 1983, and was largely responsible for persuading the Canadian government to relax immigration regulations to permit unimpeded entry of Tamils from Sri Lanka.

18. A. Balasingham, *The Politics of Duplicity*.

Chapter 4

1. For an excellent study of the early years in the phases, and current position, with regard to social welfare in the country, see G.H. Peiris, *Development and Change in Sri Lanka: Geographical Perspectives*, Macmillan, New Delhi, 1996.

2. Lord Mountbatten was the commander-in-chief of Allied forces under the South East Asia Command. His stay in Kandy is reviewed in Philip Zieglar's biography, *Mountbatten*, Alfred Knopf, New York, 1985, pp. 278–80; and in Philip Zieglar (ed.), *The Personal Diary of Admiral Lord Louis Mountbatten, 1943–1946*, Collins, London, 1988, pp. 96–166.

3. Donald R. Horowitz, *Coup Theories and Officers' Motives: Sri Lanka in Comparative Perspective*, Princeton University Press, Princeton, New Jersey, 1980, Chapter 15.

4. Horowitz, *Coup Theories*, pp. 67–68.

5. K.M. de Silva, 'Politics and the Political System' in K.M. de Silva (ed.), *Sri Lanka: Problems of Governance*, Konark, New Delhi, 1993, pp. 11–24.

6. The first major work on the island's politics was published in 1960, against the background of the political changes of the mid 1950s and the first phase of the ethnic conflict in the island. This was W. Howard Wriggins's *Ceylon: The Dilemmas of a New Nation*. More recent works include: Stanley Tambiah, *Sri Lanka: Ethnic Fratricide and the Dismantling of Democracy* (2nd ed.), University of Chicago Press, Chicago, 1995; and K.M. de Silva, *Managing Ethnic Tensions in Multi-Ethnic Societies: Sri Lanka, 1880–1985*, University Press of America, Lanham, Maryland, 1986, and *Reaping the Whirlwind: Ethnic Politics, Ethnic Conflicts in Sri Lanka*, Penguin Books India, New Delhi, 1998.

7. James Manor, *The Expedient Utopian: Bandaranaike and Ceylon*, Cambridge University Press, Cambridge, 1989, p. 260.

8. Tarzie Vittachi, *Emergency '58: The Story of the Ceylon Race Riots*, Andre Deutsch, London, 1958. The Governor General was Sir Oliver Goonetilleka.

9.   Ibid.

10. Ibid., pp. 114–15.

11. K.M. de Silva, *Managing Ethnic Tensions*, pp. 268–71.

12. For a discussion of these attempted coups d'état see K.M. de Silva and Howard Wriggins, *J.R. Jayewardene of Sri Lanka: A Political Biography*, vol. 2, Leo Cooper, London, 1994, pp. 107–24, 154–59.

13. For a study of the abortive coup of 1962, see K.M. de Silva and Howard Wriggins, *J.R. Jayewardene of Sri Lanka*, pp. 107–20.

14. In his article 'Sri Lanka: The Challenge of Post-War Peace Building, State Building and Nation Building' in *National and Ethnic Politics*, 15, 2009 (p. 437), S.W.R. de A. Samarasinghe shows this situation continued even in 2009. There is no change even today.

15. A.C. Alles, *Insurgency 1971*, Colombo, 1976. For a comprehensive and insightful study of the JVP in later years, see C.A. Chandraprema, *Sri Lanka: The Years of Terror: The JVP Insurrection, 1987–1989*, Colombo, 1991.

16. Support for the beleaguered Sri Lankan government took the form of an international 'joint venture', with arms coming in from a remarkable number of countries: US, the Soviet Union, Yugoslavia, Pakistan and Egypt, among others.

Chapter 5

1.   Thomas Sowell, *Preferential Policies: An International Perspective*, Morrow, New York, 1990, p. 14.

2.   Robert Oberst, 'Policies of Ethnic Preference in Sri Lanka' in Neil Nevitte and Charles H. Kennedy (eds), *Ethnic Preference and Public Policy in Developing States*, Lynne Reinner, Boulder, Colorado, 1986, pp. 95–118.

3.   Oberst, 'Tigers and the Lion: The Evolution of Sri Lanka's Civil War', *Harvard International Review*, XVIII (3), Summer 1996, pp. 32–35, and p. 80. This essay was one of several ones on the special theme of 'The Politics of Identity in South Asia' in that issue of the journal.

4.   Ibid., p. 33.

5.   Esman, Milton J., *An Introduction to Ethnic Conflict*, Polity Press, Cambridge, UK, and Malden, MA, USA, 2004.

Chapter 6

1.   The 1987 report was published by the UGC. The 1993 report was handed over to the then minister, higher education, Anura Bandaranaike, but was never published because of the change of government that occurred in 1994.

2.   It is to the credit of the academic community at the then University of Ceylon, Peradeniya, that they criticized this change from the moment it was proposed. Its implications were reviewed in discussions organized by the Ceylon Studies Seminar, and in several well-researched articles on its basic unfairness, and its potential political dangers. See for example, C.R. de Silva, 'Weightages in University Admission: Standardisation and District Quotas in Sri Lanka, 1970–75', *Modern Ceylon Studies*, V (2), pp. 152–78.

3.   In a long obituary on the recently deceased Badi-ud-din Mahmud, an anonymous writer sought to assign the blame for the initiative in the unilateral change in university admissions policy on a Sinhalese activist group, the Sinhala Tharuna Sanvidhanaya. While this group did play a role in highlighting this issue, it could not have succeeded in securing this fateful change of policy without the active support of the minister of education, Badi-ud-din Mahmud. The obituary on Badi-ud-din Mahmud appeared in the *Sunday Leader*, 22 June 1997.

4.   C.R. de Silva, 'The Politics of University Admissions: A Review of Some Aspects of University Admissions Policy in Sri Lanka, 1971–1978', *Sri Lanka Journal of Social Sciences*, vol. I, no. 2, 1978, pp. 89–90.

5.   Ibid., p. 90.

6.   K.M. de Silva, 'University Admissions and Ethnic Tension in Sri Lanka, 1977–83' in R.B. Goldmann and in A.J. Wilson (eds),

From Independence to Statehood: Managing Ethnic Conflict in Five African and Asian States, London, 1984, pp. 97–110.

7.   C.R. de Silva, 'The Politics of University Admissions', op. cit., p. 99.

8.   Ibid., pp. 100–01.

9.   Report of the Committee to Review University Admissions Policy, University Grants Commission, Colombo, 1987, pp. 7–8.

10. Report from the Select Committee appointed to inquire into and Report on the Grave and Unsettled Conditions Prevailing in all the University Campuses in Sri Lanka and to make Recommendations with Regard to the further Functioning of the University Campuses. Parliamentary series, no. 107, 16 December 1987, published in mimeographed form. The proceedings of the committee and the minutes of evidence referred to on the cover were not published. Indeed, the report itself was not printed.

11. K.M. de Silva, 'The Sri Lankan Universities from 1977 to 1990: Recovery, Stability and the Descent to Crisis', *Minerva*, 1990, pp. 156–216, see particularly p. 202.

12. Ibid., p. 203.

13. Ibid.

Chapter 7

1.   G.P. Malalasekera's articles, Ceylon *Daily News*, 10–12 October 1955.

2.   Ibid.

3.   On opposition to assimilation, see G.G. Ponnambalam's speech in the state council, *Hansard* [state council], 1939, column 960. See also S. Nadesan, *Ceylon's Language Problems*, Colombo, 1955, passim.

4.   While students entered the universities on the basis of the language medium in which they sat for the qualifying examination in order to gain admission to the universities, they had a free choice with regard to the medium of instruction through which they preferred to read for the university examinations once they gained admission.

5. On the significance of this change, see the assessment by N. Satyendra, 'Language in the New Constitution', *Ceylon Daily News*, 4 October 1978. Nadesan's son Satyendra, like his father, is a lawyer.

6. Sessional Paper [SP] V of 1980, Report of the Presidential Commission on Development Councils, pp. 86–87, for a memorandum by two Muslim members of the commission pointing out the importance of changes made to the benefit of Tamil speakers in the island.

7. See for example, S. Nadesan, *Ceylon's Language Problems*, Colombo, 1955.

8. Carol L. Schmid, *Conflict and Consensus in Switzerland*, University of California Press, Berkeley and Los Angeles, 1982, p. 21.

9. Hughes, *Switzerland*, Ernest Benn, London, 1975, p. 59.

10. Cynthia H. Enloe, *Ethnic Conflict and Political Development*, Little Brown, Boston, 1973, p. 97.

11. Schmid, op. cit.

12. Hughes, op. cit.

13. Article 21(1) of the Constitution of 1978.

14. Schmid, op. cit., p. 20.

15. Ibid.

Chapter 8

1. Quoted in Mavis Puthucheary, 'Indians in the Public Sector in Malaysia' in K.S. Sandhu and A. Mani (eds), *Indian Communities in South East Asia*, Singapore, 1993, p. 337. The document cited Report on the General and Economic Conditions etc. of the Ceylonese in Malaya as prepared by V. Coomaraswamy for the then Ceylon government and was published in June 1946 as SP (Sessional Paper) IX of 1946.

2. Soulbury Report, 1945, p. 49.

3. Ibid., p 50.

4. Ibid.

5. S.W.R. de A. Samarasinghe, 'Ethnic Representation in Central Government Employment and Sinhala–Tamil Relations in Sri Lanka: 1948–1981' in Robert B. Goldmann and A.J. Wilson (eds), *From Independence to Statehood*, 1984, pp. 179–80.

6. In the twenty-year period 1973–92 there were over 40,000 immigrants to Canada from Sri Lanka, of whom the vast majority came in after 1984. The great bulk of them were Tamils from the Jaffna peninsula. See *Refuge*, XIII (3), June 1993, Special Issue on Sri Lanka, p. 36. *Refuge* is Canada's principal periodical on refugees, published by the Centre for Refugee Studies, York University, Ontario. The current estimate is that around 1,25,000 Tamils, almost all of them from Jaffna and the north of Sri Lanka, live in and around Toronto.

7. On the Tamil emigration to Switzerland, see Christopher McDowell, *A Tamil Asylum Diaspora: Sri Lankan Migration, Settlement and Politics in Switzerland*, Berghan Books, Oxford and Providence, Rhode Island, 1996.

Chapter 9

1. John Gooneratne, *Negotiating with the Tigers (LTTE), 2002–2005: A View from the Second Row*, Colombo, 2007.

2. On the CFA, see Austin Fernando, *My Belly is White*, Colombo, 2008. Fernando was defence secretary in Ranil Wickremasinghe's short-lived administration. G.H. Peiris takes a more critical view of the CFA in his *Twilight of the Tigers: Peace Efforts and Power Struggles in Sri Lanka*, Oxford University Press, New Delhi, 2009.

3. While the CFA is seen as a largely Norwegian initiative, there is substantial evidence that the Norwegians had the support of India in this, and that Indian support was a crucial, if hidden, factor.

4. It is argued that the acceptance of regional autonomy and regional government was an initiative of the LTTE's chief

negotiator, Anton Balasingham, and did not have the support of Prabhakaran. The LTTE very early repudiated this suggestion of regional autonomy. Prabhakaran adhered to his commitment to a separate state.

5.   Gooneratne, *Negotiating with the Tigers*.

6.   Ibid.

7.   Rajapaksa's emergence as prime minister was part of an effort to overcome President Kumaratunga's bid to retain her influence within the SLFP through a more acceptable—i.e., acceptable to her—successor.

8.   The Wickremasinghe administration adhered to an orthodox neo-liberal economic policy.

Chapter 10

1.   While the Rajapaksa government claimed to have taken a political decision on this occasion, to use force, the army under Lt. Gen. Fonseka was intent anyway on using force against the LTTE at Maavil-Aru.

2.   At this time, I and my co-author Howard Wriggins were writing our two-volume political biography of J.R. Jayewardene and were made aware by him about this Indian pressure. At the Colombo end, the Indian pressure was managed by the Indian high commissioner to Sri Lanka, J.N. Dixit.

3.   The north-eastern province was an amalgamation of the northern and the eastern provinces.

4.   It is important to remember that the eastern province had been part of the Kandyan Kingdom and that those villages were in existence from that time.

5.   This is not to exonerate the Rajapaksa government from its own role as manipulators of the electoral system.

6.   See particularly, Cyril Ranatunga, *Adventurous Story: From Peace to War, Insurgency to Terrorism*, Vijitha Yapa, Colombo, 2009. Hereafter C. Ranatunga, *Memoirs*.

Chapter 11

1. C. Ranatunga, *Memoirs*, pp. 125–43, 143–59.
2. Under President Chandrika Kumaratunga, the army had taken over Jaffna and parts of the northern province then under the control of the LTTE. Jaffna fell to the army without much of a fight. There were no civilian casualties. This is partly because the LTTE compelled en masse the people of those areas to move further south in a brutal campaign.
3. See particularly K.M. de Silva, *Regional Powers and Small State Security: India and Sri Lanka 1977–90*, The Woodrow Wilson Center Press, Washington DC, 1995.
4. For an excellent survey of these problems, see Nitin A. Gokhale, *Sri Lanka from War to Peace*, Har-Anand Publications, New Delhi, 2009.
5. This is reviewed by Dr Micheal Roberts in *Fire and Storm: Essays in Sri Lankan Politics*, vol. 1, Colombo, 2010, in which Chapter 25 carries the title 'Dilemmas at War's End: Thoughts on Hard Realities'.
6. Gokhale, op. cit. See also Sinharaja Tammita-Delgoda, 'Sri Lanka: The Last Phase in Eelam War IV, from Chaundikulam to Pudumattalan', Manekshaw Paper, New Delhi, no. 13, 2009.
7. Gokhale, op. cit. All LTTE soldiers, sailors and other supporters carried cyanide vials and were trained to use these and to commit suicide rather than surrender. Many of them actually did so. It is therefore surprising that Prabhakaran and the rest of the LTTE high command did not adhere to this policy. They made an attempt to break through the lines established by the army and navy so as to prevent these forces from getting through, and paid the penalty.

   Reddy B. Muralithar, *The Hindu*, 27 May 2009, 'Multiple Displacements, Total Loss of Identity'. See also Reddy B. Muralithar, 'Nowhere People', *Frontline*, 14 February 2009, vol. 27 (4).

I am much obliged to Dr Michael Robert's *Fire and Storm*, for reminding me of these articles by Reddy.

8. Although there is no evidence on war crimes, the Tamil diaspora made these accusations, and these were taken up by some western politicians.

9. There was a dwindling Tamil population in the north and the east of the island then under the control of the LTTE. The LTTE kept a tight control on the sale of property in the areas they controlled. As a general rule, they imposed a levy of 25 per cent on these transactions.

10. This was before the navy established control over the coasts in the north and the east of the island.

11. Among those killed was the prominent LTTE leader Tamilchelvam.

12. Gokhale, *Sri Lanka: From War to Peace*, op. cit.

13. Ibid.

14. Ibid., chapters XII and XIII.

Chapter 12

1. On diasporas, see William Saffran, 'Diasporas in Modern Societies: Myths of Homeland and Return', *Diaspora* 1(1), 83–99 (1991); Robin Cohen, *Global Diaspora: An Introduction* (London, 1997). See also, *Nationalism and Ethnic Politics*, vol. 17 (1), January–March 2011 'Special Issue on Diaspora and Citizenship.

2. *The Economist*, 4 June 2011, p. 40.

3. See particularly S.W.R. de A. Samarasinghe, 'Sri Lanka: The Challenge of Post-War Peace-Building, State-Building and Nation-Building' in *National and Ethnic Politics*, 15, 2009, p. 437.

Chapter 13

1. K.M. de Silva, *Regional Powers and Small State Security*, pp. 130–32.

2. For discussion on this, see Tarzie Vittachi, *Emergency '58*, op. cit., passim.

3. This additional expenditure included the costs of General Cyril Ranatunga's Vadamarachchi campaign of 1987 in which he routed the LTTE and sent them fleeing to Tamil Nadu and, most of all, to the areas around Mullaitivu in the northern province. The Indian government intervened to save the LTTE on this occasion.

4. J.W. Bjorkman, 'Health Policy and Politics in Sri Lanka', *Asian Survey*, XXV (5), May 1985, p. 547.

5. Saadet Deger, *Military Expenditure in Third World Countries: The Economic Effects*, London, 1986, p. 232.

6. For further discussion on this, see Saadet Deger, *Military Expenditure*, op. cit., pp. 41–43. Deger argues that the International Monetary Fund's definition of defence is 'probably the most comprehensive and explicit'. See ibid., pp. 41–42, for the IMF definition. For purposes of this present chapter, we have relied on the figures provided in the annual budgets of the Sri Lankan government. These figures at that time were reasonably 'comprehensive and explicit'.

7. The expansion of the security services was largely due to General Cyril Ranatunga's successful Vadamarachchi campaign against the LTTE in 1987. On the Vadamarachchi campaign, see Cyril Ranatunga, *Memoirs*, 2009, particularly pp. 109–58.

8. K.M. de Silva, *Regional Powers and Small State Security*, for a comprehensive review of the Indo-Sri Lanka accord of 1987. See particularly pp. 221–44.

9. On the military aspects of the IPKF in Sri Lanka, see Rajesh Kadian, *India's Sri Lanka Fiasco: Peacekeepers at War*, Vision Books, New Delhi, 1990; and *India and its Army*, New Delhi, 1989, see particularly pp. 65–69; Major Shankar Bhaduri and Major General Afsir Karim, *The Sri Lankan Crisis*, Lancer Paper 1, Chanakya, New Delhi, 1990; and Ravi Rikhye, *The Militarization of Mother India*, New Delhi, 1990, particularly pp. 77–90. Rikhye's estimate of the size of the IPKF at 1,50,000 is the largest we have.

10. Stephen Cohen, 'Marching in Step: Politics-free Military and Military Style Policies', *India Today*, 16 November 1998, p. 68, a review of Apurba Kundu's *Militarism in India*. The then deputy minister of defence, A. Ratwatte, the man in charge of the campaign against the LTTE, had been retired from the army in 1977 when the UNP came to power, but in 1995 was promoted, controversially, to the rank of General after the PA captured power in the general election of that year. Equally controversially, he wore a military uniform when he visited the battle front. His right to wear it was challenged.

11. Ratwatte was the minister for lands, irrigation and power. He was also the chief organizer of the SLFP in its electoral campaigns. Currently (i.e., 2011), Ratwatte is facing charges at the high court in Colombo of accumulating cash and property far beyond anything he could have managed on his salary from the state and any other resources he could claim legitimately.

12. Like General Sarath Fonseka, G. Rajapaksa was a Lt. Col. at the time of General Cyril Ranatunga's Vadamarachchi campaign of 1987. G. Rajapaksa left the island a few years after this campaign and moved to the USA. He did not return to the island till Mahinda Rajapaksa became President in the year 2000. He had been away from Sri Lanka for fifteen years or so.

13. This well-publicized seminar was conducted in Colombo between 29 May and 2 June 2011.

Chapter 14

1. For an account of the upsurge of nationalism in the defeat of the LTTE, see Robert D. Kaplan, 'Buddha's Savage Peace' in *The Atlantic*, September 2009, pp. 56–61, especially pp. 60–61. Kaplan reports the upsurge of nationalism in the defeat of the LTTE as an eye witness.

2. Saman Kelegama, *Development under Stress: Sri Lankan Economy in Transition*, Sage Publications, New Delhi, 2006.

3. Ibid.

4. Sri Lanka was a good example of the benefits that accrued to the people in a plantation economy—indeed a controversial statement but one that needs to be made. As Kelegama, *Development under Stress*, op. cit., shows, Sri Lanka, at Independence, was one of the most prosperous parts of Asia, second only to Japan in terms of annual per capita income.
5. On this episode of ethnic cleansing, see K.M. de Silva, *Reaping the Whirlwind*, pp. 268–71.
6. The High Security Zones (HSZ) occupy about 10 per cent of the land area in the Jaffna peninsula.

Chapter 15

1. G.G. Ponnambalam was a member of the Cabinet from 1949 to 1953.
2. The Rajapaksa government's record, in the construction of houses in the northern and the eastern provinces after the Tsunami, is dismal. The construction of 50,000 houses is a formidable undertaking, well beyond the capacity of the Rajapaksa government unless active Indian assistance is available.
3. When the district councils were established in the 1980s and later on the provincial councils, the TULF persuaded the Sri Lankan government to abolish the village councils and to transfer their functions to provincial and later provincial councils.
4. This has been especially so over the last twenty years.
5. For an excellent introduction to this problem, see Robert D. Kaplan, 'The Geography of Chinese Power', *Foreign Affairs*, May–June 2010, pp. 22–41.

Conclusion

1. President Premadasa not only provided the LTTE with arms and money, he also permitted the LTTE to return to areas in the north of the island which they had been compelled to abandon under pressure from the IPKF.

2. Swamy, *Tigers of Lanka*. See particularly the 2nd edition with epilogue, 1996, and his *Inside an Elusive Mind: Prabhakaran*, 2003. This is the only biography so far on Prabhakaran.

3. K.M. de Silva (ed.), *Conflict and Violence in South Asia: Bangladesh, India, Pakistan and Sri Lanka*, ICES, Kandy, 2000.

4. Premadasa must take the blame for this quixotic order. He was aided and abetted in this by his minister for higher education, A.C.S. Hameed, who was one of the principal figures in the government's negotiations with the LTTE (personal knowledge).

5. *Adventurous Journey: From Peace to War, Insurgency to Terrorism*, Colombo, 2008.

6. Particularly within the officer corps of the army. The publisher Vijitha Yapa had a 'launch' party attended by virtually every significant officer in the army. There were also almost all former commanders of the Sri Lankan army.

7. Peiris, *Twilight of the Tigers*.

8. The killing of Alfred Doraiyappah, the SLFP Mayor of Jaffna, the principal Tamil politician who supported the SLFP-led government of the day, was the work of Prabhakaran, the future leader of the LTTE. But at the time the killing took place Prabhakaran was a non-entity carrying out a proclaimed political objective of the Federal Party that had announced that any Tamil who did not support the objectives of the FP or opposed it faced the risk of physical elimination.

9. There has been nothing on the lines of Jane Jacob's study of separatism in Canada. See Jane Jacobs, *The Question of Separatism, Quebec and the Struggle over Sovereignty*, Random House, New York, 1980.

10. K. M. de Silva, *The Traditional Homelands of the Tamils*, revised 2nd reprint, 1990.

11. The LTTE established their dominance over the Sri Lankan government officials who worked in the north and the east. These officials, including professionals such as doctors, had no choice but to carry out instructions from the LTTE.

12. We have very few details, from independent sources, on the capture of this individual. We do know that he is under the control of the Sri Lankan government, and occasionally permitted to play a secondary role under government supervision—in what passes for Tamil politics.

13. The reference is to Rajiv Gandhi.

14. President R. Premadasa.

15. The LTTE assassinated the then foreign minister of Sri Lanka, and deputy minister of defence, Ranjan Wijeratne, in 1991. Wijeratne was also the administrative secretary of the governing UNP. Had he lived he would have been a challenger to the post of President of Sri Lanka. The other prominent politicians, and potential executive Presidents of Sri Lanka, included Gamini Dissanayake (1995) who was the UNP candidate in the contest with the SLFP Chandrika Kumaratunga. This list should also include Lalith Athulathmudali who had been for long the deputy minister of defence, under President J.R. Jayewardene. Athulathmudali was assassinated in April 1993, a week or so before the LTTE assassinated R. Premadasa. Athulathmudali was a distinguished lawyer and an aspirant to the position of executive President of Sri Lanka.

16. For discussion on this, see K.M. de Silva, *Reaping the Whirlwind*, particularly pp. 302–03.

17. On the expulsion of the Muslims from the Tamil areas in the north of the island, see *Reaping the Whirlwind*, pp. 268–71.

18. This policy failure on the part of the Indian government attracted a protest from virtually all the Muslims in the Sri Lankan Parliament, both government and Opposition MPs—a unanimity unusual in Sri Lankan politics.

Select Bibliography

PART ONE

GENERAL WORKS ON ETHNICITY, POLITICS AND CONFLICT

Alter, Peter. *Nationalism*. London: Edward Arnold, 1989.

Anderson, Benedict. *Imagined Communities: Reflections on the Origin and Spread of Nationalism*. London: Verso, revised edition, 1991.

Austin, Dennis. *Democracy and Violence in India and Sri Lanka*. London: Royal Institute of International Affairs, 1994.

Azar, Edward E. *The Management of Protracted Social Conflict: Theory and Cases*. Aldershot: Hampshire, Dartmouth, 1990.

Banton, Michael. *Racial and Ethnic Competition*. Cambridge: Cambridge University Press, 1983.

Barnett, Marguerite R. *The Politics of Cultural Nationalism in South India*. Princeton: Princeton University Press, 1976.

Barth, F., ed. *Ethnic Groups and Boundaries: The Social Organization of Culture Difference*. London: Allen and Unwin, 1969.

Berdal, Mats, and David M. Malone, eds. *Greed and Grievance: Economic Agendas in Civil Wars*. Boulder: Colorado, 2000.

Bjorkman, James W., ed. *Fundamentalism, Revivalists and Violence in South Asia*. New Delhi: Manohar Publications, 1988.

Brass, Paul, ed. *Ethnic Groups and the State*. Totowa, NJ: Barnes and Noble, 1985.

—.*Ethnicity and Nationalism: Theory and Practice*. New Delhi: Sage Publications, 1991.

Breuilly, John. *Nationalism and the State*. Manchester: Manchester University Press, 1982.

Brown, Sherlyn J., and Kimber M. Schraub. *Resolving Third World Conflict: Challenges for a New Era*. Washington DC: United States Institute of Peace, 1992.

Burton, John W. *International Conflict Resolution, Theory and Practice*. Boulder: Colorado, Wheatsheaf, 1986.

Connor, Walker. *The National Question in Marxist Leninist Theory and Strategy*. Princeton: Princeton University Press, 1984.

—. *Ethnonationalism: The Quest for Understanding*. Princeton: Princeton University Press, 1994.

de Silva, K.M., et al., eds. *Ethnic Conflict in Buddhist Societies: Sri Lanka, Thailand and Burma*. London: Pinter Publishers, 1988.

Deutsch, Karl W. *Nationalism and its Alternatives*. New York: 1969.

—.ed. *Nationalism and Social Communication*, Cambridge, MA: 1966.

Edwards, J. *Language, Society and Identity*. Oxford: Blackwell, 1985.

Emerson, R. *From Empire to Nation: The Rise to Self-Assertion of Asian and African Peoples*. Cambridge, MA: 1960.

Enloe, Cynthia H. *Ethnic Conflict and Political Development*. Boston: Little Brown & Co., 1973.

—. *Ethnic Soldiers: State Security in a Divided Society*. Harmondsworth: Penguin, 1980.

Esman, Milton J. *Ethnic Politics*. Ithaca: Cornell University Press, 1994.

—. *An Introduction to Ethnic Conflict*. Cambridge: Polity, 2004.

Gellner, Ernest. *Nations and Nationalism*. Oxford: Blackwell, 1983.

—. *Encounters with Nationalism*. Oxford: Blackwell, 1994.

Ghosh, Partha. *Cooperation and Conflict in South Asia*. New Delhi: Manohar Publications, 1989.

Glazer, Nathan, and Daniel P. Moynihan, eds. *Ethnicity: Theory and Experience*. Cambridge, MA: Harvard University Press, 1975.

Gurr, Ted Robert. *Why Men Rebel*. Princeton: Princeton University Press, 1971.

Heraclides, Alexis. *The Self-Determination of Minorities in International Politics*. London: Frank Cass, 1991.

Hobsbawm, E.J. *Nations and Nationalism since 1780*. Cambridge: Cambridge University Press, revised edition, 1993.

Horowitz, Donald L. *Ethnic Groups in Conflict*. Berkeley: University of California Press, 1985.

Isaacs, Harold R. *Idols of the Tribe: Group Identity and Political Change*. New York: Harper and Row, 1975.

Kedourie, Elie. *Nationalism*. London: Hutchinson, 1966.

—. (ed.) *Nationalism in Asia and Africa*. London: 1970.

Kellas, James G. *The Politics of Nationalism and Ethnicity*. London: Macmillan, 1991.

Lijphart, Arend. *Democracy in Plural Societies*. New Haven, CT: Yale University Press, 1977.

Little, Richard. *Intervention: External Involvement in Civil Wars*. London: 1975.

May, R.J. eds. *Internationalization of Ethnic Conflict*. London: Pinter Publishers, 1991.

Montville, Joseph V., ed. *Conflict and Peacemaking in Multiethnic Societies*. Lexington, MA: Lexington Books, 1991.

Moynihan, Daniel P. *Pandemonium: Ethnicity in International Politics*. New York: 1993.

Myall, P. *Nationalism and International Society*. Cambridge: Cambridge University Press, 1990.

Nash, Manning. *The Cauldron of Ethnicity in the Modern World*. Chicago: University of Chicago Press, 1989.

Nordlinger, Eric A. *Conflict Regulation in Divided Societies*. Harvard, MA: Harvard University, 1972.

Patterson, Orlando. *Ethnic Chauvinism: The Reactionary Impulse*. New York: Stein and Day, 1977.

Periwal, Sukumar ed. *Notions of Nationalism*. Budapest: Central European Press, 1995.

Porter, J.N. and T. Taplin. *Conflict and Conflict Resolution*. New York: 1978.

Premdas, Ralph; S.W.R. de A. Samarasinghe; and Alan B. Anderson, eds. *Secessionist Movements in Comparative Perspective*. London: Pinter Publishers, 1990.

Rothschild, Joseph. *Ethnopolitics: A Conceptual Framework*. New York: Columbia University Press, 1981.

Ryan, Stephen. *Ethnic Conflict and International Relations*. Aldershot, Dartmouth: 1990.

Samarasinghe, S.W.R. de A. and K.M. de Silva *Ethnic Peace Accords and Ethnic Conflicts*. London: Pinter Publishers, 1993.

Samarasinghe, S.W.R. de A., and Reed Coughlan, eds. *Economic Dimensions of Ethnic Conflict*. London: Pinter Publishers, 1991.

Schaeffer, Robert. *Warpaths: The Politics of Partition*. New York: Hill and Wang, 1990.

Seton-Watson, H. *Nations and States: An Enquiry into the Origins of Nations and the Politics of Nationalism*. London: 1977.

Smith, A.D. *Theories of Nationalism*, 2nd ed. New York: Holmes and Meier, 1983.

—. *The Ethnic Revival in the Modern World*. New York: Cambridge University Press, 1981.

—. *The Ethnic Origin of Nations*. Oxford: Basil Blackwell, 1987.

—. *Myths and Memories of the Nation*. Oxford: 1999.

—. *National Identity*. Harmondsworth: Penguin: 1991.

—. *Nations and Nationalism in a Global Era*. Oxford: Polity Press and Blackwells Publishers, 1995.

Smith, D.E., ed. *South Asian Politics and Religion*. Princeton: Princeton University Press, 1966.

Stavenhagen, Rodolfo. *The Ethnic Question: Conflicts, Development and Human Rights*. Tokyo: United Nations University, 1990.

Stone, John. *Racial Conflict in Contemporary Society*. London: 1985.

Suhrke, Astri, and Lela Garner Noble, eds. *Ethnic Conflict in International Relations*. New York: Praeger, 1977.

Sureda, A. Rigo. *The Evolution of the Right to Self Determination*. Leiden: 1973.

Tambiah, S.J. *Leveling Crowds: Ethnonationalist Conflicts and Collective Violence in South Asia*. Berkeley and Los Angeles: University of California Press, 1996.

Tinker, H. *The Banyan Tree: Overseas Emigrants from India, Pakistan and Bangladesh*. Oxford: Oxford University Press, 1977.

Tonnesson, Stein, and Hans Antlov. *Asian Forms of the Nation*. London: Curzon Press for the Nordic Institute of Asian Studies, 1996.

van den Berghe, P.L. *The Ethnic Phenomenon*. New York: Elsevier, 1991.

Weiner, Myron. *Sons of the Soil: Migration and Ethnic Conflict in India*. Princeton: Princeton University Press, 1978.

Wriggins, W. Howard, ed. *Dynamics of Regional Politics: Four Systems on the Indian Ocean Rim*. New York: University of Columbia Press, 1992.

Young, Crawford. *The Politics of Cultural Pluralism*. Madison: 1976.

Young, Oran R. *The Intermediaries: Third Parties in International Crises*. Princeton: Princeton University Press, 1967.

PART TWO

GENERAL WORKS: ARTICLES

Ayoob, Mohammed. 'The Primacy of the Political: South Asian Regional Cooperation in Comparative Perspective'. *Asian Survey,* 25 (1985): 443–57.

—. 'India in South Asia: The Quest for Regional Predominance'. *World Policy Journal* 7, 1 (1989): 107–33.

Birch, A.H. 'Minority Nationalist Movements and Theories of Political Integration'. *World Politics*, Vol. 33 (1978): 325–44.

Chengappa, Raj. 'Return of the Tigers'. *India Today.* 25, 21 (2000): 28–34.

Collier, Paul. 'Doing Well Out of War: An Economic Perspective'. In *Greed and Grievance: Economic Agendas in Civil Wars*, edited by Mats Berdal and David M. Malone. Boulder, Colorado, 2000: 91–111.

Connor, Walker. 'Nation Building or Nation Destroying?'. *World Politics*, XXIV, 3 (1972): 319–55.

—. 'The Politics of Ethnonationalism'. *Journal of International Affairs* Vol. 27 (1973): 1–21.

—. 'Ethnonationalism in the First World'. In *Ethnic Conflict in the Western World*, edited by Milton J. Esman. Ithaca: Cornell University Press, 1977, 19–45.

—. 'A Nation is a Nation, is a State, is an Ethnic Group, is a ...' *Ethnic and Racial Studies* 1, 4 (1978): 377–400.

—. 'The Impact of Homelands upon Diasporas'. *Modern Diasporas in International Politics* edited by Gabriel Sheffer (1986): 16–68.

Esman, Milton J. 'The Management of Ethnic Conflict'. *Public Policy* XXI, 1 (1973): 49–78.

—. 'Perspectives on Ethnic Conflict in Industrialized Societies'. In *Ethnic Conflict in the Western World*, edited by M. J. Esman. Ithaca: Cornell University Press, 1977, pp. 371–90.

—. 'Ethnic Pluralism and International Relations', *Canadian Review of Studies in Nationalism* XVII, 1–2 (1990): 83–93.

Fishman, Joshua A. 'Nationality-Nationalism'. In *Language Problems of Developing Nations*, ed. Joshua A. Fishman, et al., pp. 39–51.

Geertz, C. 'The Integrative Revolution'. In *Old Societies and New States: The Quest for Modernity in Africa and Asia*, edited by C. Geertz. New York 1963: pp. 105–57.

Gladstone, Jack A. 'Theories of Revolution: The Third Generation', *World Politics*, XXXII 3, (1980): pp. 425–53.

Gurr, Ted Robert. 'Theories of Political Violence and Revolution in the Third World' in Francis M. Deng and I. William Zartman (eds), *Conflict Resolution in Africa*, Washington DC: Brookings Institution, (1991): 153–89.

Halsey, A.H. 'Ethnicity: A Primordial Social Bond', *Ethnic and Racial Studies*, 1(1) (1978): 124–28.

Hare, A.P. 'Third Party Role in Ethnic Conflict', *Social Dynamics*, 1(1), (1975): 81–107.

Hechter, Michael. 'The Political Economy of Ethnic Change', *The American Journal of Sociology*, 79(5) (1973): 1151–78.

Horowitz, Donald L. 'Ethnic Identity' in Glazer and Moynihan (eds), *Ethnicity: Theory and Experience*, 1975, pp. 111–40.

Juergensmeyer, Mark. 'Sri Lanka Rebels: An Ominous Presence in Tamil

Nadu', *India Today*, 31 March (1984) 85–99. 'What the Bhikkhu Said: Reflections on the Rise of Militant Religious Nationalism', *Religion*, 20 (1990): 53–75.

Kelegama, Saman, 'Economic Costs of Conflict in Sri Lanka' in Robert I. Rotberg (ed.), *Creating Peace in Sri Lanka*, Washington DC: 1999, pp. 71–88.

Keyes, Charles F. 'Towards a New Formulation of the Concept of Ethnic Group', *Ethnicity*, 3 (1976): 203–13.

Lijphart, Arend. 'Consociational Democracy', *World Politics*, XXI (1969): 207–25.

Lustick, Ian. 'Stability in Deeply Divided Societies: Consociationalism versus Control', *World Politics*, XXXI (3) (1979): 325–44.

McKay, James, and Frank Lewins, 'Ethnicity and the Ethnic Group: A Conceptual Analysis and Reformulation', *Ethnic and Racial Studies*, 1(4) (1978): 412–27.

Mitchell, C.R. 'Civil Strife and the Involvement of External Parties', *International Studies Quarterly*, XIV (2) (1970): 166–94.

—. 'External Peace-Making Initiatives and Intra-National Conflict' in M. Midlarsky (ed.) *The Internationalization of Communal Strife*, London: 1992, pp. 274–97.

Mwanasali, Masifsky. 'The View from Below' in Berdal, Mats and David M. Malone (eds), *Greed and Grievance: Economic Agendas in Civil Wars*, Boulder: Colorado, 2000, pp. 137–53.

O'Sullivan, Beghan. 'Household Entitlements during Wartime: The Experience of Sri Lanka' in *Oxford Development Studies*, 25(1), (1997): 95–121.

Petersen, William. 'Ethnicity in the World Today', *International Journal of Comparative Sociology*, XX (1 & 2) (1979): 3–13.

Roberts, Michael. 'Nationalism, the Past and The Present: The Case of Sri Lanka', (review essay) *Ethnic and Racial Studies*, Vol. 16, No. 1, January (1993): 133–66.

Ross, Marc Howard. 'A Cross-Cultural Theory of Political Conflict and Violence', *Political Psychology*, 7(3) (1986): 427–69.

—. 'The Role of Evolution in Ethnocentric Conflict and its Management', *Journal of Social Issues*, 47, (1991): 167–85.

—. 'Ethnic Conflict and Dispute Management' in Austin Sarat and Susan Silbey (eds), *Studies in Law, Politics and Society*, Vol. 12, Greenwich Ct. (1992): 107–146.

Rotberg, Robert I., 'Sri Lanka's Civil War: From Mayhem toward Diplomatic Resolution' in Robert I. Rotberg (ed.), *Creating Peace in Sri Lanka*, Washington DC: 1999, pp. 1–16.

Rothchild, Donald. 'Ethnicity and Conflict Resolution', *World Politics*, XX (1) (1969): 597–616.

—. 'An Interactive Model for State-Ethnic Relations' in Francis M. Deng and I. William Zartman (ed.), *Conflict Resolution in Africa*, Washington DC: The Brookings Institution, 1991, pp. 190–215.

Smith, A.D. 'The Diffusion of Nationalism', *British Journal of Sociology*, Vol. 29 (1978): 234–48.

Snodgrass, Donald R. 'The Economic Development of Sri Lanka: A Tale of Missed Opportunities' in Robert I. Rotberg (ed.), *Creating Peace in Sri Lanka*, Washington DC: 1999, pp. 89–108.

Stavenhagen, Rodolfo. 'Ethnic Conflicts and Their Impact on International Society', *International Social Science Journal*, 127 (February 1991), 117–32.

Tammita-Delgoda, Sinha Raja. 'Sri Lanka: The Last Phase in Eelam War IV', *Manekshaw Paper 13*, (2009) New Delhi: K.W. Publishers.

Touval, Saadia. 'Biased Intermediaries', *Jerusalem Journal of International Relations*, 1(1) (1975): 51–69.

—. 'Gaining Entry to Mediation in Communal Strife' in M. Midlarsky [ed.], *The Internationalization of Communal Strife*, London: 1992, pp. 255–73.

van Dyke, Vernon. 'Self-Determination and Minority Rights', *International Studies Quarterly*, 111(3) (1969): 226–33.

Wibers, Hakan. 'Self-Determination as an International Issue' in I.M. Levis (ed.), *Nationalism and Self-Determination in the Horn of Africa*, London: 1983, pp. 43–65.

Wittman, Donald. 'How a War Ends—A Rational Model Approach', *Journal of Conflict Resolution*, 23(4) (1979): 743–63.

Wood, John R. 'Secession: A Comparative Framework', *Canadian Journal of Political Science*, 1(1) (1981): 107–34.

White, N.R. 'Ethnicity, Culture and Cultural Pluralism', *Ethnic and Racial Studies*, Vol. (2) (1978): 139-53.

Yapp., Malcolm. 'Language, Religion and Political Identity: A General Framework' in D. Taylor & M. Yapp. (eds), *Political Identity in South Asia*, London: Curzon Press, 1979, pp. 1–34.

Young, Crawford. 'The Temple of Ethnicity', *World Politics*, XXXV(4) (1983): pp. 652–62.

PART THREE

BOOKS AND MONOGRAPHS ON SRI LANKA: HISTORY AND POLITICS

Alles, A.C. *Insurgency 1971*. Colombo: Colombo Apothecaries, 1976.

—. *The JVP 1969–1989*. Colombo: Lake House, 1989.

Balasuriya, Mahinda. *The Rise and Fall of the LTTE*. Colombo: 2011.

Bandarage, Asoka. *The Separatist Conflict in Sri Lanka: Terrorism, Ethnicity, Political Economy*. England: Routledge, 2009.

Bhaduri, Shankar, and Afsir Karim. *The Sri Lankan Crisis, Lancer Paper 1*. New Delhi: Lancer International, 1990.

Bond, George. *The Buddhist Revival in Sri Lanka: The Religious Tradition, Reinterpretation and Response*. Columbia, S.C.: University of South Carolina, 1988.

Bullion, Alan J. *India, Sri Lanka and the Tamil Crisis 1976-1994: An International Perspective*. London: Pinter, 1995.

—. Gota's War: *The irushing of Tamil Tiger Terrorism in Sri Lanka*. Colombo: Ranjan Wijeratne Foundation, 2012.

Chandraprema, C.A. *Sri Lanka: The Years of Terror. The JVP Insurrection 1987–1989*. Colombo: Lake House, 1991.

de Silva K.M., ed. University of Ceylon, *History of Ceylon*, vol. III, University of Ceylon, Peradeniya, 1973 and University of Peradeniya, *A History of Sri Lanka*, vol. II, Peradeniya, 1995.

—. (ed.) *Sri Lanka, A Survey*. London: C. Hurst, 1977.

—. *A History of Sri Lanka* (revised edition). New Delhi: PBI, 2005.

—. (ed.). *Universal Franchise, 1931–1981: The Sri Lankan Experience.* Colombo: Department of Information, 1981.

—. *Managing Ethnic Tensions in Multi Ethnic Societies: Sri Lanka, 1880–1985.* Lanham: Md., University Press of America, 1986.

—. (ed.). *Sri Lanka: The Problems of Governance.* New Delhi: Konark, 1993.

—. *Regional Powers and Small State Security. India and Sri Lanka, 1977–1990.* Washington DC: Woodrow Wilson Center Press, 1995.

—. *Reaping the Whirlwind: Ethnic Conflict, Ethnic Politics in Sri Lanka.* New Delhi: PBI, 1998.

—. *The Traditional Homelands of the Tamils. Separatist Ideology in Sri Lanka. A Historical Appraisal.* Kandy: International Centre for Ethnic Studies, 2nd revised ed., 1994.

DeVotta, N. *Blowback: Linguistic Nationalism, Institutional Decay and Ethnic Conflict in Sri Lanka.* Palo Alto: Stanford University Press, 2004.

Dharmadasa, K.N.O. *Language, Religion and Ethnic Assertiveness: The Growth of Sinhalese Nationalism in Sri Lanka.* Ann Arbor: Michigan University Press, 1992.

—. ed. *National Language Policy in Sri Lanka, 1956-1996: Three Studies in Its Implementation.* Kandy: ICES, 1996.

Dissanayaka, T.D.S.A. *The Agony of Sri Lanka: An In-depth Account of the Racial Riots of July 1983.* Colombo: Swastika (Pvt) Ltd., 1983.

Fernando, A. *My Belly is White.* Colombo: 2008.

Frerks, G., and B. Klem, eds. *Dealing with Diversity: Sri Lankan Discourses on Peace and Conflict.* The Netherlands: Clingendael Institute of International Relations, 2005.

Fernando, Tissa., and Robert N. Kearney, eds. *Modern Sri Lanka: A Society in Transition.* Syracuse: Maxwell School of Citizenship and Public Affairs, 1979.

Ghosh, P.A. *Ethnic Conflict in Sri Lanka and Role of Indian Peace Keeping Force.* Delhi: APH Publishing Corporation, 1999.

Ghosh, Partha S. *Ethnicity versus Nationalism: The Devolution Discourse in Sri Lanka.* India: Sage, 2003.

Gokhale, Nitin A. *Sri Lanka from War to Peace.* New Delhi: 2009.

Gunaratna, Rohan. *Sri Lanka: A Lost Revolution? The Inside Story of the JVP*. Colombo: Institute of Fundamental Studies, 1990.

—. *Indian Intervention in Sri Lanka: The Role of India's Intelligence Agencies*. Colombo: South Asian Network on Conflict Research, 1993.

Jayatilleka, Dayan. *Sri Lanka. The Travails of a Democracy: Unfinished War, Protracted Crisis*. New Delhi: Vikas, 1995.

Kaarthikeyan, D.R. and Radhavinod Raju. *Triumph of Truth: The Rajiv Gandhi Assassination, the Investigation*. Colombo: Vijitha Yapa, 2004.

Kadian, Rajesh. *India's Sri Lanka Fiasco: Peace Keepers at War*. New Delhi: Vision Books, 1990.

Kapferer, Bruce. *Legends of People, Myths of State: Violence, Intolerance and Political Culture in Sri Lanka and Australia*. Washington DC: Smithsonian Institution Press, 1967.

Kearney, Robert N. *Communalism and Language in the Politics of Ceylon*. Durham, NC: Duke University Press, 1967.

—. *The Politics of Ceylon (Sri Lanka)*. Ithaca, NY: Cornell University Press, 1973.

Kelegama, Saman. *Development under Stress: Sri Lankan Economy in Transition*. New Delhi: Sage, 2006.

Kemper, Steven. *The Presence of the Past: Chronicles, Politics and Culture in Sinhala Life*. Ithaca, NY: Cornell University Press, 1991.

Little, David. *Sri Lanka: The Invention of Enmity*. Washington DC: United States Institute of Peace, 1994.

Manogaran, Chelvadurai. *Ethnic Conflict and Reconciliation in Sri Lanka*. Honolulu: University of Hawaii Press, 1987.

Manor, James, ed. *Sri Lanka in Change and Crisis*. London: Croom Helm, 1984.

—. *The Expedient Utopian: Bandaranaike and Ceylon*. Cambridge: Cambridge University Press, 1989.

McDowell, C. *A Tamil Asylum Diaspora: Sri Lankan Migration, Settlement and Politics in Switzerland*. Providence RI and Oxford: Berghan Books, 1996.

McGilvray, Dennis B. *Crucible of Conflict: Tamil and Muslim Society on the East Coast*. Durham: Duke University Press, 2008.

Mohandas, K. *MGR: The Man and the Myth*. Bangalore: Panther, 1992.

Muni, S.D. *Pangs of Proximity: India and Sri Lanka's Ethnic Crisis*. Oslo: PRIO, 1993.

Narayan Swamy, M.R. *Tigers of Lanka: From Boys to Guerrillas*, 8th edition. New Delhi: Konark, 2008.

—. *Inside an Elusive Mind: Prabhakaran*. Colombo: 2003.

—. *The Tiger Vanquished: LTTE's Story*. New Delhi: 2010.

O'Ballance, Edgar. *The Cyanide War: Tamil Insurrection in Sri Lanka 1973–88*. London: Brassey's, 1989.

Peiris, G.H. *Twilight of the Tigers: Peace Efforts and Power Struggles in Sri Lanka*. New Delhi: Oxford University Press, 2009.

Pfaffenberger, Brian. *Caste in Tamil Culture: The Religious Foundations of Sudra Domination in Tamil Sri Lanka*. Syracuse: Syracuse University, 1982.

Ranatunga, Cyril. *Adventurous Journey: From War to Peace, Insurgency to Terrorism*. Colombo: Vijitha Yapa, 2009.

Ratnatunga, Sinha. *The Politics of Terrorism: The Sri Lanka Experience*. Canberra: International Fellowship for Social and Economic Development, 1988.

Richardson, J. *Paradise Poisoned: Learning about Conflict, Terrorism and Development from Sri Lanka's Civil Wars*. Kandy: ICES, 2005.

Robert, I. Rotberg, ed. *Creating Peace in Sri Lanka: Civil War & Reconciliation*. Washington DC: 1999.

Roberts, Michael W. *Exploring Confrontation. Sri Lanka: Politics, Culture and History*. Victoria: Harwood Academic Publishers, 1994.

—. *Confrontations in Sri Lanka: Sinhalese, LTTE and Others*. Colombo: Vijitha Yapa, 2009.

Ross, Russell R., and Andrea Matles Savada, eds. *Sri Lanka: A Country Study*. Washington DC: 1991.

Russell, Jane. *Communal Politics under the Donoughmore Constitution, 1931–1947*. Colombo: Tisara Press, 1983.

Ryan, Bryce. *Caste in Modern Ceylon*. New Brunswick: Rutgers University Press, 1953.

Sardeshpande, S.C. *Assignment Jaffna*. New Delhi: Lancer, 1992.

Seevaratnam, N., ed. *The National Question and the Indo-Sri Lanka Accord.* New Delhi: Konark, 1989.

Sharma, Rajeev. *Beyond the Tigers: Tracking Rajiv Gandhi's Assassination.* New Delhi: Kaveri Books, 1998.

Singh, Depinder. *The IPKF in Sri Lanka.* New Delhi: Trishul, 1992.

Suriyanarayana, P.S. *The Peace Trap: An Indo-Sri Lankan Political Crisis.* New Delhi: Affiliated East-West Press, 1988.

Tambiah, Stanley J. *Sri Lanka: Ethnic Fratricide and the Dismantling of Democracy.* Chicago: University of Chicago Press, 1986.

—. *Buddhism Betrayed? Religion, Politics and Violence in Sri Lanka.* Chicago: University of Chicago Press, 1992.

Tiranagama, R., et al. *The Broken Palmyra: The Tamil Crisis in Sri Lanka, An Inside Account.* California: The Sri Lanka Studies Institute, 1990.

Tiruchelvam, N. 'Devolution and the Elusive Quest for Peace in Sri Lanka', Rotberg, Robert I. *Creating Peace in Sri Lanka*, pp. 89–202.

Vanniasingham, Somasundaram. *Sri Lanka: The Conflict Within.* New Delhi: Lancer, 1988.

Weiss, Gordon. *The Cage: The Fight for Sri Lanka and the Last Days of the Tamil Tigers.* London: 2011.

Wickremaratne, L.A. *Buddhism and Ethnicity in Sri Lanka: A Historical Analysis.* New Delhi: Vikas, 1995.

Wijewardena, D. *How LTTE Lost the Eelam War.* Colombo, 2010.

Wilson, A. Jeyaratnam. *Politics in Sri Lanka, 1947–1979.* London: Macmillan, 1979.

—. *The Gaullist System in Asia, The Constitution of Sri Lanka, 1978.* London: Macmillan, 1980.

—. *The Break-up of Sri Lanka: The Sinhalese–Tamil Conflict.* Honolulu: University of Hawaii Press, 1988.

—. *Sri Lankan Tamil Nationalism: Its Origins and Development in the Nineteenth and Twentieth Centuries.* London: C. Hurst, 2000.

Wriggins, W. Howard. *Ceylon: Dilemmas of a New Nation.* Princeton, NJ: Princeton University Press, 1960.

PART FOUR

ARTICLES AND PAMPHLETS ON SRI LANKA

Amunugama, Sarath. 'Buddhaputra and Bhumiputra? Dilemma of Modern Sinhala Buddhist Monks in Relation to Ethnic and Political Conflict', *Religion* XXI (1991): 115–39.

de Silva, C.R. 'The Constitution of the Second Republic of Sri Lanka (1978) and its Significance', *The Journal of Commonwealth and Comparative Politics*, XVII(2), pp. 192–209.

de Silva, H.L. 'The Indo-Sri Lanka Agreement (1987) in the Perspective of Inter-State Relations', *Ethnic Studies Report*, vol. X, No. 2, July (1992): 10–17.

de Silva, K.M. 'Buddhist Revivalism, Nationalism and Politics in Modern Sri Lanka' in James W. Bjorkman (ed.). *Fundamentalism, Revivalists and Violence in South Asia*, New Delhi: Manohar, 1988, pp. 107–58.

—. 'Multi-Culturalism in Sri Lanka—Historical Legacy and Contemporary Political Reality', *Ethnic Studies Report*, 15 (1) (January 1997): 1–44.

—. 'Post-LTTE Sri Lanka: The Challenge of Reconstruction and Reconciliation', *India Quarterly*, 66, 3 (2010): 237–50.

Fernando, Tissa. 'Elite Politics in the New States. The Case of Post-Independence Sri Lanka', *Pacific Affairs*, XLVI: 361–83.

Halliday, F. 'The Ceylonese Insurrection' in *New Left Review*, in October 1971, reprinted in R. Blackburn (ed.), *Explosion in a Sub-Continent*, Harmondsworth, 1975, 151–220.

Kearney, R.N. 'Ethnic Conflict and the Tamil Separatist Movement in Sri Lanka', *Asian Survey*, XXV (9), pp. 898–917.

—. 'Sinhalese Nationalism and Social Conflict in Ceylon', *Pacific Affairs*, XXXVII, 125–136.

J. Jiggins, 'The Ceylon Insurrection of 1971', *The Journal of Commonwealth and Comparative Politics*, XIII (1), 40–64.

Peiris, G.H. 'An Appraisal of the Concept of a Traditional Tamil Homeland in Sri Lanka', *Ethnic Studies Report*, IX (1), 13–39.

—. 'Irrigation, Land Distribution and Ethnic Conflict in Sri Lanka: An Evaluation of Criticisms, with Special Reference to the Mahaveli Programme', *Ethnic Studies Report*, XII(1), 43–88.

—. 'The Federal Option for Sri Lanka', *Faultlines*, Vol. 17, 2006, 72.

Pfaffenberger, Brian. 'The Cultural Dimension of Tamil Separatism in Sri Lanka', *Asian Survey*, XXI (12), 1145–57.

Roberts, Michael. 'Elites, Nationalism, and The Nationalist Movement in Ceylon', xxix–ccxxii, introduction to Michael Roberts (ed.), *Documents of the Ceylon National Congress*, Vol. 1, Colombo: 1978.

—. 'Ethnic Conflict in Sri Lanka and Sinhalese Perspectives: Barriers to Accommodation', *Modern Asian Studies*, VII (3), 353–76.

Samarasinghe, S.W.R. de A. 'Ethnic Representation in Central Government Employment and Sinhala–Tamil Relations in Sri Lanka, 1948–81' in R.B. Goldmann and A. Jeyaratnam Wilson (eds). *From Independence to Statehood*, London: Frances Pinter, 1984, pp. 86–108.

Schwarz, W. *The Tamils of Sri Lanka*, Minority Rights Group Report No. 25, (revised ed.), London: 1979.

Smith, Donald E. 'The Political Monks and Monastic Reform' in Donald E. Smith (ed.), *South Asian Politics and Religion*, Princeton: Princeton University Press, 1965, pp. 489–501.

—. 'The Sinhalese-Buddhist Revolution', ibid., pp. 453–88.

Stiratt, R.L. 'The Riots and the Roman Catholic Church in Historical Perspective' in James Manor (ed.), *Sri Lanka in Change and Crisis*, London, Croom Helm, 1984, pp. 196–213.

Wilson, A.J. 'The Tamil Federal Party in Ceylon Politics', *The Journal of Commonwealth Political Studies*, IV (2), 117–39.

Wriggins, W. Howard. 'Impediments to Unity in New Nations: The Case of Ceylon', *The American Political Science Review*, LV (2), 313–21.

Acknowlededgments

This book benefitted from discussions, seminars and conferences at the International Centre for Ethnic Studies held at Kandy and the conferences on 'Ethnicity and Ethnic Conflict' held in Sri Lanka and India, as also in institutions and universities in the United States and various parts of Europe at which, quite often, Sri Lanka's affairs were the focus of attention. I am grateful for the discussions I have had with a variety of scholars, journalists, soldiers and others in Sri Lanka. They are too many to identify; and indeed some would prefer to remain anonymous.

Iranga Silva of the ICES set many of the chapters of this book with her characteristic professional competence. She has helped me immensely in the preparation of this volume for publication. I also need to thank professor G.H. Peiris for his assistance in the preparation of maps and illustrations for this volume. I am very grateful to them for their assistance.

Index

absorption of princely states into India, 20
affirmative action policies, 102, 104, 106, 110, 132, 134, 147, 153, 249
Afghanistan, 20, 36
    mujahideen, 23–24
    Soviet invasion, 22, 23, 68, 225
agriculture sector, 259–60, 261
    plantation, 147, 150, 248
Amirthalingam, A., 17, 31
Amnesty International, 209
Amunugama, Sarath, 179
Anthony, Charles, 205
Anuradhapura, 34, 182
arms build-up, social and economic costs, 230
armed forces, 3, 13, 68, 70, 74, 75, 88, 90, 91, 165, 191, 199, 202, 229, 232, 234
    civilian control, 95
    ethnic and religious composition, 94
    as a percentage of population, 95–96

in post-LTTE Sri Lanka, 211
Tamil separatism, 221–25
Ashraff, M. H.M., 44, 167
Asian Development Bank (ADB), 251, 261
Assam, 67, 225, 234
assassinations in South Asia, 15
    Alfred Durayappah, 27
    Benazir Bhutto, 17
    Gamini Dissanayake, 32, 72, 228
    Indira Gandhi, 1984, 16, 22
    Lakshman Kadirgamar, 178
    R. Premadasa, 1993, 17, 79, 157, 217, 227, 275
    Rajiv Gandhi, 1991, 16, 64–65, 78, 164, 204, 255, 287–88
    S.W.R.D. Bandaranaike (1959), 17, 18–19, 90, 91
    Sheikh Mujibur Rahman, 17
    Zulfiqar Ali Bhutto, 16
Athulathmudali, Lalith, 33
Azad Jammu and Kashmir, 21

Balasingham, A., 79

Bandaranaike, Anura, 168, 178

Bandaranaike, S.W.R.D., 6, 17–19, 89–91, 231

Bandaranaike, Sirimavo, 18, 19, 90, 92, 93, 97, 137, 162, 167–68, 220, 231

Bangladesh, 17, 21, 23, 53, 85, 94, 95
    independence struggle, Indian intervention, 68, 99
    emergence of, 21
    military rule, 86

Bhutto, Benazir, 17, 19

Bhutto, Zulfiqar Ali, 16

bilingualism. *See* language policy

Bjorkman, J.W., 223

Bogollagama, Rohitha, 184

British rule, 48, 85
    administrative structure, 282
    content of the Indian army of the Raj, 225
    social engineering, 283, 285
    Tamils under, 241, 249

Buddhism, Buddhists, 34
    and Christianity, conflict, 92–94

bureaucracy, 89, 213, 214, 215, 219, 266

Canada : Tamil diaspora, 42, 76–77, 152, 187, 197, 198, 199, 202, 207, 208, 209, 213, 255

Cease Fire Agreement (CFA), 158, 173, 179, 180, 182–84, 187

censorship law on foreign media, 165

Ceylon University, 109–12

Ceylon Workers' Congress (CWC), 45–46

Chandrakanthan, Sivanesathurai (Pillayan), 188

Chelvanayakam, S.J.V., 5, 30, 47

Christians, 89–90

Christians-Roman Catholics and Protestants, 92, 94

civil disobedience, 14, 26

civil–military relations, 86, 93

Cleghorn, Hugh, 48

Cohen, Stephen P., 230

Colebrooke–Cameron reforms, 1832, 282

Colombo University, 125, 145

Constitution
    1972, 53, 138–39
    1978, 57–58, 138–39, 140
    2000, 74–75, 138, 163, 166–70, 175

constitutional
    changes, reforms, 75, 149, 163, 169, 171, 175
    crisis, 170
    structure of the island, 54
    system, 71

corrupt practices in Sri Lankan elections, 269

Coup attempts
    1962, 91, 93–95
    1966, 93–95

Crown colony, 42, 85

Dalada Maligawa (Temple of Tooth), Kandy, 34

de A. Samarasinghe, S.W.R., 151–52

de Silva, Chandananda, 219
de Silva, Colvin R., 53, 112, 117
defence expenditure, 69, 71, 97–98, 223, 224, 226–27, 230
Deger, Saadet, 223
demilitarization to militarization, 85–99
democracy, democratic practices, 5, 11, 42, 46, 91, 143, 218, 244
indirect form, 94
restoration in the Tamil areas, 263–69
Democratic People's Liberation Front, 166
demographic profile, 43
destruction years 1620 and 2009, 281–86
development agenda for the northern and the eastern provinces, 258–62
devolution of power, 53–62
Dissanayake, Gamini, 32, 72, 228, 311
Dissanayake, S.B., 171
District Development Councils Act, 1980, 58
Dravida Kazhagam (DK), 52, 99
Dravida Munnetra Kazhagam (DMK), 27, 52, 99
Durayappah, Alfred, 27

Eastern University of Sri Lanka, 145
economic
growth and development, 94, 244–45, 252, 256–57, 285
effects of military expenditure, 223
reconstruction, 252, 255, 257, 259
refugees, 152, 202
resources, 147, 148, 244–45, 256, 257
education
reforms, 135–36, 151
right to, 144
scientific and technical education streams, 111
school system, 137, 147, 261
Eelam People's Democratic Party (EPDP), 166–67
Eelam People's Revolutionary Liberation Front (EPRLF), 31
Eksath Bhikkhu Peramuna (EBP), 101
electoral
politics, 250, 265–66, 268
violence, 162
electronic media, 162, 171
Elephant Pass, 73–74, 163, 165, 193, 260
Ellalan Force, 77
Emergency, 178, 221
English. See also language policy
as official language, 51, 109
Only, 140
replacement by Sinhala and Tamil as official language, 101
speaking minority of Quebec, 143
Esman, Milton J., 104, 106, 107

ethnic
     cleansing, 182, 249–50, 286
     conflict, 13–38, 57, 65, 69, 83,
          89, 111, 152, 215, 218, 234,
          263, 269, 286
          appraisals, 100–07
          negotiating a settlement,
               39–62
     preferences in university
          admissions, 118
     and religious composition
          of the police and armed
          forces, 91–95
     violence in the mid 1950s–in
          1956 and 1958, 26, 98, 221
ethnicity and the security
     services, 13, 232–36

Federal Party (FP), 30, 43, 47,
     49–50, 52, 58, 267–68, 279
Federation of Associations of
     Canadian Tamils (FACT), 77
Fernandopulle, Jeyaraj, 188
fisheries, 177, 258–59
Fonseka, General Sarath, 3, 159,
     165, 187, 190–91, 201, 205,
     216–18, 239, 242, 255, 269,
     276–78, 281, 288
     hour of glory, 202–04
     prosecuted on a number of
          charges, 273–74

Gandhi, Indira, 16, 41, 64, 69
Gandhi, Rajiv, 16, 18, 19, 32, 37,
     64–65, 67, 69, 78, 164, 204,
     225, 255, 274, 287–88
parliamentary elections;

General Elections
     1956, 100
     1994, 44, 71
     2000, 2, 6, 44, 73–75, 167
     2001, 172
     2004 and a quarrelsome
          coalition, 174–75
     2011, 206
Golden Triangle, 75, 199
Gross National Product (GNP),
     223
guerilla forces, 31, 220–21
Gunaratna, Clement V., 163

Hakeem, Rauf, 169
Hameed, A.C.S., 109, 131
High Security Zones (HSZs),
     174, 252–53
Hughes, Christopher, 143–44
human rights violations, 190, 289

Ilankai Thamil Arasi Kachchi
     (ITAK), 50
Illankai Tamil Sangam in the
     USA, 78
Indian
     assistance for development,
          251
     diplomatic or political
          intervention and security
          services, 23, 57, 63–79, 98–
          99, 225–27, 270, 274, 287
     failure, 40, 286
     and the rehabilitation
          programme, 262–63
Indian Parliament attacked 2001,
     19–20

Indian Peace Keeping Force (IPKF), 61, 67–70, 73, 75, 157, 163, 193, 200, 205, 216, 225–27, 229, 275, 287–88

Indian system of provincial governments, 271

Indian Tamils, 44–46, 72, 109, 120–21, 126, 152, 214, 228

Indo-Sri Lanka Accord, 1987, 57, 64–68, 75, 225, 275

International Crisis Group, 209

International Federation of Tamils (IFT), 78

Internationalization of Sri Lanka's ethnic conflict, 27, 36

Inter-Services Intelligence Directorate (ISI), Pakistan, 24, 30

Islamic Socialist Front, 113

Jaffna College, 262

Jaffna University, 145, 261

Jammu and Kashmir, 3, 15, 234

Jammu and Kashmir Liberation Front (JKLF), 23

Janatha Vimukthi Peramuna (JVP), 28, 67, 69–70, 93, 96–98, 162, 167, 170–72, 174–75, 177, 179, 180, 184, 189, 220, 226–27, 230

Jathika Hela Urumaya (JHU), 174, 179

Jayasikuru Operation, 73, 229

Jayasuriya, Karu, 184

Jayewardene, J.R., 1–2, 55, 65, 68, 109, 130–31, 141, 159, 183, 216, 219, 225, 271, 275–76

Johnson, Samuel, 148

Kadirgamar, Lakshman, 178

Kandyan Kingdom, 113, 282

Kankesanthurai port, 251

Karunanidhi, Muthuvel, 164–65, 196

Khan, Ayub, 93–94

Kilinochchi, 73, 192, 193, 195, 229, 280

Kumaratunga, Chandrika, 19, 71, 79, 93, 158, 161, 201–02, 217, 228, 274–75

language policy, 6, 51, 90–91, 101–03, 105–06, 134–46, 147, 151, 215, 241–42
  bilingualism, 135, 140, 142
  linguistic nationalism, 51
  'official', national language' and 'link language', 140–41
  reforms (1956), 134
  rights of Tamil minority, 134, 139
  standardization, 117–19
  Swiss, 142–46
  three language media–Sinhala, Tamil, English, 137, 145

Lanka Sama Samaja Party (LSSP), 53, 135, 138

Liberation Tigers of Tamil Eelam (LTTE)
  administrative structures, 1, 216, 279
  ban on, 78, 162, 164–65, 170, 173, 181–82, 187 Cease Fire Agreement (CFA), 158,

173, 179, 180, 182–84, 187
collapse, 192–204
controlled political structure,
    254
after defeat, 205–36
domination, 7–8, 29, 201, 243,
    250, 264, 268, 284
last phase, no war no peace,
    180–91
political aims and objectives
    of potential successors, 11,
    208, 279
rout, 2006 to 2009, 274–78
surrender of police forces in
    eastern province, 276
transnational 'government' of
    the LTTE, 208

Maavil-Aru system, 182–83, 190,
    203, 205, 217, 288
Mahajana Eksath Peramuna
    (MEP), 101
Mahmud, Badi-ud-din, 109, 110,
    113, 137
Malalasekera, G.P., 135
Malaysia, 148–49, 150
    Malays of South East Asia, 76
Mannar district, 256, 259
Marxism, Marxist trade unions,
    45, 96
Media-wise standardization, 112
Memorandum of Understanding
    (MoU), 170, 184
militarization, 85–99, 210–15,
    245
    challenges 1986–2011, 219–36
    and its problems, 230–31

minorities, 65, 94, 127, 135,
    212–13, 272. See also Muslims,
    Tamils
    lack of concern for, 241–42
    rivalries, 108, 242
moderates and extremists, 11,
    278–81
Moor-Malay group, 113–14, 120
Moratuwa University, 125
mother tongue, 135. See also
    language policy
Mujahidin in Afghanistan, 23
Mullaitivu, 73, 192, 195, 204, 229
    capture by LTTE and the
        humanitarian problem,
        196–201
Musharraf, Pervez, 86
Muslims minority, 111, 182, 186,
    187, 247, 263, 265, 266, 272,
    282–83, 285
    expelled by LTTE, 33, 61,
        249–50, 286
    language policy and, 136–37
    massacre, 33, 183
    in politics, 44, 62
    in private sector, 153
    university admissions policy
        and, 111, 121–22
    and Tamils, rivalry, 6, 41, 49,
        58, 61–62, 108, 242–43,
        286

Nanthikadal, 217
Narayan Swamy, M.R., 275
national census
    2001, 212–13
    2011, 212–14

national consciousness, 47
National Language Act No. 33,
    1956, 134
National Planning Council, 114
National Unity Alliance (NUA),
    167–68
non-governmental organizations
    (NGOs), 190
north central provincial council
    (NCPC), 189
Norwegian intervention, 39, 78,
    152, 163, 168, 173, 174, 207

Oberst, Robert, 102, 104, 107,
    134, 147
Official Language Commission
    Act No. 18, 1991, 141

Pakistan, 36, 86, 99, 269
partition of Pakistan 1971, 53
People's Alliance (PA), 45,
    71–72, 74–79, 93, 227–29; and
    LTTE, 71–79
People's United Front (PUF), 101
Peradeniya University, 125, 145
plantation industry, 214–15, 248,
    256
political
    assassination. See assassination
        in South Asia
    changes and their impact
        on the security services,
        89–96, 134
    class, 100
    crisis, 90–91, 225
    establishments, 57
    groupings, 15, 268

hierarchy, 72
    marginalization, 61
    and military challenges,
        162–73
    negotiation, 63
    participation in decision-
        making, 58
    parties and groups, 41, 44,
        66, 79
    system in India, 64
    violence, 3, 4, 11, 26, 28
    will, lack of, 56, 142
politics, 32, 35, 67
    domestic, 98
    in Tamil Nadu, 64
Ponnambalam, G.G., 257, 267
Post-Tsunami Operations
    Management Structure
    (P-TOMS), 177, 179
power-sharing and those who
    shared power, 42–46
Prabhakaran, Velupillai, 1, 3, 7,
    27, 30, 35, 78, 173, 181, 191,
    196, 201–02, 204, 205–06,
    208, 209, 212, 215–17, 246–
    47, 255, 273, 275–77, 288
Premadasa, R., 17, 32, 69, 70,
    72, 79, 140, 157–58, 216–17,
    226–28, 274–75;
provincial autonomy and states'
    rights, distinction, 60
provincial council of the eastern
    province, 265–66
Provincial Councils Act 42 of
    1987, 57–58
Public Security Act, 90, 164, 221
public security, threat and role of

the armed services, 96–99

Rajapaksa, Gotabhaya, 6, 203, 235, 276
Rajapaksa, Mahinda, 6, 158, 169, 174, 178–79, 182, 189–90, 202, 203, 205, 207, 217–18, 220, 235, 239, 242, 245, 246, 248–49, 254–55, 262, 265, 271, 273–74, 276, 285, 288
Ranatunga, Cyril, 1–2, 66, 157, 191, 192, 196, 204, 205, 215–16, 255, 269, 274–77, 281, 284, 287–88
Ratwatte, Anurudha, 93, 220, 230, 235
reconciliation and reconstruction policies, 210, 241–53, 254–72, 284–86
Reconciliation Commission, 246–50
regime, change, 227–29
regional
     autonomy, 48, 52, 57, 173
     merit quotas, 120
     political systems, 255
     rivalries, 269–72
Research and Analysis Wing (RAW), 30, 34, 209, 221

security forces, 26, 30, 37, 63, 70, 72, 85, 97, 157, 165, 188, 211–13, 217, 222, 224, 227–28, 231, 242, 252–53, 258
Senanayake, Dudley Shelton, 43, 46, 145
separatism and terrorism in

South Asia and Sri Lanka, 3–5, 13–38, 74, 78
     in Kashmir, 68
     in Myanmar, Thailand, and the Philippines, 25
Sharif, Nawaz, 86
Simla Accord, 1972, 22
Singh, V.P., 69
Sinhala Tharuna Sanvidhanaya (Sinhala Youth Organization), 117
Sinhala-only demand, 101, 103, 105–06, 135–36, 138–40, 146, 241
     medium of instruction, 111–12
Sinhalese-Buddhist majority, 43, 89, 91, 114, 117, 119, 213. *See also* Tamils
     dominated government and polity, 105, 135, 137, 147, 212, 241, 250
     identity of the armed services, 92–95, 212
     national politics, 114
     resistance to western colonial powers, 54
     rural values and traditions, 242
South Asian Association for Regional Co-operation (SAARC), 189–90
South East Asia Command (SEAC), 86
Sowell, Thomas, 102, 104, 107, 134
Sri Lanka Freedom Party

(SLFP), 6, 26–27, 43, 44, 53, 55, 58, 67, 71, 91, 92, 109, 135, 137, 168, 171, 174, 178, 179, 186, 188, 217, 226, 274
Lanka Sama Samaja Party (LSSP) coalition, 135
Sri Lanka Muslim Congress (SLMC), 44, 62, 167–69, 172, 189
suicide bombers, 15, 31–32, 161–62, 182
Swiss Federation of Tamil Associations, 78

Tamil(s), Tamil minority, 8, 26, 45–46, 63, 75, 99, 105, 119, 142–44, 150, 153, 227, 271
of Batticoloa, 277
cultural identity, 59
diaspora. *See* Tamil diaspora
domination, 52, 58, 62, 179, 267
in Public sector, 149, 248–49
language, subordinate role, 138–39
medium of instruction, 111–12, 119, 135
and the Muslims. *See* Muslims
plantation workers, 264
political assertiveness, 44, 47–48, 207
politics, political parties, 4, 5, 7, 39–41, 46, 50, 59, 118, 146, 247, 267
population, 25, 113
separatism in Sri Lanka, 25, 30, 41, 46–53, 59, 76–77, 98, 220–25, 230, 279

and Sinhalese majority, relations, 94, 109, 242, 244, 249, 281, 286
role in Sri Lankan democratic system, 7
state creation in Sri Lanka, 279
from Jaffna, 25, 45, 149, 213, 215, 277, 281–85
Tamil Congress, 52, 257, 267–68
Tamil Co-ordinating Committee, Norway, 78
Tamil Diaspora, 76, 206–10, 245, 258, 261, 280, 289
in Australia, 76, 152, 202, 207, 209, 213
in Canada, 42, 76–77, 152, 187, 197, 198, 199, 202, 207, 208, 209, 213, 255
in France, 207, 209
in Malaysia, 143, 145, 207, 209
in United Kingdom, 206–09
in western Europe, 210
Tamil Eelam Liberation Organisation (TELO), 30
Tamil Kingdom Party (Tamil State Party), 52
Tamil Language (Special Provisions) Act No. 28, 1958, 138–39
Tamil Nadu factor, 63–64, 209, 221
Tamil National Alliance (TNA), 7, 172, 206, 254, 265, 267
Tamil United Front's (TUF), 27, 28, 47

Tamil United Liberation Front
    (TULF), 4–5, 7, 17, 27–31, 43,
    44, 46, 47, 49, 54, 55, 56, 58,
    60, 61, 66, 119, 166, 244, 270,
    278, 279, 281
Tamileela Makkal Viduthalai
    Pulikal (TMVP), 188
terrorism
    and civil disobedience,
        distinction, 14
    a feature of politics, 15
    in Jammu and Kashmir, 15,
        19–24, 36
    in north-east of India, 15
    and ordinary criminal acts,
        distinction, 13–14
    a feature of politics, 15
    and separatism in Sri Lanka,
        25–35, 36
    in South Asia, 16–19
    and war, distinction, 13–14
Thondaman, S., 45, 214
traditional homelands of the
    Tamils, 4, 46, 47–48, 49, 279
tsunami and a government in
    crisis, 176–84
    rehabilitation policies, 176
Tutu, Desmond, 247

United Front (UF), 26, 27, 29,
    53, 92, 97, 106, 109, 110, 113,
    116, 117, 138
United National Front (UNF),
    172–73, 174–75, 180
United National Party (UNP),
    32–33, 43–45, 55, 58, 72, 74,
    92, 101, 109, 135, 137, 140,

158, 161–63, 166–70, 172,
    174–75, 176–79, 180, 184,
    186, 188–89, 227–28, 242
United Nations (UN), 77, 218
    Human Rights Commission
        (UNHRC), 198
    sub-committees, 63, 224
United People's Freedom
    Alliance (UPFA), 174, 176,
    239
United States Federal Bureau of
    Investigation (FBI), 187
universal suffrage, 11, 42, 100,
    244, 268
university admissions,
    controversial issue, 6, 83, 102,
    103, 105, 106, 107, 108–33,
    242
    an abortive attempt at change,
        125–33
    differential qualifying marks
        for Sinhalese and Tamil
        students, 112
    district quota system (district
        preferences), 116, 122,
        126–29, 132
    preferential policies, 108
    standardization by language,
        110, 112, 113, 115, 117–19,
        123
    educationally backward
        districts quota, 120, 131,
        132
    national merit quota, 132
    two-tier system, 121
    three-tier admissions policy,
        1977 and after, 116–33

University Grants Commission (UGC), 108, 120, 122, 125, 127, 129, 130–3, 261

Vadamarachchi campaign, 1–3, 66, 215–16, 236, 275–77, 281, 284, 286–87

Wajed, Sheikh Hasina, 19
welfare policies, 86, 100, 223–24

Wickremanayake, Ratnasiri, 167, 179
Wickremasinghe, Ranil, 161– 62, 163, 172, 173, 179
Wijeratne, Ranjan, 33, 311
Wijetunga, D.B., 227
World War II, role of Sri Lanka, 86–88
Zardari, Asif Ali, 18
Zia, Khaleda, 19
Zia-ul-Huq, 16